Research Methods in Law
Second Edition

Explaining in clear terms some of the main methodological approaches to legal research, the chapters in this edited collection are written by specialists in their fields, researching in a variety of jurisdictions.

Covering a range of topics from Feminist Approaches to Law and Economics, each contributor addresses the topic of 'lay decision-makers in the legal system' from their particular methodological perspective, explaining how they would approach the issue and discussing the suitability of their particular method. This focus on one main topic allows the reader to draw comparisons between methods with relative ease.

The broad range of contributors makes *Research Methods in Law* well suited to an international audience, and it is ideal reading for PhD students in law, undergraduate dissertation students in law, LL.M research students and early year researchers.

Dawn Watkins is an Associate Professor of Law at the University of Leicester.

Mandy Burton is Professor of Socio-Legal Studies at the University of Leicester.

Research Methods in Law
Second Edition

Edited by Dawn Watkins
and Mandy Burton

Routledge
Taylor & Francis Group

LONDON AND NEW YORK

Second edition published 2018
by Routledge
2 Park Square, Milton Park, Abingdon, Oxon, OX14 4RN

and by Routledge
711 Third Avenue, New York, NY 10017

Routledge is an imprint of the Taylor & Francis Group, an informa business

First edition published by Routledge 2013

British Library Cataloguing-in-Publication Data
A catalogue record for this book is available from the British Library

Library of Congress Cataloging-in-Publication Data
Names: Watkins, Dawn (Dawn Elizabeth), editor. | Burton, Mandy, editor.
Title: Research methods in law / [edited by] Dawn Watkins, Mandy Burton.
Description: Second edition. | Abingdon, Oxon [UK] ; New York : Routledge, 2017. | Includes bibliographical references and index.
Identifiers: LCCN 2017004557 | ISBN 9781138230187 (hbk) | ISBN 9781138230194 (pbk)
Subjects: LCSH: Legal research.
Classification: LCC K85. R47 2017 | DDC 340.072—dc23
LC record available at https://lccn.loc.gov/2017004557

ISBN: 978-1-138-23018-7 (hbk)
ISBN: 978-1-138-23019-4 (pbk)
ISBN: 978-1-315-38666-9 (ebk)

Typeset in Garamond
by Keystroke, Neville Lodge, Tettenhall, Wolverhampton

Printed and bound by CPI Group (UK) Ltd, Croydon. CR0 4YY

Contents

Notes on contributors

Anthony Bradney is Professor of Law at Keele University. His research ranges over a wide area, including law and popular culture, the legal profession, university legal education and religion and law. He has published extensively, including *Conversations, Choices and Chances: The Liberal Law School in the Twenty First Century* (Hart, 2003) and *Law and Faith in a Sceptical Age* (Routledge/GlassHouse Press, 2009). He is a Fellow of the Academy of Social Sciences and of the Royal Society of Arts, a former Vice Chair of the Socio-Legal Studies Association and a member of the Advisory Editorial Board of the *Journal of Law and Society*.

Mandy Burton is a Professor of Socio-Legal Studies at the University of Leicester. Her research interests are in criminal justice, family law and socio-legal studies, with a particular focus on legal responses to domestic violence. She has carried out numerous empirical research projects, many of them commissioned by UK Government departments. She teaches criminal law and justice to undergraduates and socio-legal research methods to postgraduate students.

Steven Cammiss is a Senior Lecturer in Law at the University of Leicester. He has a long-standing interest in law and language, with a particular focus on language use in interaction in legal settings. His PhD utilised narrative analysis to examine narrative production in the courtroom within the mode of trial hearing. A recent project (with Colin Manchester of the University of Warwick) adopted a socio-linguistic and ethnomethodological approach to explore the language of complaining in a legal setting (objecting to a licensing application).

Fiona Cownie is Professor of Law and Pro Vice Chancellor (Education & Student Experience) at Keele University. A former Vice Chair of the Socio-Legal Studies Association, she is a Fellow of the Academy of Social Sciences and of the Royal Society of Arts. She has published widely in her specialist field of legal education, including *Legal Academics: Culture and Identities*

(Hart, 2004) and (with Ray Cocks), *'A Great and Noble Occupation!' The History of the Society of Legal Scholars* (Hart, 2009).

Anthony Good is Emeritus Professor of Social Anthropology at the University of Edinburgh. His overseas field research focuses on South India and Sri Lanka. He has acted as expert witness in over 600 asylum appeals involving Sri Lankan Tamils, and has done ESRC- and (with Robert Gibb) AHRC-funded research on the asylum processes in France and the United Kingdom. Books include *Anthropology and Expertise in the Asylum Courts* (Routledge, 2007) and (with Daniela Berti and Gilles Tarabout) *Of Doubt and Proof: Ritual and Legal Practices of Judgment* (Ashgate, 2015).

Philip Handler is a Senior Lecturer in Law at the University of Manchester. He has published widely on criminal law and modern English legal history. With Henry Mares and Ian Williams, he is editor of *Landmark Cases in Criminal Law* (Hart, 2017). He currently serves as Book Review Editor and Co-Editor of *Legal Studies*.

Terry Hutchinson held the position of Associate Professor in Law at Queensland University of Technology, being a member of Faculty 1987–2016. She taught criminal law and legal research, and has published widely in the areas of youth justice and postgraduate legal research training, including *Researching and Writing in Law* (Thomson Reuters, 4th edn, forthcoming 2017). She has served as a full-time member of the Queensland Law Reform Commission and has had an active involvement in the Queensland Law Society's Equity and Diversity and Children's Committees, as well as in the Law Council of Australia's Equalising Opportunities in the Law Committee. Terry was also Editor of the Australasian Law Teachers' Association's (ALTA) journal *Legal Education Review* 2004–2011, and remains a member of the journal's Advisory Board.

Panu Minkkinen is Professor of Jurisprudence at the Faculty of Law, University of Helsinki, Finland. Over the years his research has focused on philosophical and theoretical perspectives in law (especially the critique of Kantian and neo-Kantian jurisprudence) and critical legal scholarship, as well as interdisciplinary themes at the intersection of law and the humanities. His major publications in English include the monographs *Thinking without Desire* (Hart, 1999) and *Sovereignty, Knowledge, Law* (Routledge, 2009), and numerous articles published in leading jurisprudential and theoretical journals. His current research interests include projects on law as a human science and on constitutional theory.

Vanessa E. Munro is Professor of Law at the University of Warwick. She has published extensively on feminist legal and political theory, and has conducted a number of large-scale empirical projects exploring contemporary socio-legal responses to sexual violence. She was conferred as a Fellow of the Academy of Social Sciences in 2016, in recognition of her contribution to research and policy.

Geoffrey Samuel is a Professor at the Kent Law School and is a Professeur *affilié* at the School of Law, Sciences-Po, Paris. He holds doctorates from Cambridge, Maastricht and Nancy (*honoris causa*), and specialises in the law of obligations, comparative law, legal reasoning and legal epistemology. He publishes regularly in the leading law journals and in edited works; and his latest books are *An Introduction to Comparative Law Theory and Method* (Hart, 2014) and *A Short Introduction to Judging and to Legal Reasoning* (Edward Elgar, 2016).

Albert Sanchez-Graells is a Senior Lecturer in Law at the University of Bristol. He takes a law and economics approach to his research and specialises in European economic law, with a focus on competition law and public procurement, on which he has published the leading monograph *Public Procurement and the EU Competition Rules*, (Hart, 2nd edn, 2015). His working papers are available at http://ssrn.com/author=542893 and his analysis of current legal developments is published in his blog, http://www.howtocrackanut.com.

Dawn Watkins is an Associate Professor at the University of Leicester. Her research interests are in law and humanities and legal education; particularly public legal education. She has recently completed an ESRC-funded research project using digital gaming as a research tool to assess children's legal understanding (see http://www.le.ac.uk/licl). She teaches on undergraduate law courses and has been involved in the design and delivery of training programmes for postgraduate research students, as well as supervising students through to the successful completion of their PhDs. She was awarded a university distinguished teaching fellowship in 2012 and was shortlisted for the Law Teacher of the Year Award 2013.

Acknowledgements

We wish to thank Panu Minkkinen for his encouragement in the early stages of planning the first edition of this book. We are grateful also to the team at Routledge for suggesting that we publish a second edition, and for helping us to see this through to completion. Thanks to our contributors, 'old and new'; all of whom have provided authoritative, informative and thought-provoking contributions, in spite of heavy workloads and pressing schedules. Special thanks are due to Tracey Varnava, who was involved initially in the editorial process for the first edition and who must take the credit for coming up with the 'one topic' idea which is a distinguishing feature of this book. At the time, Tracey was the Associate Director of the UK Centre for Legal Education and her remit included responsibility for the UKCLE's research strategy, focusing on issues such as providing funding and online resources to support the teaching of legal research skills. Tracey is now Deputy Director of the Undergraduate Laws Programme at the University of London.

Introduction

Dawn Watkins and Mandy Burton

Our motivation for publishing the first edition of this book came primarily from our experiences of supervising PhD candidates and from being involved in the design and delivery of training sessions for postgraduate research students. Our aim was to provide an overview of some of the many methods that constitute legal research; so as to assist postgraduate research students and early career researchers in gaining not only an understanding of each of the methods discussed, but, more importantly, to gain an understanding of the inter-relationship between these methods and the advantages and disadvantages of relying on one method in preference to another, or on a particular combination of methods, in the pursuit of any given research question. In short, our intention has been to give readers an idea of the vast array of possibilities that are open to them in the planning, development and pursuit of any research project in law. We are therefore delighted to have extended this edition to include three further chapters covering law and anthropology, law and economics and feminist approaches to legal research.

We envisage that readers will benefit most from reading the book as a whole and, in order to facilitate this holistic approach, we have asked all of our contributors to focus on just one research topic.[1] There were, of course, a host of possible topics, but we opted for 'lay decision-making in the legal system' as it offered sufficient opportunity for consideration across a variety of disciplines and jurisdictions. Contributors have drawn on their own work and upon the work of others in order to provide examples of research carried out via a particular method, or combination of methods, within this single topic.

On method and methodology

The terms 'method' and 'methodology' are used frequently in the context of legal research. They are sometimes used interchangeably to mean the same

---

1 As stated in our Acknowledgements, credit must be given to Tracey Varnava for this 'one topic' idea, which is a distinguishing feature of this book.

thing, but they are often used also to mean slightly different things. In the current context, we are concerned with method as an approach to the practice of legal research: 'what you *actually do* to enhance your knowledge, test your thesis, or answer your research question'.[2] The term 'methodology' can also be used in this way; most commonly to refer collectively to a group of chosen methods. By contrast, however, the term 'methodology' can also be employed to refer more critically to 'the study of the direction and implications of empirical research, or of the suitability of the techniques employed in it'.[3] In this sense, it refers to the thinking that takes place *about* methods; or the thinking that takes place *outside* of the practical aspects of a research project and which determines its design. Cryer et al. explain this as follows:

> Every legal research project begins from a theoretical basis or bases, whether such bases are articulated or not. The theoretical basis of a project will inform how law is conceptualised in the project, which in turn will determine what kinds of research questions are deemed meaningful or useful, what data is examined and how it is analysed (the method). Often these are arrived at unconsciously . . . We believe, however, that it is better to be open about the bases of research and to think about them than to leave them unaddressed and uncritically accepted . . . For us, methodology has theoretical connotations. Moreover, methodology is closely related to what we understand the field of enquiry . . . to be. Methodology guides our thinking or questioning of, or within, that field or both.[4]

For this reason, readers of this text will discover that an appreciation and understanding of methodology, as it is defined here, is an essential precursor to the pursuit of legal research of any kind. Whether or not the researcher is aware of it, her 'world view' will influence every aspect of her research, not least her choice of method.

Readers will discover that the approaches of our contributors tend to vary in their use of the terms 'method' and 'methodology'. Nevertheless, all of them agree that establishing an appropriate theoretical basis for a research project is as important as determining the appropriate method(s) for carrying out the research. Handler, for example, warns against projecting our modern conceptions of law onto the past when carrying out research in legal history. Instead, he argues, 'the task is to understand and perceive the limitations on

2 Cryer, R., T. Hervey and B. Sokhi-Bulley, *Research Methodologies in EU and International Law*, Oxford: Hart, 2011, 5 (emphasis in the original).
3 This is a standard *Oxford English Dictionary* definition.
4 Cryer et al., *Research Methodologies in EU and International Law*, 5.

what could be asked then in order to grasp the questions that can be asked now'.[5] Cownie and Bradney note that socio-legal empirical scholars have been accused of producing poorly theorised or methodologically weak work and they remind us that 'choosing the appropriate theoretical approach and the method of investigation is just as important for the socio-legal researcher as all the other aspects of socio-legal research'.[6] This is a theme which is taken up by Burton in her chapter on empirical studies, where she states that 'developing and testing research theory is a significant part of the empirical research process . . . The kind of research done will depend to an extent on the theory underpinning it.'[7] Taking this one stage further, Samuel seeks to demonstrate that it is neither possible nor appropriate to draw a distinction between 'method' and 'perspective' in the field of comparative law. He states: 'method is in fact central to comparative law but . . . in understanding what is meant by "method" in this domain one must have a commitment both to theory and to interdisciplinarity'.[8] He then goes on to demonstrate this with considerable expertise in his comparison of the institution of the jury in English and French law. In our experience, it is not uncommon to read a proposal from a prospective PhD student that states an intention to compare the law or practice of one country with the 'equivalent' law or practice of another. Comparing the law or legal systems of two different countries is not, in itself, a method of legal research. As Samuel explains, the researcher must avoid 'the great danger of legal imperialism' that assumes that the 'other' shares the same understanding of a given term; even 'law' itself. There is a great deal more expected of the comparative lawyer than an abstract analysis of the respective functions of two similar laws in two different countries. The researcher must appreciate that the law operates within the distinctive legal culture of each jurisdiction, a culture that the researcher will need to fully engage with in the course of her project. The researcher must ask herself not only *what* she wishes to compare, but *how* and *why* she wishes to draw comparisons.

Knowing your field and justifying your approach

As well as providing discrete examples of research on the topic of lay decision-making in the legal system, all of our contributors have provided readers with

---

5 See Chapter 5, p. 106
6 See Chapter 2, p. 46 Cownie and Bradney provide two interesting examples of the development of theory in socio-legal research: Layard's study of planning and the social production of space, and Bradney's study of the *Buffy the Vampire Slayer* series.
7 See Chapter 3, p. 68.
8 See Chapter 6, p. 123.

an overview of their particular method or approach to legal research, and it is our hope that readers who are in the early stages of planning a research project can draw on this more general information to 'situate' their research within an appropriate field.[9] This is not to say that an academic discussion must take place within any pre-established confines; indeed, Cammiss and Watkins argue that (in the field of law and humanities at least) 'the possibilities for research are not only endless, but boundless'.[10] Readers will also observe that although our contributors' discussions of the various research methods are presented in discrete chapters, these methods are not always clearly defined and they are seldom exclusive. Cownie and Bradney, for example, highlight the lack of consensus as to what constitutes 'socio-legal' research. The term is used to cover a variety of different approaches, including critical legal studies and empirical research, both of which have distinct chapters in this book. As Cownie's research has shown, 'socio-legal' is an inclusive label that many academics working in law schools would now apply to themselves, yet they might also fall easily into a number of other descriptive categories. One example of research that Cownie and Bradney refer to is Cane's non-empirical, historical/comparative approach to studying tribunals. This research identified different models of administrative adjudication in different jurisdictions and across different times, revealing, inter alia, the changing attitudes to lay participation in the United Kingdom. In this book, we have separate chapters on legal history and comparative approaches. Nevertheless, scholars adopting these methodological approaches might claim the label 'socio-legal' just as easily as their empiricist colleagues. So when we speak of 'situating' research, we refer primarily to the view that in the early stages of any research project, the researcher must seek to ensure that she familiarises herself with the relevant literature, so as to enter into an academic debate on level terms. In other words, as Minkkinen states, in order to argue successfully for a departure from tradition, the researcher must first engage with a critical dialogue within that tradition.

---

9 Allied to this is the need to recognise the distinction between 'curiosity-driven' research and policy-driven, government-funded research, where the agenda is at least partly set by the funder and with possible limitations on publication. There are particular lessons to be learnt from this – for example, relating to the potential limitations on academic freedom, although as Cownie and Bradney observe, this was not particularly evident in the study of tribunals which they include in their chapter. Nevertheless, it is a theme returned to by Burton in her chapter and one of which early career researchers embarking down a path of government-funded research should be mindful.

10 See Chapter 4, p. 98.

Importantly, we seek to emphasise that a decision to pursue research via a 'traditional' doctrinal research method still requires explanation and justification. In the opening chapter to this book, Hutchinson sets out a comprehensive explanation of this method and while she concedes that the view will be criticised, Hutchinson contends that doctrinal research 'still necessarily forms the basis for most, if not all, legal research projects'.[11] Readers will note that this is a claim that is countered immediately and explicitly by Cownie and Bradney, whose subtitle to the second chapter of this book is 'A challenge to the doctrinal approach'. Later, Cammiss and Watkins explain that a significant feature of research in law and humanities has been its capacity to challenge the traditional approach to legal research that Hutchinson appears to defend. Are Hutchinson's claims for doctrinal supremacy, then, unfounded? Before concluding whether or not this is the case, it is necessary to acknowledge the differences in the perspectives of our contributors. Hutchinson writes from the perspective of researching and teaching law in Australia, and from her experience as a full-time member of the Queensland Law Reform Commission. And when she speaks of legal research, Hutchinson has in mind not only academic legal research, but also the research carried out by legal practitioners. By contrast, the focus of Cownie and Bradney's discussion is upon English legal scholarship, carried out within the academic community. Cammiss and Watkins, too, refer to academic research, but mainly in the context of English and American scholarship. This does not mean that it is impossible to challenge Hutchinson's claims. But it does demonstrate that care must be taken when we seek to engage in any debate about the claims of a fellow researcher.

Sanchez-Graells concedes that doctrinal legal research has a place in ensuring that researchers' analyses 'are technically sound from a legal perspective', yet he calls for legal scholars to broaden their views and to consider such analyses in context. In particular, Sanchez-Graells contends that:

> . . . carrying out legal research without assessing its economic implications and without incorporating the insights of economic theory is ultimately unsatisfactory, just as it is equally faulty not to incorporate the insights derived from political science and other social sciences such as sociology or anthropology, or even beyond, from evolutionary theory and psychology.[12]

Clearly, and as Sanchez-Graells concedes, this is just one view and his firm adherence to economically informed legal research is itself countered by other contributors.

11 See Chapter 1, p. 10.
12 Chapter 8, p. 173.

Interestingly, Minkkinen does not focus his attention on disputing the claims made by his positivist counterparts. Rather, in the most subversive of all our chapters, Minkkinen turns his attention to his own 'tradition', arguing that:

> . . . all legal methods, be they conventional or allegedly 'critical', impose limitations into the ways in which the researcher produces legal knowledge . . . A 'critical legal method', if there is such a thing, would, then, be no different. Textbooks in the area are cluttered with the nomenclature of acceptable frameworks for critical 'methods', and in its insistence on complying with them, critical legal research can often be just as orthodox in its approach as its more conformist cousins.[13]

Consequently, Minkkinen rejects the notion of there being a 'critical legal method' and argues instead that 'a "critical" perspective to law can only be more like an "attitude" than a scientifically motivated methodic approach'.[14]

While she cautions us that 'there is no such thing as a unified feminist jurisprudence, nor a universally shared feminist legal method', Munro explains that attending to law *in context* has been 'a prominent theme' in this field of scholarship. Drawing on case studies on lay decision-making in jury trials and asylum cases, Munro demonstrates that legal decision-makers do not apply legal rules neutrally; and how unequal gender power relations can influence how the law operates in these and other areas. She alerts the researcher, too, to the fact that the way in which empirical work is carried out, the chosen methods and the practicalities of the research, may either enable or inhibit the voices of women being heard. Both the jury and asylum studies described by Munro stem from her own empirical work with others and she demonstrates how a feminist approach can influence both the choice of empirical methods and the interpretation of empirical findings.

Finally, in the closing chapter of the book, Anthony Good's explanation of legal pluralism and 'lay' decision-making (discussed within the broader context of law and anthropology) calls us to take a step even further beyond the discussions of legal research that we have encountered in previous chapters. Through his comprehensive and critical account of legal pluralism, Good requires us to question our hitherto unquestioned assumptions about what constitutes 'the law' and, consequently, to reconsider even the apparently non-controversial distinction between legal and lay decision-making that we make

13 See Chapter 7.
14 *Ibid.*

in this book. And so, for researchers who are planning to conduct legal research from *any* perspective, Good's analysis represents an irresistible invitation to question, interrogate and challenge the assumptions upon which their research is based.

In conclusion, the aim of legal research is to contribute to the body of knowledge in a given field and our hope is that the critical explanation of legal research methods provided by this book, when combined with an appropriate theoretical approach, will equip the reader to do so more effectively.

1 Doctrinal research

Researching the jury

Terry Hutchinson*

> The training of lawyers is a training in logic. The processes of analogy, discrimination, and deduction are those in which they are most at home. The language of judicial decision is mainly the language of logic . . . But certainty generally is illusion . . . Behind the logical form lies a judgment as to the relative worth and importance of competing legislative grounds, often an inarticulate and unconscious judgment, it is true, and yet the very root and nerve of the whole proceeding. You can give any conclusion a logical form. You always can imply a condition in a contract. But why do you imply it? It is because of some belief as to the practice of the community or of a class, or because of some opinion as to policy, or, in short, because of some attitude of yours upon a matter not capable of exact quantitative measurement, and therefore not capable of founding exact logical conclusions.
>
> Oliver Wendell Holmes Jnr[1]

The collection of essays in this book attests to the array of research methodologies that are used to research the law. This chapter examines the doctrinal methodology which many lawyers consider best typifies a distinctly legal approach to research. Legal research skills have been identified as a core skill for lawyers,[2] and within the profession, such skills are regarded as synonymous

* My thanks to John Pyke for comments on the manuscript and to Edward Bowden for work on the brainstorming diagram.

1 O. Wendell Holmes Jnr, 'The Path of the Law', *Harvard Law Review* 10, 1897, 457.
2 See, generally, T. Hutchinson, *Legal Research in Law Firms*, Buffalo, New York: W. S. Hein, 1994, ch. 3; MSJ Keys Young Planners, *Legal Research and Information Needs of Legal Practitioners: Discussion Paper*, Surrey Hills, New South Wales: MSJ Keys Young, 1992; A. Sherr, *Solicitors and their Skills: A Study of the Viability of Different Research Methods for Collating and Categorising the Skills Solicitors Utilise in their Professional Work*, London: Law Society, 1991; K. Economides and J. Smallcombe, *Preparatory Skills Training for Trainee Solicitors*, London: Law Society, 1991; D. Benthall-Nietzel, 'An Empirical Investigation of the Relationship between Lawyering Skills and Legal Education', *Kentucky Law Journal* 63, 1975, 373; R. A. D. Schwartz, 'The Relative Importance of Skills used by Attorneys', *Golden Gate*

with the doctrinal research method. Good legal research skills are a necessary step in attaining the ability to 'think like a lawyer' and achieving valid legal reasoning outcomes.[3] For lawyers, therefore, the doctrinal method is an intuitive aspect of legal work.[4] Yet, as this chapter demonstrates, the doctrinal methodology is not without its detractors. There have been serious criticisms of the method put forward by exponents of the various critical legal theories, as well as a perception in some academic circles that the doctrinal research method is nothing more than mere 'scholarship' and as a result less compelling or respected than the research methods used by those in the sciences and social sciences.[5] Despite these attacks, and the incursions on the method posed by the

Law Review 3, 1973, 321–33; J. de Groot (1993) 'Producing a Competent Lawyer', DPhil thesis, University of Queensland, 199, 201; J. Smillie, 'Results of a Survey of Otago Law Graduates 1971–81', *Otago Law Review* 5(3), 1983, 442–57, 442–50; F. Zemans and V. Rosenblum, 'Preparation for the Practice of Law – the Views of the Practicing Bar', *American Bar Foundation Research Journal* 1, 1980, 3; L. L. Baird, 'A Survey of the Relevance of Legal Training to Law School Graduates', *Journal of Legal Education* 29, 1978, 264–73; The Committee on the Future of the Legal Profession (The Marre Committee), *A Time for Change: Report of the Committee*, 1988, 113; and J. Peden, 'Professional Legal Education and Skills Training for Australian Lawyers', *Australian Law Journal* 46, 1972, 157–67. And, more recently, Council of Australian Law Deans (CALD), *The CALD Standards for Australian Law Schools*, 2009, 3; Australian Learning and Teaching Council, *Learning and Teaching Academic Standards Project – Bachelor of Laws, Learning and Teaching Academic Standards Statement*, 2010, 11, 22; S. Christensen and S. Kift, 'Graduate Attributes and Legal Skills: Integration or Disintegration?', *Legal Education Review* 11(2), 2000, 207–37; and Australian Qualifications Framework Council for the Ministerial Council for Tertiary Education and Employment, 'Australian Qualifications Framework', http://www.aqf.edu.au/wp-content/uploads/2013/05/AQF-1st-Edition-July-2011.pdf (accessed 3 March 2017).

3 A quote from Professor Kingsfield in the film *The Paper Chase*: 'You come in here with a head full of mush and you leave thinking like a lawyer' (writer/director J. Bridges, Twentieth Century Fox, 1973), which was based on the novel by J. Jay Osborn, Jr, *The Paper Chase* (1970). See also, for example, L. O. N. Gantt II, 'Deconstructing Thinking Like a Lawyer: Analyzing the Cognitive Components of the Analytical Mind', *Campbell Law Review* 29, 2007, 413–81; I. Baghoomians, 'Review of F. Schauer, Thinking Like a Lawyer: A New Introduction to Legal Reasoning', *Sydney Law Review* 31, 2009, 499; M. Sanson, T. Anthony and D. Warwick, *Connecting with Law*, South Melbourne, Victoria: Oxford University Press, 2010, 10.

4 D. W. Vick, 'Interdisciplinarity and the Discipline of Law', *Journal of Law and Society* 31(2), 2004, 163, 177.

5 See, for example, the discussions in R. Cotterrell, 'Why Must Legal Ideas be Interpreted Sociologically?', *Journal of Law and Society* 25(2), 1998, 171, 173; and in J. M. Balkin, 'Interdisciplinarity as Colonization', *Washington and Lee Law Review* 53, 1996, 949–70.

growth in the use of non-doctrinal and interdisciplinary research work by lawyers, the argument put forward in this chapter is that the doctrinal method still necessarily forms the basis for most, if not all, legal research projects.[6] Valid research is built on sound foundations, so before embarking on any theoretical critique of the law or empirical study about the law in operation, it is incumbent on the researcher to verify the authority and status of the legal doctrine being examined. The way to accomplish this is by using a doctrinal legal research method. The first step prior to any empirical work is to check that the doctrine, properly interpreted, is being complied with, so the researcher can decide whether any perceived defects are a result of poor doctrine or lack of compliance with the doctrine.

This discussion commences with an examination of the history and basis of the doctrinal research methodology – what it is, who uses doctrinal research and for what purpose, followed by a consideration of the criticisms of this research method. This book uses the broad subject area of lay decision-makers in the legal system as a research example in order to facilitate the examination of research methodologies. Lay decision-makers include, for example, non-lawyer members on tribunals or justices of the peace. In this chapter, discussion is focused on 'the jury system' as an example of a pivotal group of lay decision-makers working within the legal system. The jury system as a topic is a 'resource-rich' area being well covered in the legal literature.[7] The jury system lends itself to a plethora of interesting research questions, some of which are best pursued using non-doctrinal methodologies, for example whether the institution works well in practice and how it can be changed.[8] Therefore, this chapter also canvases the steps required to refine a larger topic such as this into a feasible research project. This process includes uncovering your main objective in undertaking the research, together with any relevant goals or aims, and, most importantly, developing a guiding argument or hypothesis for the thesis.

The principal examples of doctrinal research on the jury chosen for discussion in this chapter are the Queensland Law Reform Commission (QLRC)

6 See the discussion in S. Bartie, 'The Lingering Core of Legal Scholarship', *Legal Studies* 30(3), 2010, 345–69, 351–52.
7 See, for example, the literature on juries extensively noted in P. Rogers, 'Supporting the Right to Fair Trial with Reforms to Jury Directions and Jury Selection', *Queensland Lawyer* 32(1), 2012, 26.
8 See N. Vidmar, 'Lay Decision-Makers in the Legal Process' in P. Cane and H. M. Kritzer (eds), *The Oxford Handbook of Empirical Legal Research*, Oxford: Oxford University Press, 2010.

Report and Discussion Paper on jury selection.[9] These reports commence with a doctrinal statement of the law on the jury system.[10] The reports present proposals for reform based on doctrinal research, as well as other research methodologies such as community consultation. However, the basis and beginning of the reports is of necessity a review of the secondary literature together with a statement of the law based on the primary sources. The main body of the discussion and recommendations in the reports then emanate from that solid doctrinal foundation.

The context for this discussion

Historically, the methodology lawyers use to determine the law has been the subject of discussion within the legal community, with conversation in recent years moving beyond the doctrinal methodology to encompass the challenges and pitfalls of multidisciplinary, interdisciplinary and comparative research. A workshop at the University of Canberra in 1995, for example, dealt with research on corporate law using various methodologies such as comparative legal research, law and economics, historical methods and theoretical critique.[11] In some ways that subject-specific approach mirrors the objective of this present collection of essays, in that here we are investigating the variety of methods that can be used to undertake legal research on 'the role of lay decision-makers in the legal process'. In 2009, the Research Group for the Methodology of Law and Legal Research at Tilburg University organised a similar workshop to examine the use of doctrinal and non-doctrinal methodologies to enhance legal research outcomes.[12] Both of those academic workshops aimed to extend the methodologies dialogue beyond the core doctrinal research method.

The approach taken in the Canberra workshop was innovative in the Australian context of the mid-1990s. Legal education at that time was

---

9 See, for example: QLRC, 'A Review of Jury Selection', Report No. 68, February 2011; QLRC, 'A Review of Jury Selection', Discussion Paper WP No. 69, June 2010, http://www.qlrc.qld.gov.au/ (accessed 3 March 2017).
10 See, in particular, QLRC, Report No. 68, Chapter 3.
11 The papers from that one-day workshop on corporate law research methods and theories organised by the National Centre for Corporate Law and Policy Research and the Corporate Law Teachers' Association were published in a special issue of the *Canberra Law Review* – 'Special Issue on Corporate Law Research Methods and Theory', *Canberra Law Review* 3(1), 1996.
12 The revised papers were included in an edited text – M. Van Hoecke, *Methodologies of Legal Research: Which Kind of Method for What Kind of Discipline?*, Oxford: Hart Publishing, 2011.

predominantly 'black letter' with a particular focus on doctrinal study at most of the law schools.[13] Up until the early 1990s, legal research training, when it was present in the curriculum, tended to focus on legal bibliography, that is, how to use the research sources in order to locate the primary materials of the law – the legislation and case law.[14] Legal research texts also followed this bibliographic model.[15] In that era, the lawyer's research tools were dense, and students needed initiation in using the hardcopy sources in order to be able to locate legal documents. This step was involved, and acted as a precursor to engaging with the literature and analysing the law. Thankfully, this threshold step of locating the law has become less arduous and time-consuming as a result of the technological revolution that has taken place in the last two decades.

In the late 1980s, the Wrens, writing primarily for the US market, highlighted the need to move away from simply teaching law students about 'how to use' the research sources.[16] The Wrens proposed an instructional method that focused on 'the legal research process (i.e. gathering and analysing facts, identifying and organising legal issues, finding legal authorities, reading and synthesising authorities, and determining whether the law is still valid)'.[17] They explained that 'through process-oriented instruction, students acquire

13 The term 'black letter' refers to research about the law included in legislation and case law. It is defined in B. Gardner, *Black's Law Dictionary*, St Paul, MN: Westlaw International, 2009, as: 'One or more legal principles that are old, fundamental, and well settled.' In addition, the definition notes: 'The term refers to the law printed in books set in Gothic type, which is very bold and black.'

14 See, generally, T. Hutchinson, 'Where to Now? The 2002 Australasian Research Skills Training Survey', *Legal Education Review* 14(2), 2004, 63–91.

15 E. Campbell, P. Lee and J. Tooher, *Legal Research: Materials and Methods*, Sydney: LBC Information Services, 1996; J. Castel, *The Practical Guide to Canadian Legal Research*, Scarborough, Ontario: Carswell, 1996; P. Clinch, *Using a Law Library*, London: Blackstone, 2001; C. Cook et al., *Laying Down the Law*, Sydney: Butterworths, 2001; J. Jacobstein, R. Mersky and D. Dunn, *Fundamentals of Legal Research*, New York: Foundation Press, 2002; A. Mitchell and T. Voon, *Legal Research Manual*, North Ryde, New South Wales: LBC Information Services, 2000; I. Nemes and G. Coss, *Effective Legal Research*, Chatswood, New South Wales: Butterworths, 2001; A. Sloan, *Basic Legal Research: Tools and Strategies*, New York: Aspen Publishers, 2003; P. Thomas, *Dane and Thomas, How to Use a Law Library: An Introduction to Legal Skills*, London: Sweet & Maxwell, 2001; and R. Watt, *Concise Legal Research*, Annandale, New South Wales: Federation Press, 2004.

16 C. G. Wren and J. R. Wren, 'The Teaching of Legal Research', *Law Library Journal* 80, 1988, 7–61; C. G. Wren and J. R. Wren, 'Reviving Legal Research: A Reply to Berring and Vanden Heuvel', *Law Library Journal* 82(3), 1990, 463–93, 466.

17 Wren and Wren, 'Reviving Legal Research', 466.

not a narrow conception of how to use law books, but a broad understanding of how to draw creatively and comprehensively on various law books in developing a problem-solving strategy'.[18] In doing this, they highlighted the importance of providing training for law students in research methodology or process rather than simply focusing on an ability to use the reference sources. Since that time, technology and the Internet have resulted in researchers having the ability to access an overabundance of legal materials. By and large, these sources are full text and poorly indexed. Good planning and methodology are therefore even more essential for efficient legal research.

What do we mean by doctrinal research?

What, then, is doctrinal research? Doctrinal research lies at the heart of any lawyer's task because it is the research process used to identify, analyse and synthesise the content of the law. The term 'doctrinal' is derived from the Latin 'doctrina', which means instruction, knowledge or learning,[19] but the word 'doctrine' has many derivations and layers of meaning. Another explanation of the term 'doctrinal' is that it emanates from the 'doctrine' of precedent in that 'legal rules take on the quality of being doctrinal because they are not just casual or convenient norms, but because they are meant to be rules which apply consistently and which evolve organically and slowly'.[20] Doctrine has been defined as 'a synthesis of rules, principles, norms, interpretive guidelines and values', which 'explains, makes coherent or justifies a segment of the law as part of a larger system of law'.[21] In this method, the essential features of the legislation and case law are examined critically and then all the relevant elements are combined or synthesised to establish an arguably correct and complete statement of the law on the matter in hand.

Legal training developed from a rhetorical tradition handed down from the Greek and Roman philosophers. The Catholic monasteries, the main centres of learning during the Middle Ages, kept this tradition alive. The first university in Bologna was established around 1088 as a centre for the study of canon law, and instruction initially took place in Latin. According to the history of legal training in the medieval universities, doctrinal textbooks were used at that time – with Aristotle being studied in the faculty of arts and Justinian in

18 *Ibid.*
19 T. Hutchinson and N. Duncan, 'Defining the Doctrinal', *Deakin Law Review* 17(1), 2012, 84.
20 *Ibid.*, at 85.
21 T. Mann, *Australian Law Dictionary*, South Melbourne, Victoria: Oxford University Press, 2010, 197.

law.[22] In Europe, the universities concentrated on teaching civil law, and prior to codification in the nineteenth century, learned writings, or 'doctrine', were fundamental sources of law.[23] It was not until Blackstone's lectures at Oxford between 1753 and 1765, which were later published as the *Commentaries*, that an attempt was made to document and teach English common law in Britain.[24] This method, including the 'inductive pedagogy of teaching from cases', was further developed in the late nineteenth century by Christopher Langdell at Harvard University.[25] Doctrinal researchers in common law jurisdictions continue to undertake this process of analysis aimed at incorporating new elements of the law, whether legislation or principles from recent case law, into the existing system of law. Doctrinal researchers undertake a constant search for legal coherence.

Despite the differences in context and meaning between the use of the term 'doctrine', Van Gestel and Micklitz have identified three core features of doctrinal research, 'both in European countries and even across the Atlantic in the U.S.'.[26] The most important characteristic is that in doctrinal work, 'arguments are derived from authoritative sources, such as existing rules, principles, precedents, and scholarly publications'. Secondly, 'the law somehow represents a system' so that 'through the production of general and defeasible theories, legal doctrine aims to present the law as a coherent net of principles, rules, meta-rules and exceptions, at different levels of abstraction', and, thirdly, 'decisions in individual cases are supposed to exceed arbitrariness because they have to (be) fit into the system. Deciding in hard cases implies that existing rules will be stretched or even replaced but always in such a way that in the end the system is coherent again.'[27]

These cornerstones of the method are also identified in the definitions of legal method emanating from the various government and institutional reviews of law schools. In 1987, the Pearce Committee reviewed the research emanating from Australian law schools. The Committee categorised this research as encompassing doctrinal research, and in addition, reform-oriented

22 M. Asztalos, 'The Faculty of Theology' in *A History of the University in Europe*, Vol. 1, Cambridge: Cambridge University Press, 1992, 409.

23 J. Farrar, *Legal Reasoning*, Pyrmont, New South Wales: Lawbook Co., 2010, 191.

24 W. Blackstone, *Commentaries on the Laws of England in Four Books*, London: A. Strahan, 1809.

25 B. Kimball, *The Inception of Modern Professional Education: C.C. Langdell, 1826–1906*, Chapel Hill, NC: University of North Carolina Press, 2009.

26 R. van Gestel and H. Micklitz, *Revitalizing Doctrinal Legal Research in Europe: What about Methodology?* (European University Institute Working Papers Law 2011/05), 2011, 26.

27 *Ibid.*

and theoretical research. The Committee defined doctrinal research as 'Research which provides a systematic exposition of the rules governing a particular legal category, analyses the relationship between [the] rules, explains areas of difficulty and, perhaps, predicts future developments'.[28] Both the other categories of research identified by the Pearce Committee include aspects of the doctrinal. Reform-oriented research is that which 'intensively evaluates the adequacy of existing rules and which recommends changes to any rules found wanting'.[29] Similarly, theoretical research 'fosters a more complete understanding of the conceptual bases of legal principles and of the combined effects of a range of rules and procedures that touch on a particular area of activity'.[30] In most instances, a researcher would need to use doctrinal research to identify the pertinent law (legislation, rules and principles) before, for example, embarking on any empirical work on the policy or context behind the implementation of the law, or the subsequent effects of the law on the community.

Doctrinal research is intrinsically important to the discipline of law.[31] The 2009 Council of Australian Law Deans (CALD) Standards state that students must be able to achieve 'the intellectual and practical skills needed to research and analyse the law from primary sources, and to apply the findings of such work to the solution of legal problems, and the ability to communicate these findings, both orally and in writing'.[32] Similarly, Martha Minow, Dean of Harvard Law School, has indicated that 'doctrinal restatement' and 'recasting' are some of the intellectual contributions achieved through legal scholarship:[33]

'Doctrinal Restatement' – 'Organize and reorganize case law into coherent elements, categories, and concepts'; 'Acknowledge distinction between settled and emerging law'; and 'identify difference between majority and "preferred" or "better" practices with an explanation of the criteria utilized'.

'Recasting Project' – 'Gather more than one "line" of cases across doctrinal fields and show why they belong together or expose unjustified discrepancies'; and 'offer a new framework or paradigm'.

---

28 D. Pearce, E. Campbell and D. Harding, *Australian Law Schools: A Discipline Assessment for the Commonwealth Tertiary Education Commission*, Canberra: Australian Government Publishing Service, 1987.
29 *Ibid.*
30 *Ibid.*
31 Consultative Group on Research and Education in Law, *Law and Learning: Report to the Social Sciences and the Humanities Research Council of Canada* (The Arthurs Report) (Information Division of the Social Sciences and Humanities Research Council of Canada), 1983.
32 CALD, *The CALD Standards for Australian Law Schools*, at 10.
33 M. Minow, 'Archetypal Legal Scholarship – A Field Guide', *Journal of Legal Education*, 63(1), 2013, 65–69.

But it is the CALD description which most succinctly 'delineates the sophisticated higher level thinking which is the hallmark of doctrinal work' and permeates all quality legal research.[34] The CALD 'Statement on the Nature of Legal Research' states:[35]

> To a large extent, it is the doctrinal aspect of law that makes legal research distinctive and provides an often under-recognised parallel to 'discovery' in the physical sciences. Doctrinal research, at its best, involves rigorous analysis and creative synthesis, the making of connections between seemingly disparate doctrinal strands, and the challenge of extracting general principles from an inchoate mass of primary materials. The very notion of 'legal reasoning' is a subtle and sophisticated jurisprudential concept, a unique blend of deduction and induction, that has engaged legal scholars for generations, and is a key to understanding the mystique of the legal system's simultaneous achievement of constancy and change, especially in the growth and development of the common law. Yet this only underlines that doctrinal research can scarcely be quarantined from broader theoretical and institutional questions. If doctrinal research is a distinctive part of legal research, that distinctiveness permeates every other aspect of legal research for which the identification, analysis and evaluation of legal doctrine is a basis, starting point, platform or underpinning.

The CALD statement makes some important points about doctrinal research. It emphasises that this research method is equivalent to scientific research in that it is intellectually rigorous when undertaken properly. The statement describes doctrinal research as involving 'creative synthesis', together with the challenge of extracting principle from diverse sources of the law. The statement echoes Oliver Wendell Holmes' views regarding the importance of the expert use of logical analysis and the 'unique blend of deduction and induction' which go to make up the doctrinal research process.[36] It also underscores the pivotal importance of doctrinal research to the lawyer's task. The 'conceptual analysis of law'[37] recognised in this statement lies at the heart of 'black letter law',[38] and is the basis upon which legal scholarship is built.

---

34 Hutchinson and Duncan, 'Defining the Doctrinal', at 104.
35 CALD, 'Statement on the Nature of Legal Research', 2005, 3, http://www.cald. asn.au/docs/cald%20statement%20on%20the%20nature%20of%20legal%20 research%20-%202005.pdf (accessed 3 March 2017).
36 Holmes Jr, 'The Path of the Law', at 457.
37 T. Mann, *Australian Law Dictionary*, South Melbourne, Victoria: Oxford University Press, 2010, 501.
38 Bartie, 'The Lingering Core of Legal Scholarship', at 345, 350.

Variations in the doctrinal method

The degree of complexity of doctrinal legal research varies, with 'the more simple versions of that research being the necessary building blocks for the more sophisticated ones'.[39] Research takes place at various levels – and the following is by no means a determinate list. There is the research law students undertake for assignments. There is research undertaken by law librarians either to locate specific documents or to answer reference questions or to provide bibliographies and to locate specific documents to assist others' analysis. Postgraduate students undertake research for research project papers and higher degree theses. Law academics undertake research to ensure their teaching materials are up to date for their students, but they also research in order to discuss new or difficult issues with their peers by way of conference papers. Academics undertake doctrinal (and theoretical and non-doctrinal) funded and unfunded research either alone or as part of interdisciplinary research teams investigating aspects of law in society. Lawyers research and write monographs, peer-reviewed journal articles, practitioner information pieces, submissions to government and reports for government and corporations. Legal practitioners undertake research to ensure the advice they provide to their clients is based on a current and correct reading of the law. And judges read and analyse the law in order to formulate wise decisions and worthy precedents.

The simple problem-based doctrinal research methodology used by practitioners and undergraduate students adheres to a fundamental pattern also followed to some extent in aspects of higher-level research. It is predicated on efficiency and the solving of a specific legal problem in the minimum amount of time and usually includes the following steps:

1 assembling relevant facts;
2 identifying the legal issues;
3 analysing the issues with a view to searching for the law;
4 locating and reading background information (including legal dictionaries, legal encyclopaedias, textbooks, law reform reports, policy papers, looseleaf services, journal articles);
5 locating and reading the primary sources (including legislation and delegated legislation and case law);
6 synthesizing all the issues in context; and
7 arriving at a tentative conclusion.

39 M. Van Hoecke, *Methodologies of Legal Research: Which Kind of Method for What Kind of Discipline?*, Oxford: Hart Publishing, 2011, vi.

This research design, to some extent, mirrors that of a social science study, but with one important exception. The information or data collected is not quantifiable, but rather it is legislation and case law – the primary materials of the law – as well as relevant secondary commentary. As a result, the information-based or 'library-based' research design, which is often directed to identifying the resolution to a specific legal problem, has had a detrimental effect on the status of the doctrinal methodology in the broader (interdisciplinary) academic context. Therefore, some argue that the doctrinal methodology is simply 'legal puzzle solving', and little more than a process used in order to achieve pragmatic solutions. Pragmatism may play a role in problem-solving, but of necessity it is based on sound legal analysis and a defensible or arguably correct view of the law.

Like all research, doctrinal research requires a critical analysis of the existing literature to inform the researcher of 'what is known and not known' about the topic.[40] In other disciplines, secondary research (also known as desk research) involves the summary, collation and/or synthesis of existing research for a literature review rather than primary research, where data are collected from research subjects or through the conduct of experiments.[41] However, the scholarship involved in undertaking doctrinal research is much more than a literature review of secondary sources.[42] In doctrinal research, the primary data consist of the sources of the law. Primary research is the intricate step of locating and then 'reading, analysing and linking' the new information to the known body of law.[43]

The doctrinal method is normally a two-part process involving both locating the sources of the law and then interpreting and analysing the text. In undertaking a doctrinal study, the researcher must initially access 'the law'. Depending on the topic, this step might simply involve locating one section of the Criminal Code or, at the other end of the spectrum, it could involve months of detailed work locating current and historical legislation along with administrative regulations, covering three or four different but related legal subjects, together with any existing judicial interpretation of those rules and statutes. Once located, the researcher needs to read and analyse the material to

---

40 M. Walter, *Social Research Methods*, South Melbourne, Victoria: Oxford University Press, 2010, 485.

41 S. Crouch and M. Housden, *Marketing Research for Managers; The Marketing Series; Chartered Institute of Marketing*, Boston, MA: Butterworth-Heinemann, 2003, 19.

42 A. Fink, 'Conducting Research Literature Review: From the Internet to Paper', in M. McConville and W. H. Chui (eds), *Research Methods for Law*, Edinburgh: Edinburgh University Press, 2007, 22–23.

43 T. Hutchinson, *Researching and Writing in Law*, 3rd edn, Pyrmont, New South Wales: Lawbook Co., 2010, 38.

determine a meaning and pattern so as to condense the writing to its essence. This step involves the use of reasoning and problem-solving skills such as deductive logic, inductive reasoning and analogy – the 'common law devices which allow lawyers to make sense of complex legal questions'.[44]

In making sense of the complexities of new court decisions, the doctrinal researcher must fit new material into the existing legal framework because 'one of the basic claims of or assumptions of the black-letter tradition is that legal doctrine possesses logical coherence'[45] or an underlying rationale.[46] This means that 'one vital task for students conducting dissertation research from a black letter approach is to carefully disclose the existence and operation of this underlying systematic order, which both integrates and "makes sense of" the otherwise unwieldy mass of case-law decisions'.[47] New fact situations must be integrated with the relevant law and underlying legal principles applicable to a legal area. Some suggest that a way of achieving this is through using mental algorithms:

> the optimal algorithm will at each step ask the question which if negative eliminates the most remaining possibilities, and which step by step asks for each material fact necessary to support the legal conclusion that a particular black letter rule or principle applies or does not apply to the problem presented.[48]

This process may be successful at times. However, if legal reasoning was always this exact, there would be no dissenting judgments in the higher appellate courts. Hofheinz concedes this point – one that every common lawyer appreciates:[49]

> Only rarely will there be a rule that directly and unambiguously determines the outcome of the problem presented. Seldom will the applicable black letter rule (precedent) have been determined in a case with identical facts and circumstances and near in time ('on all fours') to the problem

44 I. Baghoomians, 'Review of Frederick Schauer, *Thinking like a Lawyer: A New Introduction to Legal Reasoning*, Boston, MA: Harvard University Press, 2009', *Sydney Law Review* 31, 2009, 499.
45 M. Salter and J. Mason, *Writing Law Dissertations: An Introduction and Guide to the Conduct of Legal Research*, Harlow: Longman, 2007, 68.
46 *Ibid.*, at 75.
47 *Ibid.*, at 68.
48 W. Hofheinz, 'Legal Analysis', 1997, available via http://archive.is/www. hofheinzlaw.com (accessed 20 March 2017).
49 *Ibid.*

under consideration. Seldom will legislation or regulations unambiguously determine the outcome of problems which arise.

Reasonable people can differ regarding the outcome which should arise from particular facts when no rule unambiguously determines the outcome. It is essential that you be able to determine the differences between your analysis, and that of another choosing a different outcome. The questions you develop to apply the facts to the black letter law can enable you to identify agreement and disagreement in analysis and focus your attention on resolving disagreement.

There are other accepted ways of approaching legal discussion. In areas covered by legislation, the researcher must consider the accepted rules of statutory interpretation. In considering criminal law in the Code states, the doctrinal researcher needs to begin with a statement of the elements of the offence, or the requirements for an excuse or defence, before discussing any judicial consideration or legal definitions or tests propounded in the courts.

The solutions to any legal question or dilemma are rarely unambiguous, and as Christopher McCrudden has commented: 'If legal academic work shows anything, it shows that an applicable legal norm on anything but the most banal question is likely to be complex, nuanced and contested.'[50] Richard Posner also observed that:[51]

> The messy work product of the judges and legislators requires a good deal of tidying up, of synthesis, analysis, restatement, and critique. These are intellectually demanding tasks, requiring vast knowledge and the ability . . . to organize dispersed, fragmentary, prolix, and rebarbative material.

There is more potential to increase the scope of investigation so as to achieve a greater depth of enquiry with academic and higher degree legal research. At that level, researchers have different time constraints or practical limitations than practitioners, and there are more opportunities to confront the conundrums and uncertainties at the frontiers of the law. Not all doctrinal research begins with a legal problem. Doctrinal research may be used to determine the law on a specific topic or in a broader legal geographic jurisdictional context. Law reform and comparative perspectives may be used to examine the law in a wider framework. At the higher levels of analysis, the doctrinal research can provide significant challenges.

50 C. McCrudden, 'Legal Research and the Social Sciences', *Law Quarterly Review* 122, 2006, 632–50, 648.
51 R. Posner, 'In Memoriam: Bernard D, Meltzer (1914–2007)', *University of Chicago Law Review* 74, 2007, 409–45, 435, 437.

In addition, the value of the outcomes of the doctrinal study depends on the expertise, knowledge and experience of the individual researcher. The task of doctrinal legal research is commonly acknowledged as requiring immense skill. Doctrinal research requires the use of specific language. Words can have special legal meanings. The definitions of legal terms are often at odds with their use in everyday social language. Terms derived from Law French are used as shorthand for quite abstruse legal principles. Doctrinal analysis requires an ability to work within accepted discipline standards and rules to achieve a high level of interpretation and critique. Researchers must be able to identify the principle or *ratio decidendi* which is often buried in the verbiage of multiple decisions within a single judgment. The researcher needs a recognised skill set. Therefore, the value of the research output is to a great extent predicated on the author's identity. The esteem and reputation of the doctrinal 'voice' is paramount in judging quality, and the quality of the outcome of the research can vary according to the expertise of the individual scholar. It is in many respects a hermeneutic discipline where scholars are interpreting authoritative texts. Therefore, the anonymity and lack of order and indexing of the Internet poses a risk to researchers relying on interpretations located online. John Farrar has warned that 'we are at risk of entering a new Dark Age when reputation has been replaced by fame, and fame is ephemeral'.[52] Simply because an interpretation or text is available and published on the Internet does not mean that it is correct or authoritative. The value given to doctrinal research and writing is still dependent on the identity and reputation of the researcher.

Criticism of the doctrinal method

As with all research endeavours, the individual doctrinal scholar's theoretical stance towards the topic can be a pervasive influence in determining the questions being researched. Unfortunately, though, the doctrinal researcher's underlying views are often not articulated. Pauline Westerman has argued that within the dominant paradigm, 'the legal system itself functions as a theoretical framework that selects facts and highlights them as legally relevant ones',[53] so that in fact the researcher's view is narrowly confined within the box labelled 'law' and not concerned with the effects of the law in the world external to the black letter box. Westerman suggests that the function of

---

52 J. Farrar, *Legal Reasoning*, Pyrmont, New South Wales: Lawbook Co., 2010, 205; see also R. Posner, *Cardozo: A Study in Reputation*, Chicago: University of Chicago Press, 1990.

53 P. Westerman, 'Open or Autonomous? The Debate on Legal Methodology as a Reflection of the Debate on Law', in M. Van Hoecke (ed.), *Methodologies of Legal Research: Which Kind of Method for What Kind of Discipline?* Oxford: Hart Publishing, 2011, 91.

the theoretical framework of research, 'namely to provide a guideline and a perspective from which the object can be described in a meaningful way, is exercised by the legal system itself'.[54] Westerman views 'legal doctrine' as research which draws on the legal system 'as the main supplier of concepts, categories and criteria'.[55] The legal doctrinal researcher therefore seeks to 'give sense and to order new cases or developments' rather than to understand the legal system as a whole.[56] This she distinguishes from research that studies law 'from an independent theoretical framework, which consists of concepts, categories and criteria that are not primarily borrowed from the legal system itself' and which includes 'historical studies, socio-legal research, philosophy, political theory and economy'.[57]

In its purist form, therefore, doctrinal research takes an insider's view of the law. This view – that the law is able to be studied in isolation from its context – emanates from the common law's underlying liberal philosophy. This view is intrinsic to the common law which developed in England, and which was imported into legal systems in Australia, Canada, New Zealand and the United States. This philosophy includes ideas of the priority of the individual, the need for a distinction to be made between regulation of the public as compared to the private spheres, limited government, liberty and freedom from individual interference, as well as personal autonomy, equality before the law and the importance of the rule of law. These values mould the legal system that has developed in these jurisdictions and other common law legal systems. There are various dimensions to liberal theory, but it is basically a conservative view of the world and therefore it is not surprising that legal critique tends to be restrained. As Salter and Mason have commented, 'it is important not to exaggerate the critical dimension to black letter analysis because, on balance, such analysis tends towards conservatism rather than radicalism'.[58]

Oliver Wendell Holmes Jr also viewed research in the law as being research from an insider's point of view. As he wrote in *The Common Law*:

> The business of the jurist is to make known the content of the law; that is, to work upon it from within, or logically, arranging and distributing it, in order, from its stemmum genus to its infima species, so far as practicable.[59]

---

54 *Ibid.*, at 90.
55 *Ibid.*, at 94.
56 *Ibid.*, at 91.
57 *Ibid.*, at 94.
58 Salter and Mason, *Writing Law Dissertations*, at 100.
59 O. Holmes Jr, 'The Common Law', 2000, 219, http://www.gutenberg.org/files/2449/2449-h/2449-h.htm (accessed 3 March 2017).

This approach has been echoed by other commentators; for example, N. E. Simmonds refers to the 'corpus of rules, principles, doctrines and concepts used as a basis for legal reasoning and justification'[60] that constitute legal doctrine and asserts that 'legal science, being itself a body of practices, can be understood only by reference to its own self-conception'.[61]

This stance exposes the serious weaknesses in the doctrinal methodology. William Twining pointed out that the central weakness of the expository tradition 'is that typically it takes as its starting point and its main focus of attention rules of law, without systematic or regular reference to the context of problems they are supposed to resolve, the purposes they were intended to serve or the effects they in fact have'.[62] At times, doctrinal researchers do no more than 'work the rules' in isolation from practice or the theory under-lying the rules, and without due consideration for how the rules might be improved or reformed. The research is not always grounded in the practice of the courts or the policy discussed in Parliament. Using this method some researchers may consider that the law can be examined effectively in a social, political, moral, economic and theoretical vacuum. Rules and case law can be reviewed by a doctrinal researcher from an undisclosed and seemingly objective viewpoint that is disguising a personal attitude which too often is deeply conservative and imbued with positivism and liberal theory. Critical legal theorists and postmodernists, of course, are quick to point out that rules can never be neutral or the law objective.[63] At its worst, doctrinal research can veer into the realms of formalism so that the views taken are excessively dogmatic and rigid.[64] Social justice, economic theory and politics are all extrinsic considerations.

Modern scholars, most notably Roger Cotterrell, would argue that true legal scholarship must also entail a sociological understanding of law.[65] Such a view would involve, for example, a study of the law in practice taken from a

60 N. E. Simmonds, *The Decline of Juridical Reason: Doctrine and Theory in the Legal Order*, Manchester, Dover, NH: Manchester University Press, 1984, 1.

61 *Ibid.*, at 30.

62 W. Twining, *Taylor Lectures 1975 Academic Law and Legal Development*, Lagos: University of Lagos Faculty of Law, 1976, 20.

63 G. Simpson and H. Charlesworth, 'Objecting to Objectivity: The Radical Challenge to Legal Liberalism', in R. Hunter, R. Ingleby and R. Johnstone (eds), *Thinking about Law: Perspectives on the History, Philosophy and Sociology of Law*, Sydney: Allen & Unwin, 1995, 86–132.

64 Salter and Mason, *Writing Law Dissertations*, at 112–18 provide a list of 42 criticisms of 'black-letter methodology'.

65 Cotterrell, 'Why Must Legal Ideas be Interpreted Sociologically?', 171–92; see also C. M. Campbell, 'Legal Thought and Juristic Values', *British Journal of Law and Society* 1(1), 1974, 13–30.

standpoint outside the legal system, and using scientific or social science methodologies.[66] There have been passionate pleas for 'more emphasis on multidisciplinary legal research' and 'an enrichment of traditional legal scholarship with empirical methods or economic insights'.[67] Eric Posner has gone so far as to argue that 'doctrinal legal research is dead', and that legal academics should be engaging in 'law and . . . research'.[68] Posner Senior has consistently taken a contrary view, and argued that doctrinal research 'is important for the vitality of the legal system and of greater social value than much esoteric interdisciplinary legal scholarship'.[69] Rob van Gestel and Hans-W. Micklitz recognise that the negative image concerning legal doctrine that Eric Posner and others share:

> has much to do with the formalism and the strong divide between the law as it is and the law as it ought to be, which are all too often associated with a dogmatic approach towards academic legal research. Especially interdisciplinarians often perceive doctrinalists to be intellectually rigid, inflexible, formalistic, and inward-looking. Other accusations include that doctrinalists show an unhealthy preoccupation with technicalities, often focus on unimportant topics, repeat existing knowledge, and fail to connect law to life by assessing the real world consequences of doctrinal frameworks. Proceeding otherwise would, according to Deborah Rhode, require significant time, money, and non-legal expertise, which she believes most authors of doctrinal work are more than happy to avoid. As a consequence, many doctrinal works are 'glutted with theory and starved for facts', according to Rhode. Pierre Schlag goes even further. He feels that much of the doctrinal research in the U.S. can be labelled as 'case law journalism'. Many scholarly legal publications offer little more than comments on recent court rulings.[70]

But by and large most doctrinal scholars would agree that the immediate first step is to understand the content of the law before being concerned about its derivation, or effects on society. As Ian Ramsay comments on this point:

---

66 W. Lucy, 'Abstraction and the Rule of Law', *Oxford Journal of Legal Studies* 29(3), 2009, 481–509.
67 Van Gestel and Micklitz, *Revitalizing Doctrinal Legal Research in Europe*, at 1.
68 *Ibid.*
69 *Ibid.* See also Richard A. Posner, 'The State of Legal Scholarship Today: A Comment on Schlag', *The Georgetown Law Journal* 97, 2009, 845–55; and Richard A. Posner, *How Judges Think*, Cambridge, MA: Harvard University Press, 2008, 211.
70 Van Gestel and Micklitz, *Revitalizing Doctrinal Legal Research in Europe*, at 2; footnotes omitted.

One of the disincentives to undertaking empirical research is that the researcher needs to spend sufficient time in order to be reasonably on top of the subject before commencing the empirical research . . . All of us no doubt spend a significant period of time reading recent cases, statutory amendments and some portion of the enormous quantity of corporate law articles published in any year. All of this is very demanding and necessarily precedes empirical research.[71]

Take as an example a research project examining the practice of plea bargaining in Australia. Such a project is necessarily predicated on the identification of the underpinning of the practice within the rules of evidence and procedure. So, it is not surprising that Van Gestel and Micklitz reiterate, 'if doctrinal legal research has ever been dead, it has until today always succeeded in rising from the grave'.[72]

Refining the topic and planning the project

A research and writing 'plan' exists on two levels. First, there is the 'idea plan' – which consists of the topic you are writing about, the aspect of the main subject you intend developing, your hypothesis and your arguments. The second plan, the 'research plan', 'hangs off' the first. Once you decide what you need, the second plan maps out how you are going to locate the relevant information – basically your research methodology.[73]

Determining the research methodology is really the second step in the research process. The first step is the idea plan. Harking back to the example of the lay decision-makers who fulfil such important functions within the legal process, none are more important than the citizens who are called to serve on jury panels. As a research topic, the jury system is a broad and 'research-rich' area with extensive coverage of every aspect, from its history in English law,[74] to US studies on jurimetrics.[75] Nevertheless, the engaged researcher is always able to perceive opportunities for additional perspectives.

---

71 I. Ramsay, 'Why Is There So Little Empirical Corporate Law Research? A Comment', *Canberra Law Review* 3(1), 1996, 110–12.
72 Van Gestel and Micklitz, *Revitalizing Doctrinal Legal Research in Europe*, at 5.
73 Hutchinson, *Researching and Writing in Law*, at 137.
74 P. Devlin, *Trial by Jury*, London: Stevens, 1956.
75 Jurimetrics is the study of law and science. 'Used primarily in academia to mean a strictly empirical approach to the law, the term *jurimetrics* originated in the 1960s as the use of computers in law practice began to revolutionize the areas of legal research, evidence analysis, and data management. A neologism whose roots suggest Jurisprudence and measurement, it was popularized by the American Bar

The process of choosing a research topic consists of gradually refining the issues to isolate those most in need of further exploration and discussion. There are a number of threshold queries. Is the research on juries to be conducted within the framework of the criminal law or the civil law? Is the research to concentrate on the methods juries use to arrive at their decisions, on the social make-up of the juries or the methods barristers use to decide which jurors on the panel to challenge so as to prevent a potential juror sitting on a particular case? The research topic needs to be tailored to the individual researcher's expertise and then refined so as to be able to be completed within the stipulated time period and resources.

There are a variety of techniques you can use to refine a broad research topic such as 'the jury system' so that it results in a research and writing project with worthwhile academic outcomes. Brainstorming is the most popular method used to 'kick-start' the creative process of generating ideas and solutions in order to refine the topic and set achievable research goals.[76] Brainstorming is a non-analytical way of setting out ideas and questioning the known and unknown aspects and the broad scope of projects in a non-judgmental fashion. Start with a blank piece of paper and write down anything you know or would like to know about the topic. At this stage, the general goal is to broaden the scope of the topic so that all the possible opportunities for further research are put on the table for discussion. At this point, you may find that you need to delve into the literature to at least scope the topic as widely as possible.

After you have filled the blank page (or several pages) with ideas and issues that push the boundaries of the topic, you might attempt to make obvious and not so obvious idea connections between the various issues. The 'brain-dump' of topics stimulates lateral thinking and unusual interconnectedness. Related issues can be grouped together for separate treatment. This brain-storming process can also be undertaken as a group project. If you are a research student, then your supervisor will assist in filling the whiteboard with additional ideas based on a more extensive knowledge from the literature of areas in need of reform and further articulation. If you are working alone, you may find it helpful to think about other people's views on the topic.

Association (ABA), whose quarterly *Jurimetrics Journal of Law, Science, and Technology* is a widely respected publication with an international focus', *The Free Dictionary*, http://legal-dictionary.thefreedictionary.com/Jurimetrics (accessed 3 March 2017). See, for example, A. Gelfand and H. Solomon, 'Considerations in Building Jury Behavior Models and in Comparing Jury Schemes: An Argument in Favor of 12-Member Juries', *Jurimetrics Journal* 17, 1977, 292–313; and J. R. Snortum et al., 'The Impact of an Aggressive Juror in Six- and Twelve-Member Juries', *Criminal Justice & Behavior* 3(3), 1976, 255–62.

76 *Ibid.*, at 137–38.

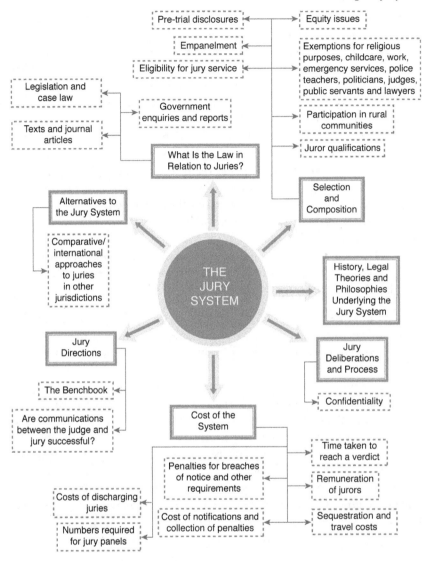

Figure 1.1: Brainstorming example

One way of doing this is to use Edward de Bono's 'Thinking Hats'.[77] This is a form of psychological role-play to coerce you, the researcher, into considering and understanding additional perspectives on your topic.

1   *White hat*: Thinking without bias. When you wear the white hat, you attempt to expunge any bias or value judgements from your view. You

---

77 E. de Bono, *Six Thinking Hats*, Toronto: Key Porter Books, 1985, 99.

become a computer and take a literal view of the world. You take a neutral, emotion-free or detached view of the situation.

2   *Red hat*: Thinking with emotion. When you put this hat on, you lay your emotions on the table. There is no need to justify your likes and dislikes. You lay bare your hunches, gut feelings and guesses based on experience.

3   *Black hat*: A negative view. The black hat gives free reign to pessimism and more critical views. This hat is usually not used first, but allows for a 'devil's advocate' approach that can often be very useful and constructive when working out the details of a plan. However, de Bono warns that 'Destruction is always much easier than construction'.

4   *Yellow hat*: An optimistic view. The yellow hat allows an opportunity for positive, constructive views on making things happen.

5   *Green hat*: Creativity and new ideas. The green hat forces lateral thinking or thinking 'outside the box'.

6   *Blue hat*: The big picture, pulling the issues together. The blue hat is the conductor who attempts to orchestrate, record and observe, and perhaps provides an overview of all the others.[78]

At its simplest level, this technique challenges you to recognise and intellectually engage with all the views on your subject including the emotional, negative and creative, alongside the optimistic, neutral and the broader 'big picture' view.

Idea generators or heuristics, such as the well-known 'who, how, what, when, where and why', are also effective.[79] Who serves on juries in the various jurisdictions? Does the legislation between the various jurisdictions in Australia or elsewhere vary to any great extent? And if so, why are there variations in the jury districts? How does a person come to be on the jury roll? What does a person need to do to be called up for jury service? How can a person be excused from serving on a jury? What is the role of the jury? When were juries first used? Where and in what jurisdictions are juries used? Historically why were juries used in the courts? Similarly, the searching questions widely attributed to Aristotle are effective idea generators:

•   Definition (What is it? What is the jury system?)
•   Comparison (What is it like and unlike? What is a jury like and unlike?)
•   Relationship (What caused it? What caused the jury system to be established?)
•   Testimony (What has been said about it? What has been written about the jury system?)

78 Hutchinson, *Researching and Writing in Law*, at 143.
79 *Ibid.*, at 139.

- Circumstance (What can come of it? How will a jury behave in different situations?)[80]

Constructing diagrammatic representations of the central issues and 'mind mapping' your topic also increases your ability to identify possible theories and solutions.[81] A legal project analysis matrix acknowledges all the varied views within the legal process beginning with the 'black letter' or content of the law as opposed to operational or theoretical aspects. It also flags the range of viable methodologies for the project – non-doctrinal as well as those based on doctrinal work.[82]

Using the quadrant, researchers can pursue the endless possibilities for researching the law and legal practice in relation to the jury system. Here are some examples for questions that might be appropriate for each of the quadrants:

Table 1.1: Legal project analysis matrix

	Critique	How would an ideal law in a particular area work in practice and what changes in motivations, behaviour and other actions would it need?	How might the relevant law be redesigned outside its existing frame of reference to create an ideal law?	What is the best theory for explaining the relevant law, why is it best, how does it explain things best?
Approaches to law	*Policy reform*	What must happen in practice to accommodate incremental changes or developments in the relevant law?	How might the relevant law be changed, reformed or developed within its existing frame of reference?	How might the theories explaining the relevant law be improved within their own frames of reference or in their application to the relevant law?
	Empirical/ doctrinal	What happens in practice in light of the relevant law?	What is the relevant law?	What theories explain the relevant law and how do they apply to it?
		Practical/operational dimension	Elements of law	Theoretical/conceptual dimension
		Content of law		

---

80 *Ibid.*, at 141.
81 *Ibid.*, at 144.
82 *Ibid.*, at 152.

The first three quadrants represent the law as it is written and practised, and the current theories or philosophies behind this situation.

Quadrant 1
'What happens in practice in light of the relevant law?'
Example: 'How do the rules relating to juries apply to persons residing within court jurisdictions?'

Quadrant 2
'What is the relevant law?'
Example: 'Who is qualified and liable to serve as a juror? Who is ineligible to serve as a juror? What legislative provisions cover the jury system?'

Quadrant 3
'What theories explain the relevant law and how do they apply to it?'[83]
Example: 'What theories explain the existence of the jury system and the development of the law relating to juries?'
The next three quadrants represent the issues that might arise in a context of reform or 'incremental' change.

Quadrant 4
'What must happen in practice to accommodate incremental changes or developments in the relevant law?'
Example: 'What practical changes must be implemented by the courts in order to accommodate changes in the law and procedures relating to juries?'

Quadrant 5
'How might the relevant law be changed, reformed or developed within its existing frame of reference?'
Example: 'What are the values and policy considerations which inform the development of the jury system? How can the jury system and process be reformed within the present framework?'

Quadrant 6
'How might the theories explaining the relevant law be improved within their own frames of reference or in their application to the relevant law?'[84]
Example: 'How might the theories on which the jury system is based be enhanced in light of the evolution of theories and newer theories such as, for example, therapeutic justice?'
The final three quadrants refer to an ideal law redesigned outside its existing framework and based on a revised theoretical premise.

83 *Ibid.*, at 48–49.
84 *Ibid.*

Quadrant 7
'How would an ideal law in a particular area work in practice and what changes in motivations, behaviour and other actions would it need?'
Example: 'Ideally how would an ideal decision-making process function in practice and what changes would be required in order for this to occur?'

Quadrant 8
'How might the relevant law be redesigned outside its existing frame of reference to create an ideal law?'
Example: 'How might the law be redesigned to create an ideal decision-making process? Would there be an ideal system to replace the jury?'

Quadrant 9
'What is the best theory for explaining the relevant law, why is it best and how does it explain things best?'[85]
Example: 'Is the legislation underlying the jury system fair and just or is it value ridden?'

Certainly, in order to achieve meaningful research objectives and research aims, or to formulate a valid doctrinal hypothesis, you need to gain sufficient familiarity and understanding of your research area. In order to achieve this depth of knowledge, you must clarify what research has been undertaken in the area, what questions other researchers have asked and assess the outcomes and results of their efforts. You must ascertain which legal areas or policies are still unclear or proving in some way problematic to practitioners, government or the public, and what type of research or information might be required to highlight any inadequacies.

This constitutes the literature review – 'a critical analysis of the existing research literature, theoretical and empirical'.[86] Any research needs a review of the secondary literature and commentary on the topic which is available from texts, journal articles, law reform commission reports, PhD theses, conference papers, online information and blogs, newspaper reports and so on. Obviously, this review takes place in stages. When you are first choosing the topic to research, you will be reading broadly and skimming the literature for ideas and an overall view of the work already completed. Once the research has a clear focus, you will need to be painstaking in your search for all the relevant and most recent publications and research activity currently under way. This

---

85 *Ibid.*
86 M. Walter, *Social Research Methods*, South Melbourne, Victoria: Oxford University Press, 2010, 485.

current awareness search is an ongoing process. Make sure you are included on all relevant mailing lists and communication sources and cultivate a good network of like-minded scholars.

When the area of law has been fine-tuned sufficiently and there is a narrower research topic, the next step is to determine your overall objective in undertaking the research. What is it that you hope to achieve in researching this topic? Have you more specific aims or goals that you want to address in doing the research? Most importantly, what is your guiding argument, your tentative hypothesis? In order to achieve this objective and provide a tentative response to your hypothesis, what data is needed? What methodology are you going to use to obtain this information? These factors – a narrower topic, an overall objective, specific aims, a clear argument or hypothesis and a sound methodology to locate the required data to achieve a conclusion – are all pivotal in ensuring successful project outcomes.

Having gained a broad contextual understanding of the area, and planned your research project, you will need to clarify the detail of the law. All of the steps taken so far, including refining the topic, deciding on objectives and a guiding hypothesis are common to any research project. However, in order to determine the law, you need to use a doctrinal research methodology. It may be that this step is simply a precursor to using another social science method to, for example, determine whether the law is having the effect that was expected or planned by the Parliament when it was passed. So, the researcher might very well follow on from the statement of law with further quantitative or qualitative methodologies used to further the stated research objective. The crux of the doctrinal research method lies in identifying the legislation and pertinent case law and stating what the law is in the area. An examination of the issue of what constitutes a 'material irregularity' during a jury's deliberations, for example, involves a discussion of applicable legislation, and a close reading of English as well as Australian authorities.[87] This is also often accompanied by a statement of any difficulties that have been encountered in applying the law because often the researcher's purpose is to identify those aspects of the law that need to be changed in order to achieve different (and more effective) outcomes for the community. The vast majority of doctrinal research projects include a reform perspective.

Time is the most precious commodity in undertaking research, and time, along with the availability of other resources including funding and research assistance, will often determine the project's ultimate methodology. The time available is dependent on external deadlines as well as the researcher's other

---

87 See *R. v. Chaouk* [1986] VR 707.

competing commitments.[88] Many student researchers begin with ambitious plans which involve complex empirical methodologies. In the majority of projects, the initial literature review and doctrinal research to establish the relevant rules and principles of law are threshold steps. However, often these two steps end up consuming all the student's available time and resources. Many legal research projects are therefore ultimately condensed to a solid doctrinal analysis of the law with a more extensive empirical study relegated to a future second stage.

In delineating the scope of the topic, it is essential to define any important terms. It is also important to establish the jurisdictional focus for the review. In the Australian context, a researcher will state whether the research focus is on the law in one state jurisdiction, or encompasses a larger national canvass with a perspective covering all state and territory jurisdictions as well as the Commonwealth. The researcher will need to decide on the legal periods or time frames being covered. The aspects of the topic being discussed may differ. In a topic dealing with the jury system, the researcher may, for example, decide to confine the discussion to juries in the criminal trial process.

Doctrinal research on the jury system

Many examples of doctrinal research on the jury system are available in the legal literature.[89] The examples of doctrinal research used in this chapter are drawn from segments of the published law reform reports on the jury system in Queensland, in particular:

Queensland Law Reform Commission, *A Review of Jury Selection*, Report No. 68, February 2011; and
Queensland Law Reform Commission, *A Review of Jury Selection*, Discussion Paper, WP No. 69, June 2010.

Law reform commission publications constitute a separate legal writing genre. However, any recommendations for reform of the law must be based initially

---

88 T. Hutchinson and N. Cuffe, 'Legal Research Project Management: Skills Extension for Upper Level Law Students', *The Law Teacher* 38(2), 2004, 159.
89 See, for example, the case note and discussion of the legal implications of a specific case in J. Stelios, '*Brownlee v The Queen*: Method in the Madness', *Federal Law Review* 29, 2001, 319; see also R. Johns, 'Trial by Jury: Recent Developments', Briefing Paper No. 4/05, NSW Parliamentary Library Research Service, 2005; N. Vidmar (ed.), *World Jury Systems*, Oxford: Oxford University Press, 2000; J. O'Leary, 'Twelve Angry Peers or One Angry Judge: An Analysis of Judge Alone Trials in Australia', *Criminal Law Journal* 35, 2011, 154.

on extensive doctrinal research. Law reform commission publications include excellent models of doctrinal analysis. Of course, law reform makes use of additional non-doctrinal research methodologies, in particular wide public consultation through public forums and focus groups, as well as public submissions prompted by published issues papers. Nonetheless, extensive doctrinal research is undertaken, much of it prior to consultation, and this research is included in both the discussion papers and reports. Recent Queensland Law Reform Commission reports cover two discrete aspects of the working of the jury system – the law and practice relating to the selection of juries, and jury directions. These areas fall squarely within this book's chosen topic of 'lay decision-makers in the law'. The doctrinal analysis within the law reform reports is expressed more formally and is more pragmatic than that in a postgraduate thesis, but these reports bear witness to how a group of career researchers and legal experts document and analyse the law. These are excellent examples and easily accessible on the Internet.[90]

Law reform consists of 'proposals for change made with full knowledge of the content and taking into account the history and development of the . . . legal system, over-arching legal policies and the interaction of the collection of rules and principles in relevant subject areas of the law'.[91] Law reform has a long history in the common-law world, beginning with committees such as that set up by Sir Matthew Hale in England from 1652 to 1657. The UK Law Revision Committee was operational from 1934 to 1939, and then from 1952 there was the Lord Chancellor's Law Reform Committee. This was followed by the English Law Commission, which was established in 1965.

The Queensland Law Reform Commission is an independent statutory body established under the Law Reform Commission Act 1968.[92] The function of the Commission, as provided in the Act, is to keep under review the law applicable to Queensland with a view to its systematic development and reform having regard to its codification, the elimination of anomalies and of obsolete and unnecessary enactments, the reduction of the number of separate enactments and generally the simplification and modernisation of the law.[93] The Commission's role is limited to reviewing particular areas of Queensland law referred to it by the Attorney-General at any given time. The mission of the Law Reform Commission is 'to meet the needs of the Queensland

---

90 See http://www.qlrc.qld.gov.au/ (accessed 26 March 2017).
91 A. Rose, 'Reform and Renovation: Reassessing the Role of the ALRC', *Reform* 67, 1995, http://www.austlii.edu.au/au/journals/ALRCRefJl/1995/2.html (accessed 3 March 2017).
92 See http://www.qlrc.qld.gov.au/ (accessed 3 March 2017).
93 Law Reform Commission Act 1968 (Qld), s 10(1).

community by reviewing areas of law in need of reform'.[94] The Commission makes recommendations for reform to Parliament through the Attorney-General. These recommendations are based on extensive research, public consultation, impartiality, equity and social justice.[95]

Report writing is a discrete writing genre with a publication format which differs significantly from a refereed journal article or a PhD thesis. However, the fundamental doctrinal research necessary for any legal project is very similar. Law reform research is undertaken collectively by research experts in an organised research unit. The reports are the product of full-time professional staff working in a group research structure. There is a focus on detail and accuracy in locating the current legislation and its history, summarising important decisions, and analysing the differences in approach between individual judges, courts and jurisdictions. In this respect, the doctrinal research undertaken in law reform agencies models good practice. Undergraduate research students or busy legal practitioners would be hard pressed to achieve a comparative depth of research coverage within their pragmatic deadlines. The research in the reports is similar to that undertaken by higher degree research students, though the writing style is much more concise. The reports have great authority because they are published under the auspices of a government statutory body and tabled in Parliament. The reports are government documents and, as a result, the extent of the legal discussion, depth of critique and the language used in the text reflects these formal constraints.

Law reform bodies adhere to strict Terms of Reference which determine and constrain the project. In this way, policy discussion papers and law reform reports differ significantly from regular academic research projects because the parameters are set externally and not determined by the individual researcher. In self-directed work, the researcher is in control and possesses the freedom to establish the limits of the research topic. It is the practice in government reports to state any aspects of the topic that are not covered by the Terms of Reference; for example, the Discussion Paper for *A Review of Jury Selection* states:

> Three areas are also expressly excluded from this review by the Terms of Reference:
>
> • consideration of whether juries should have a role in sentencing;
> • the merits or desirability of trial by jury; or
> • the requirement for majority verdicts in Queensland.[96]

---

94 'Queensland Law Reform Commission Annual Report 2010–11', State of Queensland (Queensland Law Reform Commission), 2011, 1.
95 *Ibid.* and see diagram in Hutchinson, *Researching and Writing in Law*, at 68.
96 QLRC, 'A Review of Jury Selection', WP No. 69, at 1.7; notes omitted.

In addition, it is also the practice for the reports to alert the reader to additional issues that may have been raised in the public consultations and submissions, but which are not to be covered in the Report. This becomes necessary because of the need to limit the research to those issues that are most relevant to the Terms of Reference. See, for example, this statement from the *Jury Selection* Discussion Paper:

> Other areas not covered by this reference, but which have been raised in the public media from time to time, include: the size of juries, the use of reserve jurors, access by jurors to the media (including the internet) during trials, juror misconduct and the use and admissibility of expert evidence in criminal trials. Neither is the Commission asked to review the range of criminal (or civil) cases in which juries are used.[97]

This practice of clearly delineating the parameters of a research project is also often encountered in doctrinal journal articles and theses. It is a useful device to circumvent criticism where specific aspects of a topic have not been covered because the author has deemed the issue irrelevant to the main argument or because of lack of time or resources.

Having highlighted the scope of the project, and defined any legal terms, usually the researcher's next step is to examine the background and context of the topic. The jury has a long history dating back to Periclean Athens and the Magna Carta.[98] This material would by and large be found in secondary sources (such as texts, previous law reform publications and journal articles); however, there may also be important statements on the role of the jury in case law, or in the judges' public lectures and other published presentations. Reference sources such as encyclopaedias can be helpful in the first instance; however, these are rarely completely up to date. An introduction to the topic in a legal encyclopaedia is only a doorway to a further chamber of analysis. The challenge is to confine the broader contextual discussion of the 'big picture' and background to the topic, so that it does not subsume the entire project.

The body of secondary material on the jury system is immense – so much so that the researcher would need to be extremely discerning in collecting relevant items. A basic catalogue search in the university law library, for example, will identify hundreds of potentially useful books and scores of law reform papers. In addition, there are numerous journal articles and presentations on the same topic evident from a basic legal journals index scan and millions of Google

97 *Ibid.*, at 1.10; notes omitted.
98 QLRC, 'A Review of Jury Selection', Report No. 68, at 2.14.

entries as a result of a search for the term 'Jury Selection'. Many jurisdictions have now included information for prospective jurors on their websites. These also must be reviewed. However, in order to ascertain which items are relevant and which are not, all the material must be located and read and analysed and the ideas grouped to reflect the obvious (and not so obvious) connections.

Published statistics also serve as context for the discussion. The Australian Bureau of Statistics, for example, provides useful statistical details on the resolution of criminal proceedings, as well as detailed demographics covering the age and educational background of the general population.[99] From these and other available statistics, some attempt is made to indicate who serves on juries, together with rates of excusal or exemption, and rates of non-compliance by those called in to serve on juries.[100] Any empirical research into jurors' perceptions and experience, especially Australian studies, are examined.[101] In our example, there is some discussion of the results of additional surveys and interviews prepared by social researchers at the University of Queensland.[102]

Therefore, one of the most difficult aspects of any research is a meaningful and comprehensive literature review. Much of the skill in presenting the review of the literature lies in the way it is organised. Take, for example, Chapter 5 of the *Jury Selection* Report, which contains a discussion of the guiding principles for reform of the jury selection process.[103] Most of these issues emanated from the Jury Selection Review Terms of Reference. These principles include right to a fair trial, separation of powers, representativeness, impartiality, non-specialist composition, competence and non-discrimination. This list and the analysis of each provides a neat example of how a variety of issues can be grouped and discussed in a meaningful fashion so as to form the basis for further examination of the topic.

Of most importance to our discussion is Chapter 3 of the Report, which examines the sources of the law in relation to a person's liability to serve on a jury.[104] In the example chosen, the emphasis lies on Queensland legal sources because of the jurisdictional framework for the enquiry. The research therefore covers the current Queensland legislation, together with the history of the provisions. It includes a discussion of superseded legislation, which provides an

---

99 *Ibid.*, at 2.13; and Australian Bureau of Statistics (ABS), 4513.0 *Criminal Courts, Australia*, various years; Report No. 68, Chapter 4; and ABS, 3101.0 *Australian Demographic Statistics*, June 2010.
100 Report No. 68, Chapter 4.
101 Report No. 68, at 2.27.
102 Report No. 68, at 4.14.
103 Report No. 68, Chapter 5.
104 Report No. 68, Chapter 3.

insight into the law's development. Explanatory memoranda and second reading speeches explain the forces prompting change and amendments. As Australia is a federation, applicable Commonwealth legislation is also examined, along with juries' legislation in all the Australian state and territory jurisdictions, and relevant jurisdictions outside Australia including England and Wales, Hong Kong, Ireland, New Zealand and Scotland. Judicial consideration of the legislation and earlier common law cases is also analysed.

In our chosen example, *A Review of Jury Selection*, the structure of the Report follows the Terms of Reference. So, in discussing reform of the jury selection process, the Report examines the qualifications needed for jury service including the threshold requirement of electoral enrolment and therefore citizenship, and the legislative provisions disqualifying those with criminal records, as well as the effect of any legislatively enshrined schemes that remove convictions from a person's criminal history after a 'prescribed rehabilitation period'.[105] The Report also examines exclusion on the basis of the potential juror's occupation or personal attributes (such as being the spouse of a person in an excluded category). There are comparisons of legislation in other jurisdictions on all aspects of jury service, including excusal as of right for previous jury service, excusal for cause, deferral of jury service, and any excusal and deferral guidelines. Other issues covered include jury selection and empanelment, regional issues and indigenous representation, remuneration, civil jury trials, and breaches and penalties for a range of offences from non-compliance with jury service summonses to influencing or threatening a juror.[106]

Conclusion

Doctrinal legal research is a discrete research methodology. It is more than simply scholarship or an elaborate literature review of primary materials. Doctrinal research has been the dominant method used by legal research scholars within the common-law system for the last two centuries, and this methodology constitutes the foundation or starting point of most legal research projects.

The doctrinal methodology has survived despite its limitations. The doctrinal approach to research is in harmony with legal practice. It is well suited to advocacy and finding solutions to legal problems. It mirrors the analytical decisions of the judges and provides a pathway to explore the way forward through the plethora of common-law cases. The sources for doctrinal work are by and large on the public record. Other methods may be used subsequent to the

---

105 Report No. 68, Chapter 6.
106 Report No. 68, Chapters 6–14.

doctrinal research, but it can be argued that the lawyer needs to commence any legal discussion by using this method to critically determine 'what the law is'.

Recommended reading

Bartie, S., 'The Lingering Core of Legal Scholarship', *Legal Studies* 30(3), 2010, 345.

Hutchinson, T., *Researching and Writing in Law*, 3rd edn, Pyrmont, New South Wales: Lawbook Co., 2010.

Hutchinson, T. and Duncan, N., 'Defining the Doctrinal', *Deakin Law Review* 17(1), 2012, 83.

McConville, M. and Chui W. H., *Research Methods for Law*, Edinburgh: Edinburgh University Press, 2007.

McKerchar, M., *Design and Conduct of Research in Tax, Law and Accounting*, Sydney: Lawbook, 2010, pp. 125–78.

Rubin, E., 'The Practice and Discourse of Legal Scholarship', *Michigan Law Review* 86, 1988, 1835.

Salter, M. and Mason, J., *Writing Law Dissertations: An Introduction and Guide to the Conduct of Legal Research*, Harlow: Longman, 2007.

Van Hoecke, M. (ed.), *Methodologies of Legal Research: Which Kind of Method for What Kind of Discipline?* Oxford: Hart Publishing, 2011.

2   Socio-legal studies

A challenge to the doctrinal approach

Fiona Cownie and Anthony Bradney

The doctrinal approach to teaching and researching law, focused exclusively on traditional legal materials and the techniques required to interpret them (what Margaret Thornton has termed the 'technocentric' approach to law[1]), constituted the dominant mode of law teaching and research until well into the twentieth century.[2] In the early years of the century, most law graduates came from the 'golden triangle' of Oxford, Cambridge and London universities, where the use of classic textbooks ensured that the legal education offered was doctrinal in nature.[3] Since it was graduates of these universities who became law teachers, they continued to foster the doctrinal approach to law. In addition, many provincial law schools were founded as a result of activity by local Law Societies, and as a result they were highly sensitive to the needs of the legal profession.[4] The pre-eminence of doctrinal law was also reinforced because, until the major expansion of universities brought about by the Robbins Report, many law school staff were part-time practitioners, whose orientation naturally tended to be towards the vocational aspects of law. It was not until after the mid-1960s that law schools began to employ young lecturers who were full-time academics, whose allegiance was to the development of law as an academic discipline, rather than to law as a vocational subject.[5]

---

1 M. Thornton, 'Technocentrism in the Law School: Why the Gender and Colour of Law Remain the Same', *Osgoode Hall Law Review* 36, 1998, *passim*.
2 W. L. Twining, *Blackstone's Tower: The English Law School*, London: Sweet & Maxwell, 1994, ch. 6.
3 F. Lawson, *The Oxford Law School: 1850–1965*, Oxford, Oxford University Press, 1968; at pp. 229–35 there are examples of examination papers which reflect the doctrinal nature of that which was taught.
4 D. Sugarman, 'Legal Theory and the Common Law Mind: The Making of the Textbook Tradition', in W. L. Twining (ed.), *Legal Theory and the Common Law Mind*, Oxford: Blackwell, 1986, 31.
5 C. M. Campbell and P. Wiles, 'The Study of Law in Society in Britain', *Law and Society Review* 10, 1976, 547–78, *passim*.

Evidence of the developing interest in socio-legal studies was reflected in the founding of the Socio-Legal Group of the Society of Legal Scholars (SPTL) in the early 1970s. The first conference of the SPTL's Socio-Legal Group took place in Manchester in December 1972.[6] The Group grew rapidly, with 150 members joining in its first year.[7] Over the next 20 years, the Socio-Legal Group became independent from the SPTL, and in 1990 the Socio-Legal Studies Association was established.[8] The continuing strength of the Association, which now holds an annual conference, as well as facilitating many other socio-legal events, reflects the increasing interest in socio-legal studies among the academic community.[9]

However, the influence of the doctrinal approach on both research and teaching remained strong, much to the dissatisfaction of those academic lawyers who wished to engage in legal research of a similar nature to the research emanating from other, more overtly intellectual, parts of the academy. As late as 1987, Professor Geoffrey Wilson characterised research in law in the following terms:

> The words 'English legal scholarship', though high-sounding, have a similar function to the words 'disposable plastic cup'. Each adjective strengthens the message that one cannot expect much in terms of quality or long-term utility from it.[10]

However, during the latter part of the twentieth century, a number of alternative approaches to the study of law emerged to challenge the supremacy of doctrinal law. Feminism and critical legal studies both offered alternative ways of analysing law and legal phenomena, and researchers working within these traditions made significant contributions to legal scholarship.[11] Of the various critiques that emerged, the one which has arguably gained the widest following among legal academics has been the socio-legal approach, also known as 'law in context'.[12]

6 F. Cownie and R. Cocks, *A Great and Noble Occupation! The History of the Society of Legal Scholars*, Oxford: Hart Publishing, 2009, 137.

7 *Ibid.*, 138.

8 P. A. Thomas, 'Socio-Legal Studies: The Case of Disappearing Fleas and Bustards', in P. A. Thomas (ed.), *Socio-Legal Studies*, Aldershot: Dartmouth, 1997, 9–10.

9 See http://www.slsa.ac.uk (accessed 3 March 2017).

10 G. Wilson, 'English Legal Scholarship', *Modern Law Review* 50, 1987, 819.

11 F. Cownie, *Legal Academics: Culture and Identities*, Oxford: Hart Publishing, 2004, 51–54.

12 *Ibid.*, 58.

Defining socio-legal studies

Socio-legal studies is hard to define, because of the diverse range of scholarship carried out under that name; like many other movements, it is not confined neatly within well-defined boundaries, and the term 'socio-legal' can be used to include both feminist work and critical legal studies, although these two approaches may also be seen as quite separate movements within legal scholarship.

The precise meaning of the term 'socio-legal' is contentious.[13] It has some-times been used in a relatively narrow manner.[14] For example, Campbell and Wiles distinguished 'socio-legal' work from work carried out within the 'sociology of law', seeing socio-legal work as 'anti-theoretical, concerned with social engineering through existing social order and not with explaining that order or transcending it by critique', while they saw sociology of law as theoretically sophisticated.[15] However, more frequently the term 'socio-legal' has been used very broadly. Thus, for example, Wheeler and Thomas comment that '[t]he word "socio" in socio-legal studies means to us an interface with a context within which law exists, be that a sociological, historical, economic, geographical or other context'.[16] In the Economic and Social Research Council's 1994 review of socio-legal studies, the section entitled 'What is Socio-Legal Studies?' begins by saying that '"Socio-legal studies" is an umbrella term for what is now an exciting, wide-ranging and varied area of research activity'.[17] No actual definition of the term is attempted, but socio-legal studies is referred to as an '*approach* to the study of law and legal processes' which '. . . covers the theoretical and empirical analysis of law as a social phenomenon'.[18] The Report points out that socio-legal research has been carried out by scholars from many different disciplines, including lawyers, political scientists, economists, historians, sociologists and anthropologists, so that research which can be des-cribed as socio-legal 'displays considerable eclecticism in subject-matter, theo-rising and methodology, ranging from macro-theoretical scholarship through empirical analyses designed to test and generate theoretical propositions, to

13 W. L. Twining, *General Jurisprudence: Understanding Law from a Global Perspective*, Cambridge: Cambridge University Press, 2009, 227–28.

14 A. Bradshaw, 'Sense and Sensibility: Debates and Developments in Socio-Legal Research Methods', ch. 5 in Thomas, *Socio-Legal Studies*.

15 Campbell and Wiles, 'The Study of Law in Society in Britain', 548–49.

16 S. Wheeler and P. A. Thomas, 'Socio-Legal Studies', in D. Hayton (ed.), *Law's Futures*, Oxford: Hart Publishing, 2000, 271.

17 ESRC, 'Review of Socio-Legal Studies: Final Report', Swindon, ESRC, 1994, 1.

18 *Ibid.*, emphasis in the original.

experimental designs and small-scale case studies'.[19] In many ways, it is easiest to think of socio-legal studies as an approach in this way, because this allows for the inclusion of the very diverse methods and perspectives adopted by socio-legal scholars.

The breadth of socio-legal work has increased the longer it has existed in the legal academy. Harris, writing in the 1980s, suggests that socio-legal studies begins with academic lawyers turning to sociology and argues that sociology, social policy and social administration have had the greatest impact on socio-legal studies.[20] Yet, even at this early stage in the development of this approach, Harris notes the potential importance of social history for socio-legal studies.[21] From its very beginning, socio-legal studies has encompassed the use by academic lawyers of a very wide range of disciplines, not just those belonging to the social sciences, and writing in the present day, it is now difficult to think of any discipline in the social sciences or humanities that has not been used by scholars working in a socio-legal mode. Such is its potential that interest in socio-legal studies has been characterised as '. . . the emergence of a new legal paradigm'[22] and socio-legal scholarship as '. . . the most important scholarship currently being undertaken in the legal world'.[23]

Empirical research on the legal academy indicates that the doctrinal approach to legal analysis no longer dominates legal education and research in the way it once did; Cownie's research on legal academics suggests that about half of legal academics would now describe themselves as socio-legal, while of those remaining, many who are cautious about using the term 'socio-legal' to describe their approach (generally because they associate that term exclusively with empirical investigation) are actually following an approach which is indistinguishable from their socio-legal colleagues.[24] When asked about the nature of legal research in the future, the majority of legal academics in Cownie's study (including many who described themselves as 'black-letter' lawyers) believed that socio-legal work would become more important as time went on.[25]

The very variety of the kind of work being carried out in socio-legal studies can be seen as being an intellectual advantage. Cotterrell has argued that '[a]n

19 *Ibid.*, 2.
20 D. Harris, 'The Development of Socio-Legal Studies in the United Kingdom', *Legal Studies* 3, 1983, 315.
21 *Ibid.*, 331–32.
22 Thomas, 'Socio-Legal Studies', 19.
23 R. Cotterrell, *Law's Community: Legal Theory in Sociological Perspective*, Oxford: Clarendon Press, 1995, 314.
24 Cownie, *Legal Academics*, 54–58.
25 *Ibid.*, 63–65.

important reason for the vitality of the socio-legal community in Britain . . . has surely been its rich, almost anarchic heterogeneity and its consistent openness to many different aims, outlooks, and disciplinary backgrounds'.[26]

While the strength of socio-legal studies may remain a matter of debate, with some experts arguing that it has become the dominant mode of research and teaching in university law schools, others are less optimistic about the progress of socio-legal studies (a debate analysed by Collier in 2004),[27] it is certainly the case that this challenge to the doctrinal paradigm has become firmly entrenched, not only within academic legal studies, but in the academy generally.[28]

Doing socio-legal research

Socio-legal scholars, especially those conducting empirical research, have sometimes been accused of producing research which is not particularly intellectually sophisticated and which is atheoretical and descriptive in nature. This was essentially the criticism put forward by Campbell and Wiles in the 1970s and it has been echoed since by others – for example, Nicola Lacey has argued that the approach of socio-legal studies to one of its central concerns, that of effecting policy change,

> has all too often been premised on both a poorly theorised account of social institutions and an insufficient attention to the democratic legitimacy of proposed changes. Inadequately theorized and contextualised socio-legal research . . . ignores relevant questions . . . [and] proceeds from an insufficiently thorough critique of existing legal institutional forms . . .[29]

Some of Cownie's interviewees pointed to another potential criticism of socio-legal research – that it is methodologically unsophisticated, resulting in the

26 R. Cotterrell, 'Subverting Orthodoxy, Making Law Central: A View of Socio-Legal Studies', *Journal of Law and Society* 29, 2002, 632–33.
27 R. Collier, 'We're All Socio-Legal Now – Legal Education, Scholarship and the Global Knowledge Economy: Reflections on the U.K. Experience', *Sydney Law Review* 26, 2004, 517–19.
28 See, for instance, Scott's discussion of 'trans-disciplinarity' using biotechnology and socio-legal studies as examples, without feeling the need to explain either term: P. Scott, *The Meanings of Mass Higher Education*, Milton Keynes: Open University Press, 1995, 149.
29 N. Lacey, 'Normative Reconstruction in Socio-Legal Theory', *Social and Legal Studies* 5, 1996, 143–44.

production of poor-quality data and consequent questionable analysis.[30] This is particularly true of socio-legal researchers, whose academic background lies in the discipline of Law. Cownie comments:

> Engaging in socio-legal or inter-disciplinary work is a significant challenge for academic lawyers trained in the British tradition, since doctrinal law does not engage with other disciplines . . . the Law syllabus rarely includes any significant study of the theories or research methods which are regarded as fundamental by [other disciplines]. The lack of such a background, either in social sciences or in any of the other disciplines which might usefully be employed to examine legal phenomena, was seen as a big problem for the future development of the discipline . . .[31]

Concerns about the continuing capacity of the academy to produce large-scale *empirical* socio-legal research were expressed by the authors of the Nuffield Inquiry on Empirical Legal Research, which reported in 2006.[32] However, although it raises a number of interesting issues, the Report was not uncritically received by the socio-legal community. A former Chair of the Socio-Legal Studies Association commented:

> Most importantly, I would argue that there are young scholars, in their twenties, thirties and forties, who are more confident than previous generations in critiquing and applying theories and approaches developed in disciplines other than the study of law. What this means is the problem of lack of capacity no longer involves a lack of interest in socio-legal approaches to law and legal phenomena. This adds a new dimension to the debate as it may be that those seeking to recruit to empirical work are no longer just competing with doctrinal or critical lawyers, but with socio-legal scholars who choose to approach their work through non-empirical routes. One of the stories behind the low rate of applications to funding bodies to do empirical work may be that there is a lack of sufficient capacity. Another may be that there is a lack of interest amongst socio-legal scholars in carrying out this type of project.[33]

30 Cownie, *Legal Academics*, 65–66.
31 *Ibid.*, 66.
32 H. Genn, M. Partington and S. Wheeler, *Law in The Real World: Improving Our Understanding of How Law Works*, The Nuffield Inquiry on Empirical Legal Research Final Report, London: Nuffield Foundation, 2006.
33 L. Mulcahy, 'A Crisis in Socio-Legal Studies?', *Socio-Legal Newsletter,* No. 51, spring 2007, Socio-Legal Studies Association, 3.

Overall, despite some concerns, it would appear that socio-legal studies is here to stay, and the main problem for researchers is how to do socio-legal work of high quality which will have lasting interest and value.

Thinking about method

For the researcher who is considering conducting some socio-legal research, the choice of method and approach is extensive, as is the range of theoretical work upon which the socio-legal researcher can draw. To avoid the pitfalls leading to the sort of criticisms outlined above, careful consideration has to be given to the adoption of an approach and a method which is suitable for the research question which is being investigated and to the theory or theories which can most appropriately throw light upon the relevant topic. Whatever approach is chosen, it is important to be aware of the relevant academic literature on theory and method. Choosing the appropriate theoretical approach and the method of investigation is just as important for the socio-legal researcher as all the other aspects of socio-legal research, such as the collection, analysis and dissemination of information and data. Indeed, it is important not to push on with the collection of data until the research questions, method and theoretical approach are clear in the researcher's mind. The range of theories and methods available to the socio-legal researcher make it impractical to cover in this chapter all the issues which need to be considered, but there is an extensive literature available for consultation,[34] and most institutions offer appropriate research training opportunities so that socio-legal researchers without the relevant intellectual background can acquire the knowledge and skills which they need.

The range and breadth of contemporary socio-legal research

The best socio-legal research will explicitly address issues of theory and method, and readers will be able to identify the researchers' engagement with the relevant methodological and theoretical literature, thus giving their work the intellectual rigour it needs. This section of the chapter introduces two examples of recent socio-legal research in order to illustrate the variety of work which is gathered together under the umbrella of 'socio-legal research', and to show how research questions, method and theory interact in socio-legal research. The first piece of work we look at is about property law, often

34 Some of which is referenced in Burton's chapter in this book.

thought of as a very traditional doctrinal legal subject. Here, however, it is approached from a non-traditional perspective. Conversely, the second piece we look at is about a series of television programmes (hardly a traditional 'legal' topic) which the author uses to analyse the nature of law and the role that law plays in people's lives – topics that have been addressed in traditional jurisprudence for many years.[35]

Our first piece of socio-legal work is Antonia Layard's examination of the ways in which city centres have been transformed from places with many individual spaces (streets, squares and so on) into a single homogeneous space in the form of shopping centres, carefully regulated so as to facilitate the shopping experience.[36] Adopting a case-study approach, she explores the ways in which the creation of the Cabot Circus shopping centre in Bristol and the development of the adjoining Quakers Friars area of the city has led to a change from multiple ownership of land to single ownership, with the consequent concentration of the rights of ownership into the hands of the city council and a large property development company.[37] These legally facilitated changes lead to profound consequences for the users of this space, as Layard comments:

> Uses that facilitate the shopping experience are promoted; uses that restrict it are prohibited. As a result, throughout Quakers Friars and its associated retail development Cabot Circus, 'visitors' are now unable to walk a dog, play a guitar, take a photograph or smoke a cigarette in places previously understood as being in the public realm.[38]

Using the work of de Certeau (in particular his classic text *The Practice of Everyday Life*) and that of Tuan, a human geographer, Layard draws a distinction between 'place' and 'space'. For de Certeau:

> A place (lieu) is the order (of whatever kind) in accordance with which elements are distributed in relationships of coexistence . . . A place is thus an instantaneous configuration of positions. It implies an indication of stability . . . A *space* exists when one takes into account vectors of direction, velocities and time variables.[39]

35 See, e.g., H. L. A. Hart, *The Concept of Law*, Oxford: Clarendon Press, 1961.
36 A. Layard, 'Shopping in the Public Realm: A Law of Place', *Journal of Law and Society* 37, 2010, 414.
37 *Ibid.*, 417.
38 *Ibid.*, 415–16.
39 M. de Certeau, *The Practice of Everyday Life* (1984) at p. 117, cited in Layard, 'Shopping in the Public Realm', 415 (emphasis in the original).

For Tuan, Layard notes:

> place can be distinguished from space by envisaging a sense of space as an open arena of action and movement, while place invites stopping, resting and becoming involved. While space is amenable to the abstraction of special science and economic rationality, place is amenable to discussions of things such as 'value' and 'belonging'. In short, as Carter et al succinctly summarize, place is space to which meaning has been ascribed.[40]

Layard goes on to develop the idea of the social production of space, focusing on the role played by the law in this enterprise, using the work of Lefebvre to provide 'a conceptual lens through which it is possible to explain how space is socially produced'.[41] She explores in particular how a particular sense of place is first envisaged and then created through the use of expertise and legal rules.[42] Finally, she explores the potential of Lefebvre's 'right to the city', arguing that we should conceptually and legally separate control of space and place from ownership, and that these concepts are not inevitably intertwined.[43]

From this brief description of Layard's work, it can be seen that it analyses the empirical case study of the shopping centre using a relevant theoretical perspective to question the legally facilitated transformation of space, particularly as it restricts public access and practices. Layard's work provides a clear example of the way in which a socio-legal approach can enable the researcher to examine mainstream legal concepts (in this case, those related to the ownership of real property) using ideas drawn from other disciplines (sociology and geography) to produce original research incorporating new ideas about law.

An apparently contrasting piece of socio-legal research is one example of Anthony Bradney's work on the television programme *Buffy the Vampire Slayer* (BtVS), which is a contribution to the emerging socio-legal research area of law and popular culture.[44] Bradney's article examines the changing image of law and law enforcement found in the first six series of BtVS. He is explicit about his method, which involves 'a close reading of the programmes'.[45] He

40 Layard, 'Shopping in the Public Realm', 414–15.
41 *Ibid.*, 416.
42 *Ibid.*, 417.
43 *Ibid.*, 437.
44 A. Bradney, 'Choosing Laws, Choosing Families: Images of Law, Love and Authority in "Buffy the Vampire Slayer"', *WebJCLI* 2, 2003, http://www.bailii.org/uk/other/journals/WebJCLI/2003/issue2/bradney2.html (accessed 3 March 2017).
45 *Ibid.*

goes on to give detailed information about his primary sources, noting that BtVS takes seven major forms, namely:

> a set of video tapes covering the six [TV] series, a set of DVDs (covering, in Great Britain, the first three series), a set of scripts (with the first and half of the second series being available in published form and all six series being available as unofficial transcripts on the Web), a book series and a comic book series.[46]

Not all of these forms contain exactly the same stories; there are subtle variations, so that, as Bradney points out, '[i]n this context of variant forms of BtVS, it is important to identify what constitutes BtVS'. This article is based on a reading of the official and unofficial scripts for the first six television series and the video tapes available in Great Britain for those series. It is these forms which Bradney sees as forming the heart of BtVS as an artefact of popular culture.[47] Referring to research on popular culture, television and law and literature, Bradney goes on to illuminate his argument with detailed analysis of the programmes.

'The initial premise of BtVS is that human beings share the world with vampires, demons and other supernatural creatures that are, on the whole, hostile to humanity.'[48] In every generation, however, there is a vampire slayer, who has heightened powers of agility, strength and so on, and whose task it is to kill vampires and demons. Buffy, as the vampire slayer, is responsible to a 'Watcher' who is her 'commander'. In turn, the Watcher is responsible to the Watchers' Council, which has final responsibility for deciding what Buffy and the Watcher should do; the Council bases its decisions on ancient laws. As Bradney comments: 'at the level of its basic premise, BtVS is little more than a traditional police series . . .'.[49]

For most of the first three series, Bradney notes, Buffy is portrayed as a deviant police officer – doing the job, sometimes in her own unofficial way, but nevertheless working within an established hierarchy.[50] However, unusually for a police series, Buffy forms deep emotional relationships – with Giles, her Watcher, and with other characters (her friends, the Scooby Gang). In time, the importance she attaches to these relationships leads her to

46 *Ibid.*
47 *Ibid.*
48 *Ibid.*
49 *Ibid.*
50 *Ibid.*

reject the authority of the Watchers' Council.[51] Bradney argues that at this point 'the contention in the series is not that some authority fails, but rather that hierarchical forms of authority fail'.[52] Buffy and her friends must now decide for themselves what to do. Buffy retains her role as a slayer, and Bradney goes on to argue that the focus of the programmes now becomes 'What laws, if any, should Buffy obey?' The answer, he says, is that in the end, the source of right authority is found not in conventional morality, but '. . . in the familial bond, the connections of Buffy, Giles and their friends the Scooby Gang'.[53] While the traditional biological family is always portrayed as dysfunctional in BtVS, the familial relationships between Buffy, Giles and the Scooby Gang are more than just those of a group of friends. The 'chosen family' is not romanticised; it is acknowledged that sometimes people fail to live up to their obligations to each other, but equally important are the attempts that Buffy and her friends make to rectify their mistakes and make amends for their errors; their efforts spring from the love they have for each other, which brings responsibility and the knowledge that their mission is to serve and save others who are in need.[54]

Bradney draws on the work of Bauman to analyse the new law that Buffy and her friends must live by, pointing out that in *Postmodern Ethics* Bauman argues that 'moral responsibility is unconditional and infinite' and that:

> [t]he postmodern mind does not expect anymore to find the all-embracing, total and ultimate formula of life without ambiguity, risk, danger and error . . . The postmodern mind is reconciled to the idea that the messiness of the human predicament is here to stay.[55]

Bradney argues that both of these ideas find a resonance in the law that is chosen by Buffy and her friends.[56] He concludes that the view of law articulated in the series can be analysed from a theoretical perspective in a number of different ways. At a superficial level, it moves from a simple command theory of law to the more sophisticated view of law arrived at by Buffy and her friends:

> where, alongside legal rules, there exist a set of Dworkinian legal principles which have weight rather than simple black and white application in

---

51 *Ibid.*
52 *Ibid.*
53 *Ibid.*
54 *Ibid.*
55 Z. Bauman, *Postmodern Ethics*, Oxford: Blackwell Publishers, 1993, 250 and 245, quoted in Bradney, 'Choosing Laws, Choosing Families'.
56 Bradney, 'Choosing Laws, Choosing Families'.

regulating conduct . . . Moreover, the new law reflects the Weberian tax-onomy of authority in that it involves a shift from a form of authority that is simply sanctified by tradition to one that is legitimated by an appeal to rationality, illustrated by the continual discussions that Buffy, Giles and the Scooby Gang have about how to proceed.[57]

As Bradney also notes, both the existence of the law of the Watchers' Council and the move away from it are examples of legal pluralism.[58] But more impor-tantly, as he goes on to argue, in later series of the programmes emphasis is placed upon a much more sophisticated and existential notion of law, which:

> requires a continual personal investment and engagement in deciding what it is. What to do, how to act, becomes a constantly complex ques-tion, demanding a personal response . . . for all of us obeying law, choosing to make a law our own as a model for behaviour, is precisely that, a matter of choice. Moreover, it is a choice that we make both personally and indi-vidually and, at the same time, in the context of the intimate relationships that we have . . . The programme captures that which, elsewhere, has been described as being 'the articulation of autonomy with heteronomy, freedom with regulation, love with law'.[59]

Ultimately, Bradney is able to use his analysis of a series of television pro-grammes to engage with both postmodern critical theory and Dworkinian analysis of the nature of law. In so doing, his work neatly illustrates the poten-tial of a socio-legal approach to use non-traditional materials to throw new light on traditional 'legal' questions.

   Together, these two pieces of research provide a good illustration of the breadth of socio-legal research, both in subject matter and approach. They both demon-strate, in different ways, how socio-legal research uses a range of disciplines and methods to examine legal phenomena, throwing new light on traditional legal areas, such as property law and, indeed, the nature of law itself.

Researching tribunals from a socio-legal perspective

Like all the contributors to this book, we have used one particular topic (lay decision-makers in the legal system) to illustrate the method that is under

---

57 *Ibid.*
58 *Ibid.*
59 Z. Bankowski, *Living Lawfully: Love in Law and Law in Love*, Dordrecht: Kluwer Academic Publishers, 2001, 11, quoted in Bradney, 'Choosing Laws, Choosing Families'.

examination. In the case of socio-legal studies, the area of research on which we will focus is the role of tribunals within the English legal system. Tribunals are generally made up of a legally qualified Chair and two lay 'wing-members', who frequently have knowledge about and/or experience in the field which is covered by the tribunal on which they sit.[60] The role of the wing-members is to participate fully in the procedure and decision-making, so that tribunals provide a good illustration of the role of lay decision-makers in the legal system. Tribunals have been subjected to examination from a wide variety of perspectives by researchers using a number of different research methods, and therefore the research on this topic also provides a good illustration of the breadth of socio-legal research which has been produced.

Policy-oriented research on tribunals

Some empirical socio-legal research has proved to be very attractive to policy-makers, who can draw on the data and insights of the researchers to inform social or economic policy, in an attempt to ensure that it is 'evidence-based'. A good example of this in relation to tribunals is the research report *Tribunals for Diverse Users* by Genn et al., published in 2006 by the Department for Constitutional Affairs, comparing the experience of tribunal users across three different tribunals (the Appeals Service, the Criminal Injuries Compensation Panel and the Special Educational Needs and Disability Tribunal).[61] The main aim of the research was to establish whether Black and Minority Ethnic (BME) users experience any direct or indirect disadvantage in accessing and using tribunal services.[62] The policy orientation of the research is clear from the outset: the front cover of the research report identifies it not only as sponsored by the Department for Constitutional Affairs, but as 'Government Social Research' and 'Analysis for Policy'. In addition, we learn that the research was carried out in accordance with a research specification supplied by the Department.[63]

The research specification set out five main questions which the research needed to answer:

- To what extent is there evidence of direct discrimination against ethnic minorities within the tribunal system?

---

60 F. Cownie et al., *English Legal System in Context*, 6th edn, Oxford, Oxford University Press, 2013, 63.
61 H. Genn et al., *Tribunals for Diverse Users*, DCA Research Series 1/06, London, Department for Constitutional Affairs, i.
62 *Ibid.*
63 Genn et al., *Tribunals for Diverse Users*, 12.

- Do questions of race influence tribunal decisions and if so how?
- Is there evidence of indirect discrimination within the tribunal system and if so how is it manifested?
- Do tribunal processes impact differently on different minority groups?
- Do different minority groups believe they are likely to be treated fairly within the tribunal system?[64]

One of the strengths of the report is the way in which it clearly relates its research questions to the methods used to gather the data, which is then analysed to answer those questions. Seven different methods of data collection were used:

- focus group discussions with 115 members of the general public exploring knowledge and attitudes to seeking redress for administrative disputes and grievances;
- face-to-face interviews with 529 users in tribunal waiting rooms exploring expectations and levels of preparedness for hearings;
- observation of 391 of those users during their tribunal hearing assessing the enabling skills of tribunal judiciary and users' ability to participate in hearings;
- face-to-face interviews with 374 of those users after their hearing and before their decision, focusing on reactions to the hearing and perceptions of the fairness of the process;
- face-to-face interviews with 295 of those users after receiving their decision, exploring users' understanding of the reasons for the tribunal's decision and views on the fairness of the outcome;
- a statistical modelling exercise using 3 058 tribunal decisions from the three tribunals to identify factors associated with success or lack of success at hearings, including case type, ethnic group, representation, pre-hearing advice and the presence of an observer at the hearing;
- telephone interviews with 63 tribunal judiciary, exploring approaches to delivering fair hearings, any challenges presented by users from different ethnic or cultural backgrounds, and views on the value of diversity training.[65]

The report devotes a whole chapter to a detailed discussion of its research design.[66] This enables readers to make an informed judgment about the

64 *Ibid.*, 12–13.
65 *Ibid.*, i.
66 *Ibid.*, ch. 2.

strength of the empirical data upon which the whole report is based, and thus to decide whether or not they are persuaded by the evidence and analysis included in the report. Detailed discussion of method is one of the hallmarks of high-quality, empirical, socio-legal research, just as it would be of social scientific research generally.[67]

It is sometimes the case that in policy-oriented research the parameters of the research project are not wholly within the control of the researchers. In those cases, aspects of the research may be dictated by the needs of the commissioning body – for instance, in this study, the decision about which tribunals were to be included in the study 'was influenced by DCA preferences', as well as the need to include tribunals with a substantial case load and a significant number of BME users.[68] Nevertheless, as far as the outcome of the research is concerned, this research report is clear that the conclusions drawn and views expressed are those of the researchers, which 'are not necessarily shared' by the commissioning department.[69]

Findings about tribunal membership

In terms of its findings about lay members of tribunals, a central objective of the study was to ascertain whether there was direct or indirect discrimination against minority ethnic users within the tribunal system.[70] Observations of tribunal hearings were used to collect quantitative and qualitative evidence about the behaviour of tribunal members.[71] An important issue lying behind this aspect of the study was the extent to which tribunal members should compensate for lack of representation and enable unrepresented users to present their case, particularly in the light of previous research studies which had discussed the difficulties for the judiciary in dealing with unrepresented parties.[72] The authors of the report note that:

> Anxiety about the 'limits' of judicial intervention expose some of the tensions inherent within the modern adversarial legal system and the problem of reconciling the concept of enabling and responsiveness to the diverse needs of users, with traditional conceptions of judicial neutrality or

---

67 On the importance of method, see J. Mason and A. Dale (eds), *Understanding Social Research: Thinking Creatively About Method*, London: Sage, 2011.

68 Genn et al., *Tribunals for Diverse Users*, 15.

69 *Ibid.*, Disclaimer.

70 *Ibid.*, 143.

71 *Ibid.*, 144.

72 *Ibid.*, 145.

impartiality . . . In seeking to understand how 'equal treatment' should be operationalised within the context of a tribunal hearing, it is necessary to go beyond conventional assumptions about the role of the judicial decision-maker as a neutral and impartial umpire. Equal treatment is not about neutrality during judicial proceedings . . . equal treatment or fairness in court and tribunal proceedings requires that disputants are able effectively to participate in proceedings.[73]

The report goes on to argue that tribunals must ensure that all users have a fair hearing, which involves not only refraining from negative assumptions, but also a positive duty to assist, in order to ameliorate disadvantage.[74]

In seeking to assess the ability of tribunals to deliver fair and impartial hearings, the researchers were able to draw upon the 'Competence Framework' for tribunal members drawn up by the Judicial Studies Board.[75] Critical competencies for tribunal members identified by the researchers included: awareness and respect for cultural differences (e.g. by using appropriate language); facilitating the participation of all parties (e.g. by explaining legal issues in everyday language); and demonstrating good communication skills (e.g. by active listening).[76] These competences provided the researchers with a starting point from which to assess tribunal hearings in a structured way. Overall, panels were found to perform very effectively, with little evidence that minority ethnic users were disadvantaged in any way. Introductions to the tribunal hearing were informative, with full explanations of matters such as the role of the tribunal members, the independence of the tribunal, issues to be covered in the hearing and so on.[77]

On the whole, tribunal hearings tended towards a high degree of informality, users were treated with courtesy, and panels demonstrated good listening skills, regardless of the ethnic origin of the user.[78] The report notes that:

Observers recorded copious examples of courteous behaviour displayed by tribunal panels. Courtesy was displayed through the use of polite language, sensitive language, consideration for the situation of the user, and checking whether the user might have any physical needs (breaks, drinks). Many

73 *Ibid.*
74 *Ibid.*, 146.
75 The current version of the competencies can be found in The Judicial Studies Board, *Tribunal Competencies: Qualities and Abilities in Action*, London: JSB, 2007.
76 Genn et al., *Tribunals for Diverse Users*, 147–48.
77 *Ibid.*, 155.
78 *Ibid.*, 159–68.

tribunals were seen to respect the courtesy of looking at the user while the interpreter was speaking and addressing comments and questions to the user rather than to the interpreter.[79]

Overall, the observations of tribunal hearings, carried out by nine different observers from a range of ethnic backgrounds, making detailed notes and sensitive to the objectives of the study, found no systematic difference in tribunals' behaviour towards minority ethnic users which might disadvantage them.[80]

Unsurprisingly, since this is policy-oriented research, the report ends by discussing a number of matters which could assist in improving the service offered by tribunals.[81] It is a piece of research which provides a very good illustration of well-designed empirical socio-legal research which throws light on an aspect of the legal system by using classic social scientific methods and uses the data produced to make policy recommendations.

Non-empirical research into tribunals

It is important to bear in mind that not all socio-legal research is empirical, and this is as true of work on tribunals as it is of research in other areas. In this section of the chapter, we are going to look at a socio-legal monograph published in 2009: *Administrative Tribunals and Adjudication*, by Peter Cane.[82] The object of the research was to study administrative adjudication, with especial reference to the Australian Administrative Appeals Tribunal (AAT), including both historical and comparative perspectives in the analysis.[83] This is not a narrow study of one tribunal in one jurisdiction; rather, it is an attempt to draw to the attention of scholars outside Australia some of the distinctive features of Australian public law, and in doing so to explore the general theoretical and constitutional significance of administrative tribunals. As the author explains:

One of the aims of this book is to introduce to a wider audience in the common law world some of the distinctive features of Australian public law and legal institutions. Although it has often been observed that the

---

79 *Ibid.*, 163.
80 *Ibid.*, 171.
81 *Ibid.*, ch. 9.
82 P. Cane, *Administrative Tribunals and Adjudication*, Oxford: Hart Publishing, 2009.
83 *Ibid.*, viii.

federal administrative law package was unique and extremely innovative, it is relatively little known or understood outside Australia. Although Australian public law is built on solid British foundations, at federal level it is also significantly informed by American ideas, and this dual heritage makes it a particularly fascinating and fruitful topic for study not only conceptually, but also institutionally, historically and comparatively. For many academic lawyers, tribunals are of only peripheral interest. This, I have come to appreciate after many years of ignoring them as much as I could, is a blinkered point of view and an extremely unsatisfactory state of affairs. It was not until I started to study Australian public law in earnest and to think about administrative adjudication historically and comparatively that I began to value tribunals not only for their practical importance but also for their theoretical and constitutional significance. This process has required me to negotiate some very steep learning curves.[84]

The study as a whole uses the AAT as a lens 'to sharpen analysis and redefine understanding of a particular set of governmental institutions'.[85] It looks at the American and British forms of administrative tribunals as well, not only because the Australian constitutional and governmental system reflects the influence of both those systems, but also '. . . because the American and British systems represent two quite different constitutional paradigms, while the Australian system represents a complex and fascinating hybrid of both those two basic paradigms'.[86] Some mention is also made of the French system, because 'it represents an approach distinctly different from that found in any of the major common law jurisdictions'.[87]

The approach of the book is to look at the 'big picture'; a historical/comparative perspective is used to locate administrative tribunals within a broad institutional and constitutional landscape, which enables the author to identify four models of adjudication within different legal systems. Overall, it is argued that the four models can be thought of as forming a continuum, with the UK model at one end and the French at the other. In the United Kingdom, tribunals are thought of as being 'court substitutes',[88] which are not only subject to supervision by courts, but are also understood as belonging to the same type of institution as courts, and, like courts, are separated from the Executive. In addition, many administrative adjudicators in the UK

---

84 *Ibid.*, viii–ix.
85 Cane, *Administrative Tribunals and Adjudication*, 2.
86 *Ibid.*, 18.
87 *Ibid.*, 20.
88 *Ibid.*, 69.

system are trained lawyers.[89] In the French model, however, 'administrative adjudication is the exclusive province of a set of public law institutions that are unsupervised by private-law courts'.[90] In France, these public law adjudicative institutions are staffed by public administrators and they are clearly understood to be part of the executive branch of government.[91] In between these two extremes sit the Australian and US models of tribunals. In the United States, administrative adjudicators are part of the institutions of the executive branch, but within those institutions, adjudicators and adjudication are separated from other officials and activities. Administrative adjudicators are typically legally trained and administrative adjudication is supervised both by courts and by the executive institutions within which adjudicators operate.[92] In the Australian system, tribunals are considered as categorically different from courts, but they are supervised by the courts, and the highest administrative tribunal, the AAT, has 'a strongly judicial ethos'.[93]

An important part of the discussion of the different models is an analysis of the membership of tribunals, and it is here that we find reference to the role of lay persons in delivering administrative justice.[94] In the United States, although administrative law judges (ALJs) must be legally qualified, they are greatly outnumbered by administrative judges (AJs), who review matters such as immigration and veterans' benefits decisions.[95] A large proportion of AJs are non-lawyers, who are typically appointed directly by the agency whose decisions they review.[96] In the United Kingdom, Cane argues that historically there has been a strong tradition of lay persons participating in the criminal justice system both as members of juries (triers of fact) and as adjudicators (as Justices of the Peace) so that when the decision was first made in the nineteenth century to appoint non-lawyers as administrative adjudicators, this did not prove unduly controversial.[97] Cane argues that attitudes towards lay participation in administrative adjudication in the United Kingdom has changed over time. 'In the 19th century, non-legal members were seen as having a significant contribution to make to administrative adjudication provided adequate legal input was available.'[98] However, since that time the

89 *Ibid.*, 69–72.
90 *Ibid.*, 90.
91 *Ibid.*
92 *Ibid.*
93 *Ibid.*
94 *Ibid.*, ch. 4.
95 *Ibid.*, 94.
96 *Ibid.*
97 *Ibid.*
98 *Ibid.*, 95.

United Kingdom has experienced an increasing 'judicialisation' of tribunals, culminating in the Tribunals, Courts and Enforcement Act 2007, which introduced a formal distinction between judges and members of the First-tier and Upper-tier tribunals. Cane comments:

> One of the aims of the new system is to 'encourage judicial career development'. The idea is that the grouping of specialised jurisdictions within the one (Lower-tier or Upper) Tribunal will give adjudicators the opportunity to acquire skills that are transferable from one jurisdiction to another, thus enabling them to deal with a wider variety of subject matter. However, it seems likely that the most transferable skills will be legal, and that non-legal members will have fewer opportunities for such career development than legal members (tribunal judges).[99]

In Australia, the participation of non-lawyers as adjudicators in the legal system is much less common than in the United Kingdom, although it remains a theoretical possibility. However, a significant proportion of members of the First-tier merits review tribunals, such as the Migration Review Tribunal and the Social Security Appeals Tribunal, as well as of members of the Administrative Appeals Tribunal, are either judges or have legal qualifications or experience.[100]

Cane's comparative analysis prompts him to argue that despite superficial differences between the comparator jurisdictions, persons sitting on administrative tribunals, whether or not they are legally qualified, are expected to 'act like lawyers' when they perform their decision-making function.[101] He also argues that adjudicators also contribute knowledge, information and 'narrative points of view' or 'data' to the decision-making process.[102] It is this latter feature which distinguishes tribunals from courts. In tribunals, adjudicators (especially lay members, including non-legal experts) are expected to contribute non-legal data to the decision-making process to a much greater extent than is permitted to judges in the traditional adversarial court process.[103]

Overall, Cane argues that as tribunals have increasingly come to be understood as belonging to the same genus as courts, the role of non-lawyers has diminished. Increasingly, they are valued as administrative adjudicators 'only if they possess some specific and obviously relevant expertise other than law, or in areas where governments wish to minimise the involvement of lawyers and

99 *Ibid.*, 96.
100 *Ibid.*, 96–97.
101 *Ibid.*, 97.
102 *Ibid.*
103 *Ibid.*

the promotion of legal values'.[104] Although he concludes that it is unlikely that for the foreseeable future tribunals will become as dominated by lawyers as courts are, in the light of his historical research, 'the position of non-lawyers in tribunals is now probably more precarious than it has been since the dawn of the modern tribunal system in the first half of the nineteenth century'.[105]

Cane's research draws on a wide range of sources to illuminate his comparative/ historical approach, and in doing so it falls within many of the definitions of socio-legal research discussed in this chapter. However, at the same time, drawing on the conventional 'legal' sources of reported cases and statutes, it also serves to illustrate the way in which the boundary between socio-legal and doctrinal research is not always absolutely clear-cut. This piece of research is likely to be drawn upon by scholars working within both those traditions, and would not necessarily be immediately identified as 'socio-legal' by all readers.

Curiosity-driven empirical socio-legal research

The final piece of research to which we shall turn is a monograph by Baldwin, Wikeley and Young, published in 1992, *Judging Social Security*, which examines social security policy and adjudication in Britain, in the light of considerable changes to the adjudicatory system which had been introduced in the late twentieth century, particularly during the 1980s.[106] This research was funded by the Nuffield Foundation, which is a charitable foundation working 'to improve social well-being by funding research and innovation in education and social policy'.[107] The aim of the research was to analyse the changes which had been introduced to the social security adjudication system which were intended 'to strengthen the independence, professionalism and quality of decision-making in the first two tiers of the adjudication system'.[108] It is essentially curiosity-driven research, with findings which are intended to throw light on 'the use of legal and administrative structures by government', as well as on the workings of the social security adjudication system itself. As such, although some of its findings may be of relevance to policy-makers, and have the potential to stimulate reform of the system, utility to policy-makers is not necessarily the main driver behind the research.

104 *Ibid.*, 98.
105 *Ibid.*
106 J. Baldwin, N. Wikeley and R. Young, *Judging Social Security: The Adjudication of Claims for Benefit in Britain*, Oxford: Oxford University Press, 1992, ch. 1.
107 See http://www.nuffieldfoundation.org (accessed 3 March 2017); Baldwin et al., *Judging Social Security*, Acknowledgements.
108 Baldwin et al., *Judging Social Security*, 24.

The research involved an empirical study of actors within the two initial tiers of the social security adjudication system, and included interviews with adjudication officers, appeals officers, chairpersons and members of tribunals, and presenting officers, as well as with appellants.[109] The researchers also observed tribunal hearings.[110] Although we are given some basic information about the ways in which data was collected, this is far less detailed than that in the Genn study discussed above, and apart from a brief section in the first chapter, is included throughout the book as different topics are addressed. This is somewhat more challenging for the reader interested in method. However, when quotations from interviews are included, the status of the speaker is clearly identified, and plenty of quotations are used, providing detailed empirical evidence to accompany the analysis. Although the system of social security adjudication has changed greatly since this research was published (including the abolition of Social Security Appeal Tribunals[111]), it remains a valuable and interesting piece of socio-legal research, due to its rigorous and detailed examination of the everyday experiences and working practices of actors within an adjudication system.

Lay decision-makers in Social Security Appeal Tribunals

While the Chair of a Social Security Appeal Tribunal had to be a barrister or solicitor of at least five years' standing, the two 'wing people' were lay persons, appointed for their 'knowledge or experience of conditions in the area' of the tribunal, and as being 'representative of persons living or working within the area'.[112] A significant number of members (38 per cent) were women, and over half were over 60 years of age (55 per cent were in their 60s and a further 8 per cent were over 70); by far the largest group of members had been nominated by trade unions.[113] The high numbers of elderly members uncovered by this study might be explained by the fact that the researchers focused on members who sat frequently, and they found that tribunal administrators, when seeking a member to sit at short notice, frequently contacted those who were retired, because they were much more likely to be available.[114] This then led to an overrepresentation of elderly members at tribunal hearings.

---

109 *Ibid.*, 13–15.
110 *Ibid.*
111 See Social Security Act 1998.
112 See Social Security Act 1975 s 97(2A) and Sched. 10 para. 1(2) as amended, referred to in Baldwin et al., *Judging Social Security*, 135.
113 Baldwin et al., *Judging Social Security*, 135.
114 *Ibid.*, 136.

Overall, the researchers comment that the tribunal system had 'failed to build up a broader base of membership to reflect in some measure the range of people that appear as appellants'.[115] They also found that this issue was not a matter of concern for some members, although a sizeable minority felt that panels were insufficiently representative, and that this did matter:

> I don't think that working class people, or people who have some understanding of the way in which many claimants live, are sufficiently represented. I think the quality of questioning and the quality of understanding peoples' lives is limited . . .
>
> I think that basically the members speak a different language to that the claimant does. And the claimant doesn't seem to get through to them. If he could get through to someone of his own class, then the outlook would probably be different to him, and it could be explained to him differently, in his own language. The communication between the claimant and the panel is not good . . .[116]

Although most chairmen, when interviewed, seemed broadly satisfied with the calibre of their members, the researchers comment that their own observations of tribunal hearings tended to coincide with the views of the minority of Chairs who were openly critical of members:

> A lot of those who are union reps are very good, the younger ones. Some of the older members on the panel, quite frankly, I feel they are just there to spend the morning filling their time up.
>
> They vary enormously in quality. Some are really first class. Others are frankly pretty hopeless, in the sense that they don't follow the proceedings in any great detail, or have a great deal to contribute to it . . .[117]

The researchers found that one problem was that members did not sit sufficiently often to enable them to develop their skills or to keep up with changes in the law.[118] Lack of training for tribunal members (as opposed to Chairs) was also identified as a problem.[119] Another reason that lay members failed to play a full part in hearings was that as the law became increasingly complex, the legally qualified Chairs enjoyed numerous advantages over the lay members, and observations of tribunal hearings revealed that lay members tended to be

115 *Ibid.*, 137.
116 *Ibid.*, 137.
117 *Ibid.*, 138.
118 *Ibid.*, 139.
119 *Ibid.*, 140–43.

marginalised by their Chairs.[120] Although the Chairs were encouraged to think of their members as equal partners in the decision-making process, many Chairs argued that this was very difficult to achieve in practice:

> Ideally . . . the members will have read the papers thoroughly, thought about it carefully and come prepared with specific questions to ask. More frequently it's the case that the members make some sort of feeble attempt to read the papers, or sometimes won't have done. They won't have understood them properly, they'll be relying to some extent on folklore, attitudes, prejudices . . .
>
> I mean some wing members have a very much palm tree justice approach, and they may take a very simplistic view of what they think is fair, quite regardless of what the legal position might be and regardless of what an analytical consideration of the evidence may point to . . .[121]

As the researchers comment, it is unsurprising that lay members were relatively uninvolved, and at best could play a subsidiary role to the legally qualified Chair.[122] Despite these (and other) disadvantages, such as the tendency of Chairs to dominate the questioning, and a lack of understanding by members of their role on the panel (seeing themselves as there to look after the interests of the claimant rather than as impartial adjudicators), the researchers argue that lay members should be retained, as there are occasions when they can play useful roles (such as asking supplementary questions, picking up points that are missed and contributing expert knowledge of certain issues where the precise facts are very important, such as whether someone has 'just cause' for voluntarily leaving a job).[123] The presence of lay members could also be seen as injecting a democratic element into the system. But if they were to be retained, the researchers argued strongly that attention would need to be paid to the problems uncovered by the research, so that members could be enabled to contribute more effectively to social security adjudication.[124] In the event, Social Security Appeal Tribunals were abolished, so the question did not arise. However, subsequent changes in the law do not detract from the research itself, which remains valuable for a number of reasons, not least because it addresses general questions about the lived experience of lay participation in a system of adjudication.

120 *Ibid.*, 144.
121 *Ibid.*, 145.
122 *Ibid.*, 147.
123 *Ibid.*, 152.
124 *Ibid.*, 153.

This research provides a very good example of what many people might think of as 'typical' socio-legal research. It is based on a piece of empirical research, but draws on the relevant academic literature to inform its analysis. It includes some policy-oriented conclusions which could be used to reform the legal process, such as the observation in Chapter 5 that 'urgent action' was needed to redress the imbalance (in terms of the ability to make a meaningful contribution to the adjudication process) between lay members of tribunals and the legally qualified Chairs.[125] However, the researchers also identified broader themes which emerged from their research, highlighting issues such as the difficulties of grafting on inquisitorial elements to an adversarial system, and the tensions between the increasing juridification of social security adjudication and the simultaneous erosion of claimants' substantive rights.[126] They also pointed to the way in which 'tightly drawn legal entitlements provide a mechanism by which [public] expenditure can be controlled'.[127] Throughout, as the extensive bibliography indicates, the analysis was informed by academic literature from a range of disciplines, including most notably social policy, but also politics, as well as law. It is thus a piece of research which falls squarely within the definitions of 'socio-legal' discussed at the beginning of this chapter.

Conclusion

In this chapter we have tried to illustrate the immense breadth of research which can be regarded as 'socio-legal', pointing not merely to different subject matter, but also to varying methods of research. While acknowledging the imprecise and sometimes controversial nature of the term, we have tried to emphasis that 'socio-legal' is not a synonym for 'empirical', and, indeed, that socio-legal research draws on many disciplines which are located within the Arts and Humanities, and does not confine itself to the social sciences. Not all legal scholars adopt a socio-legal approach to their research, but we have pointed to evidence which suggests that socio-legal studies is fast becoming the dominant mode of scholarship within the discipline of Law. An understanding of the rich variety of research which together can be described as forming 'socio-legal studies' is thus an important part of the education of contemporary legal scholars.

125 *Ibid.*, 153.
126 *Ibid.*, 211–12.
127 *Ibid.*, 212.

Recommended reading

Banaker, R. and Travers, M. (eds), *Theory and Method in Socio-Legal Research*, Oxford: Hart Publishing, 2005.

Collier, R., *Men, Law and Gender: Essay on the 'Man' of Law*, London and New York: Glasshouse/Routledge, 2010.

Hunter, C. (ed.), *Integrating Socio-legal Studies into the Law Curriculum*, Basingstoke: Palgrave Macmillan, 2012.

MacNeil, W., *Lex Populi: The Jurisprudence of Popular Culture*, Stanford: Stanford University Press, 2010.

Roberts, S., *Order and Dispute: An Introduction to Legal Anthropology*, Harmondsworth: Penguin Books, 1979.

3   Doing empirical research

Exploring the decision-making
of magistrates and juries

Mandy Burton

Empirical legal research is defined here to include the study of law, legal processes and legal phenomena using social research methods, such as interviews,
observations or questionnaires. Many students and early career legal academics embarking on empirical research into law come from academic backgrounds where they have had limited exposure to social research methods.
They may have completed law degrees where there was some use of empirical
legal research in the curriculum.[1] However, such exposure will probably be as
the reader of the findings of empirical studies and they may not have been
encouraged to consider the methodological issues in much depth. Very few
will have conducted their own research using methods of quantitative or
qualitative data collection and analysis. So how does a law graduate make the
transition from doctrinal legal research to carrying out their own empirical
legal studies, and what are the benefits of doing so?

Like any research method, empirical studies has both its advantages and
drawbacks. A researcher who opens a standard textbook on social research
might be put off by the number of challenges that experienced social researchers
suggest are likely to be faced. Many researchers refer to the amount of time and
effort involved in data collection, and the need for an element of good fortune
if all is to turn out well. However, there is a simple truth that not all research
questions can be answered using secondary sources or other research methods.
As Bradney observes:

> Quantitative and qualitative empirical research into law and legal processes
> provides not just more information about law; it provides information of a

---

1 Even then, it has been noted, the use of empirical legal research in teaching is the
   'exception rather than the norm'. See A. Bradney, 'The Place of Empirical Legal
   Research in the Law School Curriculum', in P. Cane and H. Kritzer (eds), *The
   Oxford Handbook of Empirical Legal Research*, Oxford: Oxford University Press, 2010,
   1031.

different character from that which can be obtained through other methods of research. It answers questions about law that cannot be answered in any other way.[2]

Thus, for example, knowing the legal rules may give us little understanding of how decisions are actually made in practice; for this, empirical research may be necessary.

The starting point, therefore, is always the research question. Once the research question has been formulated,[3] and the literature review completed, it should be clear whether or not that question can be answered without the collection and analysis of primary data. If not, the theoretical, methodological and practical issues of collecting original data must be tackled. This chapter aims to provide an overview of some of those issues. Many empirical questions arise from lay participation in the legal system, and it is an area where there has been a significant amount of empirical research, especially into criminal juries.[4] Other lay participants such as tribunal members and magistrates are under-researched by comparison, but not completely neglected. This chapter draws upon research into magistrates' decision-making in domestic violence cases and jury decision-making in rape cases. These studies illustrate some of the ways in which empirical legal research has enhanced our understanding of lay decision-making in the legal process and the methodological challenges posed by such work.

Theory and empirical research

Good empirical research involves more than formulating a research question and choosing a research method. Theory is an important part of empirical research. It is, of course, an oversimplification to say that there is more than one way of looking at the social world. It would be impossible to describe here the many different ways in which sociologists and social legal scholars have constructed theory to help them and us understand the social world they are

---

2 *Ibid.*, 1033
3 Formulating and refining a research question is not an easy task; however, there are many guides on this topic. See, e.g., N. Green, 'Formulating and Refining a Research Question', in N. Gilbert (ed.), *Researching Social Life*, 3rd edn, London: Sage, 2008, ch. 3.
4 See N. Vidmar, 'Lay Decision Making in the Legal Process', in P. Cane and H. Kritzer (eds), *The Oxford Handbook of Empirical Legal Research*, Oxford: Oxford University Press, 2010. Vidmar examines some of the research into criminal and civil juries, mixed tribunals (comprising legally trained and lay members) and lay magistrates.

researching.[5] However, developing and testing research theory is a significant part of the empirical research process. As Gilbert asserts, 'theory highlights and explains something that one would otherwise not see'.[6] The kind of research carried out will depend to an extent on the theory underpinning it. For example, some of the research studies in the field of policing have been informed by theories which focus on the culture and working rules of the police.[7] If the theory underlying the research is that the organisational culture of the police may explain a particular phenomenon, for example why black people are disproportionately stopped and searched,[8] then arguably the topic can only be effectively investigated by choosing a research method which will provide an opportunity to access organisational culture.[9] Explaining police decision-making in domestic violence cases is another example of a topic which requires a theory and method which looks beyond the legal rules and explores organisational culture.[10] These are just a few illustrations of method being influenced by theory.

As an empirical research project develops, theories are often refined, and some social researchers would recommend that the influence of existing theories should be minimal when embarking on data collection. Hammersley

5 N. Gilbert, 'Research, Theory and Method', in Gilbert, *Researching Social Life*, ch. 2. Durkheim and Goffman are just two notable examples discussed by Gilbert. See also Cownie and Bradney in this book for a discussion of the theories developed by Layard, Bradney and others to explain their research findings.
6 Gilbert, 'Research, Theory and Method', 25.
7 M. McConville, A. Sanders and R. Leng, *The Case for the Prosecution*, London: Routledge, 1989.
8 For an overview of the significance of race in police working rules, see A. Sanders, R. Young and M. Burton, *Criminal Justice*, Oxford: Oxford University Press, 2010, 177–82.
9 See A. Bryman (ed.), *Doing Research on Organisations*, London: Routledge, 1988. Qualitative methodologies are often the most useful for this type of research. Compton and Jones, for example, have asserted that access to organisational culture cannot be obtained through methods employed at a distance (such as questionnaires), because culture demonstrates itself in many ways and places requiring constant observation. See Compton and Jones in Bryman, *Doing Research on Organisations*. Ethnography is a favoured approach of many researchers of organisations because of the richness of data that can be obtained.
10 C. Hoyle, 'Being a "Nosy Bloody Cow" Ethical and Methodological Issues in Researching Domestic Violence', in R. King and E. Wincup (eds), *Doing Research on Crime and Justice*, Oxford: Oxford University Press, 2000. Hoyle found that police working rules, or 'cop' culture, was a powerful factor in arrest decisions; particularly influential was the victim's wishes, which may explain the relatively unsuccessful attempts in the 1990s to implement pro-arrest policies. See C. Hoyle, *Negotiating Domestic Violence*, Oxford: Clarendon, 1998.

and Atkinson encourage empirical researchers to go into the field with hypothesis or 'foreshadowed problems', but caution these have to be responsive to what the researcher finds; hypothesis and theories may be completely revised in the face of more interesting or conflicting data which runs counter to the researchers' expectations.[11] One of the most influential accounts of the process of developing theory from empirical data is the 'grounded theory' model of Glaser and Strauss.[12] Glaser and Strauss describe a process of theory generation and data analysis which takes place while data collection is ongoing.[13] While grounded theory is not a universally accepted approach to empirical research,[14] their exploratory approach does have features to commend it. While the literature review will set the scene for empirical research, there is arguably little point in carrying out empirical research if it is entirely dominated by existing ideas. So, for example, McConville has described how collection of empirical data on plea bargaining, first in England and later in New York, resulted in development of a theory about how guilty pleas were part of a 'social disciplinary' model of criminal justice.[15] At the time, theories of criminal justice were dominated by the 'crime control' and 'due process' models.[16] It would perhaps have been easy to see plea bargaining just through the theoretical lens of 'crime control', as it appears to have a significant amount of explanatory power. Indeed, traditional wisdom had also explained plea bargaining as the

11 M. Hammersley and P. Atkinson, *Ethnography: Principles in Practice*, 3rd edn, Abingdon: Routledge, 2007.

12 B. Glaser and A. Strauss, *The Discovery of Grounded Theory: Strategies for Qualitative Research*, London: Weidenfield & Nicholson, 1967.

13 See further A. Strauss, *Qualitative Analysis for Social Scientists*, Cambridge: Cambridge University Press, 1987.

14 Its popularity with social legal researchers has been questioned. See R. Banaker and M. Travers, 'Law, Sociology and Method', in R. Banaker and M. Travers (eds), *Theory and Method in Socio-Legal Research*, Oxford: Hart Publishing, 2005. Banaker and Travers claim to know of no examples of grounded theory being used in socio-legal empirical research. It seems realistic to say, in general, that 'the number of studies using grounded theory in a complete and precise fashion is probably relatively small' (P. Hodkinson, 'Grounded Theory and Inductive Research', in Gilbert, *Researching Social Life*).

15 M. McConville, 'Development of Empirical Techniques and Theory', in M. McConville and W. H. Chui (eds), *Research Methods for Law*, Edinburgh: Edinburgh University Press, 2010. As McConville notes, the 'social disciplinary' model has since been developed on the basis of further empirical work into policing.

16 Although alternative theoretical frameworks were being developed. See Sanders et al., *Criminal Justice*, ch. 1.

product of case load, suggesting a bureaucratic model of criminal justice.[17] As McConville asserts, the researcher should be wary of existing wisdom.[18] They need to be ready to find, and explain in theoretical terms, what is surprising in their empirical data.

Thus, when studying lay decision-makers, it would perhaps be unwise to assume, for the sake of illustration, that the decision-making of magistrates and jurors could be explained by reference to their composition alone. While a theory about the class or ethnic background of the bench or jury might have some explanatory power, an empiricist would want to be open to data and theories that might emerge from it.[19]

Considering the ethical issues

Empirical research involves studying people who have rights and interests of their own. As a result, empirical researchers have ethical and legal obligations to their research subjects. The Research Ethics Codes of the Economic and Social Research Council (ESRC) and Social Legal Studies Association (SLSA) are good starting points for socio-legal empiricists considering the basic principles of research ethics.[20] Many institutions to whom the researcher is obligated as either an employee or student will have their own codes of ethics and ethics approval procedure. Key principles in any code of ethics will be the avoidance or minimisation of harm, and the principle of informed consent.[21] Informed consent is related to the principle of avoidance of harm; if the research subjects do not know that they are being studied, and therefore do not consent, arguably the potential harms are greater.[22] Harm does not mean

---

17 Vogel has argued that the origins of plea bargaining are much more complex. See M. Vogel, *Coercion to Compromise*, Oxford: Oxford University Press, 2007.

18 McConville, 'Development of Empirical Techniques and Theory', p. 222.

19 Research on the significance of racial composition as a factor in jury decision-making has produced varying and perhaps, in some cases, surprising results. See C. Thomas with N. Bulmer, *Diversity and Fairness in the Jury System*, Ministry of Justice Research Series 02/07, London: Ministry of Justice (MoJ), 2007. See further C. Thomas, *Are Juries Fair?*, Ministry of Justice Research Series 1/10, London: MoJ, 2010.

20 ESRC guidelines, http://www.esrc.ac.uk/funding/guidance-for-applicants/research-ethics/ (accessed 27 March 2017); and SLSA guidelines, available in the resource area for members, at http://www.slsa.ac.uk (accessed 6 March 2017).

21 M. Bulmer, 'The Ethics of Social Research', in Gilbert, *Researching Social Life*, ch. 8.

22 At least the research participants are unable to take measures to protect themselves from harm.

just physical harm; it includes, for example, emotional distress and psychological harm. There is overlap between ethical and legal obligations relating to confidentiality and data security. When, for example, can promises of anonymity given to research subjects be broken if during the research it comes to light that someone, perhaps a child, is at risk of harm? A significant amount of time must be invested in the planning stages of a project to ensure that the ethical issues have been thoroughly considered and appropriate ethical clearance obtained.

When social scientists talk about research ethics, they often highlight studies where there have been alleged ethical violations – for example, covert research. In their defence, covert researchers might argue that their approach was justified because it would not have been possible to collect data had the research subjects known that they were being studied or, in cases of partial deception, what in particular was being studied. So, for example, Ditton's study of theft in a bakery was started as a covert research project when he took a job in the factory. When his co-workers became suspicious, he told them he was doing research, but not that he was studying theft.[23] This approach violates the principle of informed consent. However, most research, to lesser and greater degrees, will involve the researcher being less than candid about the exact purpose of the research. Negotiating the boundaries of what is acceptable or ethically justifiable is not an exact science, but it is arguably indefensible to adopt an outright position that the 'ends justify the means'. Particular care has to be taken if the research subjects are vulnerable or sensitive topics are being researched.

Lay magistrates, by virtue of their status,[24] might not be automatically regarded as vulnerable, in the way that a child, a person with mental impairment or perhaps a member of a socially disadvantaged social group would. However, vulnerability can be a relative concept. If a magistrate was being asked questions about a sensitive topic,[25] ethical issues would be raised. Likewise, jurors (or their mock substitutes) might be questioned about sensitive topics which will engage ethical issues. A scenario where magistrates or

23 J. Ditton, *Part Time Crime: An Ethnography of Fiddling and Pilferage*, London: Macmillan, 1977.

24 Most magistrates in England and Wales are middle-class professionals (see P. Darbyshire, 'For the New Lord Chancellor: Some Causes for Concern about Magistrates', *Criminal Law Review*, 1997, 861), and, therefore, it might be argued, are able to safeguard their own interests. Of course, the fact that the researcher is involved in researching a relatively powerful social group does not absolve him or her from observing ethical principles.

25 Sexual behaviour or drug use, for example.

jurors were deceived about the true nature of their task and/or the implications of their decision-making would also have ethical implications,[26] even though it might be suggested that the deception (or lack of it) can make a difference to the way they approach their task and the decisions taken.[27]

Selecting the research techniques

There are a number of different strategies that empirical legal researchers can adopt, which broadly fall into the qualitative and quantitative research distinction.[28] There are plenty of excellent books on qualitative and quantitative research and it would be impossible to review the various methods – interviews, observations, questionnaires, case studies, ethnography and so on – in any detail here.[29] There are certain aspects of law-related social life that have historically been popular with sociologists. These have mainly, although not exclusively, been related to criminal behaviour and criminal law enforcement. Thus, there is a vast criminology literature, which includes a healthy body of literature relating to research methods – a useful resource for socio-legal scholars.[30] The Nuffield Inquiry noted the bias towards criminal justice, with civil justice as the poor relation,[31] but even outside the field of criminal process, many socio-legal scholars have carefully documented their methods

26 See the discussion below, for an analysis of the impracticalities and ethical considerations for not deceiving mock jurors.
27 See Vidmar, 'Lay Decision Making in the Legal Process', for discussion of a study by Breau et al. (2007), where students were asked to sit on a disciplinary panel. Some of them knew the task was for research purposes; others thought it was real. The latter took longer to deliberate and, unlike the research-aware group, did not find a violation. Although the research was not statistically significant, Vidmar seems to suggest that more attention should be given to the question of whether mock jurors approach their task differently because they know the case is not real.
28 See A. Bryman, *Quantity and Quality in Social Research*, London: Routledge, 1988.
29 Gilbert's edited collection is a good starting point and has chapters on the various methods, as well as data analysis. See Gilbert, *Researching Social Life*, Parts II and III. See also D. Silverman (ed.), *Qualitative Research: Issues in Theory, Method and Practice*, 3rd edn, London: Sage, 2011; and A. Bryman and R. Burgess, *Qualitative Research*, London: Sage, 1999.
30 See, e.g., R. King and E. Wincup (eds), *Doing Research on Crime and Justice*, Oxford: Oxford University Press, 2000; and C. E. Pope, R. Lovell and S. G. Brandl, *Voices from the Field: Readings in Criminal Justice Research*, Belmont, CA: Wadsworth, 2001.
31 H. Genn, M. Partington and S. Wheeler, *Law in The Real World: Improving Our Understanding of How Law Works*, The Nuffield Inquiry on Empirical Legal Research Final Report, London: Nuffield Foundation, 2006.

and provided a useful resource for others contemplating the selection of appropriate research techniques.[32]

When empirical researchers are selecting the most appropriate methods for their research question, consideration has to be given to how that research will be evaluated in terms of reliability, representativeness and validity. This involves asking questions such as: Are the results of the study replicable? To what extent could the results of the study be generalised beyond the specific research context? Will the results be credible as a true picture of what is being studied? A worry for those who have carried out large-scale surveys at a distance from the research subject might be whether they managed to obtain a true picture of what it is they were aiming to study; it might be easy for respondents to fabricate a reply, or indeed in many instances not respond at all.[33] A concern for researchers embarking on small-scale empirical projects – for example, involving small numbers of interviews with a group of respondents drawn from a much larger potential sample – might be whether they can make any claims to representativeness.[34] Such concerns may be unfounded; often such research is not aimed at making claims of representativeness – rather the researchers may be aiming to expand knowledge about the things that can happen and how they are interpreted in a particular social world.

In the context of PhD research, especially in socio-legal studies, large-scale empirical projects seem to be rare.[35] Most large-scale, socio-legal, empirical

32 See Cane and Kritzer, *The Oxford Handbook of Empirical Legal Research*.
33 Questionnaires have notoriously low response rates, even when follow-up requests are sent. The obvious issue then becomes whether the responders are different in some way from those who did not respond. There are pros and cons to using the internet, as opposed to the traditional postal method (see C. Hine, 'The Internet and Research Methods', in Gilbert, *Researching Social Life*). Whatever the means of distribution (face to face, online, by phone or post), designing a questionnaire requires skill and testing to try to ensure the responses illicit relevant information and avoid such things as biased, leading questions. See M. Bulmer, *Questionnaires*, London: Sage, 2004.
34 There are many different types of research interview; some are more structured or standardised than others, for example. While interviews undoubtedly have their own limitations, informal interviews offer an opportunity for research which is more exploratory in nature than, perhaps, a questionnaire allows. Of course, there is skill involved in successfully interviewing and perhaps a large part of it is also down to an ability to put people at their ease and minimise interviewer effects. See A. Bryman, *Social Research Methods*, 4th edn, Oxford: Oxford University Press, 2012, ch. 20.
35 As Hutchinson in this collection observes, often a great deal of work goes into laying a doctrinal context for the empirical study, squeezing the resources available for the latter.

projects appear to be carried out by teams of researchers, often from different academic disciplines. This can be an excellent way for a law graduate to acquire some of the skills and knowledge to lead their own larger-scale empirical projects in the future. Many socio-legal researchers carrying out empirical research have learnt how to do it by actually doing it, and if they are lucky as part of a team of more experienced researchers. PhD researchers are sometimes written into the funding applications for large-scale projects. It is, however, possible to do worthwhile methodologically sound empirical research projects without a strong background in social research methods, a detailed knowledge of statistics or the various computer packages available to analyse data.[36] However, ultimately, when selecting a research technique, the researcher must consider the practicalities of their situation; what is achievable given the time, expertise and resources available to them. One of the key practicalities is gaining access to the research subjects.

Gaining access to research subjects

Any empirical legal research presents the challenge of accessing research subjects, but for some projects this is more difficult than others. The greater the level of access being required, the more difficult it will probably be to gain. Access to conduct interviews or administer questionnaires might be hard enough, but if the researcher wants to spend months observing and perhaps also examining documentation, then the problems are likely to be greater. If the research subjects are part of an informal group, then access can perhaps be negotiated through acceptance by an insider who acts as a sponsor and makes introductions.[37] If the research subjects are part of a formal group or organization, then obtaining access can be particularly difficult. Organisations, such as the police and courts, are often deluged with research requests and those in authority may be reluctant to grant permission for their staff to devote time to what they see as unproductive academic research activities.[38] It is probably advisable

36 A working knowledge of SPSS or NVivo might be an advantage for some projects, but it is not a necessity for small-scale qualitative research. Bryman (*Social Research Methods*) offers an introduction to SPSS and NVivo for those who are interested in computer-assisted data analysis.

37 For an ethnographer, blending into a group as an obvious outsider is not always an easy exercise. There are plenty of fascinating accounts of this process; for examples, see R. Burgess, 'Some Role Problems in Field Research', in R. Burgess (ed.), *Field Research: A Sourcebook and Field Manual*, London: Routledge, 1982.

38 Buchannan et al., 'Getting in, Getting on, Getting out, and Getting back', in Bryman, *Doing Research on Organisations*.

to seek access at the top of an organisation, because if access is negotiated at the bottom, it may be denied by someone with greater authority.

There is no single recipe for success in negotiating access, which experienced researchers caution may take months or even years.[39] The PhD researcher obviously does not have years to wait. Opportunistic approaches and the use of personal contacts can be valuable. Part of the negotiations for access will often centre on control of research findings. Many researchers have warned against agreeing to a restrictive research bargain, for example one which allows the research subjects to censor the findings and prevent publication. Yet many powerful institutions have reputations to protect and may not agree to access without such a condition. The temptation for a relatively powerless researcher may be to sign a restrictive research bargain and hope that the organisation will not make extensive use of its rights of censorship. A similar position may arise for researchers carrying out funded research, where the funders, particularly government departments, may wish to restrict publication of research findings.[40]

Gaining access to research subjects is one of those aspects of the empirical research process where there may be a large element of luck involved. The type and level of access achievable may relate back to the issue of the techniques selected; the researcher may start with one ideal, but have to modify their approach due to limitations on access. The process of planning and carrying out an empirical project is not linear; plans may have to be modified to reflect the reality.

Researching the decision-making of magistrates

The magistrates' court is the lowest court of criminal jurisdiction in England and Wales. There is a split between lay and professional magistracy, but the majority of cases are dealt with by lay magistrates.[41] Lay magistrates are therefore one of the primary examples of lay participation in the English legal system. Their significance, in terms of case load at least, far exceeds that of the jury.[42]

Although, on the face of it, magistrates might appear to be a less attractive topic than the jury, academics have found plenty to interest them in researching

39 *Ibid.*
40 R. Tarling, 'Relations between Government Researchers and Academics', *Howard Journal of Criminal Justice* 50(3), 2011, 307.
41 Sanders et al., *Criminal Justice*, ch. 9.
42 P. Darbyshire, 'An Essay on the Importance and Neglect of the Magistracy', *Criminal Law Review*, 1997, 627.

the magistracy. The decisions that magistrates make, not only about guilt or innocence, but also about such matters as where the case should be heard (mode of trial) and whether the defendant should be deprived of their liberty or granted bail pending trial, make them a rich topic for empirical investigation. There have been, for example, studies looking at the composition of the magistracy and whether they are representative of their communities and how this influences their approach to cases. Some of this research has been policy driven and/or funded by government departments,[43] so when evaluating this type of research, it is worth being mindful of the constraints that this may have placed on what was investigated and how it was reported. It is useful to know that lay magistrates approach their task in different ways from professional (legally trained) magistrates. Morgan and Russell highlight efficiency as one factor which can be taken into account in comparatively evaluating the performance of lay and professional magistrates.[44] Policy-orientated research need not favour a particular outcome and does not have to be devoid of theory.[45] Nevertheless, efficiency is often an underlying if not overt feature of government interest in the magistracy. One particular interest has been how it can be ensured that the magistrates keep more cases to themselves and send fewer to the significantly more expensive Crown Court. However, some of the most insightful work into magistrates' mode of trial decision-making in recent years has been undertaken by lone PhD researchers rather than government-commissioned research teams.[46]

Magistrates' decision-making in general is a very broad topic, so many research projects inevitably focus on an aspect of that decision-making, be that

43 See, e.g., R. Morgan and N. Russell, *The Judiciary in the Magistrates' Court*, Home Office and Lord Chancellor's Department, 2000. This research was commissioned with the specific aim of exploring the balance of work undertaken by the lay magistracy compared with the professional magistracy and to consider whether each was 'deployed in the most effective way'.

44 Professional magistrates deal with cases more speedily than lay magistrates, so it might be thought that on efficiency grounds greater use should be made of them. Although Morgan and Russell point out that the lay magistracy have their strengths, and their report does not point to any particular policy conclusion (see Morgan and Russell, *The Judiciary in the Magistrates' Court*).

45 A. Sanders, *Community Justice*, IPPR, London, 2001. In this report, Sanders evaluates empirical research on the magistracy in relation to 'core values' of criminal justice.

46 A. Herbert, 'Mode of Trial and the Influence of Local Justice', *Howard Journal of Criminal Justice* 43, 2004, 65; S. Cammiss, '"I Will in a Moment Give You the Full History": Mode of Trial, Prosecutorial Control and Partial Accounts', *Criminal Law Review*, 2006, 38; and S. Cammiss, 'The Management of Domestic Violence Cases in the Mode of Trial Hearing: Prosecutorial Control and Marginalizing Victims', *British Journal of Criminology* 46, 2006, 704.

type of decision (for example, bail, or mode of trial, as mentioned above), or perhaps type of case. Domestic violence is a frequent component of the work of the criminal justice system. Although many cases are lost in the early stages of the process of police and prosecution decision-making,[47] some cases do make it to the magistrates' court and so one research question is: how do magistrates' respond to cases of domestic violence and what influences their decision-making in such cases?

So how might a researcher go about accessing magistrates as research subjects for a project looking at their decision-making in domestic violence cases? In one sense, there is no need to negotiate access at all. If a researcher wants to carry out observations, then magistrates' courts are places to which the public have access and it is possible to simply go into the public gallery. However, even if this approach is taken, it is one that is likely to attract attention and possibly be subject to some kind of challenge.[48] Furthermore, if the researcher was trying to study the decision-making of magistrates, not only would this method be extremely time-consuming, but it would present only a partial picture of what was being studied.[49] The researcher would have no access to the deliberations of magistrates which take place in private in the retiring room, nor would they know what influence if any the court clerk had on that deliberation process.[50] If the researcher wanted to find out, for example, what influence particular factors, such as the personal characteristics of the offender or offence, had upon the process and outcome of the case, court observations would only go so far in generating data to answer that question. Ideally, the researcher might also like access to the deliberation process and perhaps also the ability to survey magistrates or conduct some in-depth interviews with a selection of magistrates. However, to interview or

---

47 See Hoyle, *Negotiating Domestic Violence*; and M. Burton, *Legal Responses to Domestic Violence*, London: Routledge, 2008.

48 D. McBarnet, *Conviction*, London: Macmillan, 1981. McBarnet describes how she was questioned about her presence in the courtroom and told to go to the Crown Court where she would find something much more interesting to observe. She remained in the magistrates' court and found plenty of interest.

49 McBarnet was able by this method to make significant observations about the conviction-oriented nature of magistrates – for example, their dismissive and hostile attitudes towards defendants, sometimes manifested in questioning which revealed assumptions of guilt.

50 The primary function of the justices' clerk is to give legal advice, but they have other functions and empirical scholars have in the past theorised that they approach their role as 'liberal bureaucrats'. There is no recent empirical research looking at how they perform their role in a much changed landscape. Sanders et al., *Criminal Justice*, pp. 514–18.

survey magistrates or observe their deliberations would require permission from the relevant authorities. Researchers have observed that it is increasingly difficult to obtain that permission, unless the authorities themselves are funding the research, with the associated limits on the scope of the investigation and publication of findings.

When carrying out their study of specialist domestic violence courts, Cook et al. were able to gain access to interview magistrates. This was part of a multi-method study which involved case-file analysis and observations, as well as interviews with a range of other criminal justice professionals involved in processing cases in specialist domestic violence courts, which in England and Wales usually operate only in the magistrates' courts setting. It should be noted that this research was commissioned by the Crown Prosecution Service (CPS) and carried out in conjunction with the Ministry of Justice (MoJ), and the final report was approved and published by both. It is not possible to tell whether permission to interview magistrates – for example, about their attitudes to domestic violence – would have been obtained without the research being funded by the CPS and sponsored by the MoJ.[51] The findings of the research by Cook et al. were used to inform a significant policy initiative by the then Labour Government to roll out specialist domestic violence courts nationally. However, it should be noted that the agenda of the research was not to prove that domestic violence courts 'worked'; in some respects, the research showed that domestic violence courts were failing victims (in ways that traditional non-specialist courts had) and that they were not fully holding perpetrators to account.

The multi-method approach adopted by Cook et al. revealed a certain level of disconnect between the views that magistrates expressed in interviews and the outcomes of cases in the case-file sample. Key informants from all the criminal justice agencies expressed the view in interviews that the sentencing practices of the magistrates had improved due to the training that magistrates received, which was directed at challenging stereotypical attitudes to domestic violence and making them think more carefully about appropriate penalties. Magistrates interviewed claimed that their attitudes and approach to sentencing had changed; however, while in some specialist domestic violence court settings the use of community penalties increased, in others financial penalties

---

51 In an earlier study, Gilchrist and Blisset were able to gain access to magistrates to present them with a range of different domestic violence scenarios and explore the attitudes underlying their decision-making. See E. Gilchrist and J. Blisset, 'Magistrates Attitudes to Domestic Violence and Sentencing Options', *Howard Journal of Criminal Justice* 41(4), 2002, 348.

(which were not seen as a positive outcome) increased.[52] These contradictory findings highlight the benefit of data triangulation; use of different research techniques to gather information addressing the same question. It is often claimed that a limitation of interviews is that what people say they do is not always what they do in practice. In this case, there appeared to be an element of truth in that statement. However, analysing the data in context suggested that the difference might be attributable to the options available to magistrates; in some areas, magistrates were unable to make as extensive use of community penalties as they might have liked because of lack of available supporting resources, such as perpetrator programmes. In short, the culture surrounding domestic violence in specialist courts might have been changing, as informants claimed, but the resources were struggling to keep up with cultural change.

While the decision-making of magistrates (and other criminal justice professionals) in domestic violence cases was the clear focus of the research of Cook et al., in other cases it has emerged as a perhaps unexpected element of a project focused originally on other issues. Cammiss' empirical work, based on observations in the magistrates' courts in addition to access to CPS files, is an example of domestic violence emerging as a theme from the data.[53] Cammiss set out to explore mode of trial decision-making. By his admission, this was regarded by others as a 'mundane' part of the criminal justice process, previously dominated by policy-relevant research with an efficiency agenda. However, his research revealed that there were significant differences in the way that domestic violence cases were treated by magistrates compared with non-domestic violence cases; the former were more frequently deemed appropriate for summary trial. Analysis of his data revealed to him that the explanation for this lay in the partial accounts presented to magistrates by prosecutors, which minimised the manner of the assault by focusing on lack of injury rather than the way in which violence was inflicted. Cammiss is giving us an example of the importance of the story told and the 'narratives' available to and constructed by decision-makers.[54] He is also showing the importance of not viewing various decision-makers within the criminal justice

---

52 M. Burton, 'Judicial Monitoring of Compliance: Introducing "Problem Solving" Approaches to Domestic Violence Courts in England and Wales', *International Journal of Family Law and Policy* 20(3), 2006, 366.

53 Cammiss, 'The Management of Domestic Violence Cases'; and S. Cammiss and C. Stride, 'Modelling Mode of Trial', *British Journal of Criminology* 48(4), 2008, 482.

54 He has gone on to develop his work on narratives in greater depth with this and other empirical projects. See further, Cammiss and Watkins in this book.

process in isolation. Magistrates do not operate in a vacuum; their decisions should be viewed through the lens of serial decision-making. Fully under-standing lay magistrates' decision-making requires access to a range of actors within the criminal justice process. This is something that can, to an extent, be carried out through observations, but it is a very time-consuming method and requires a great deal of discipline in recording observations. Cammiss, like countless others before him, has used the observation method as one tool in his methodology. Critics might say, how can one be sure that another observer would have recorded the same thing, or that the researcher has accurately recorded the social world of the research subjects? Data triangu-lation can help to minimise some of the concerns surrounding the reliability and validity of observational research.[55]

So far, some of the disadvantages of being a lone PhD researcher have been highlighted, but there are also advantages. While a PhD researcher might have fewer resources than a research team or established academic with research funding, they might also have fewer problems in finding an appropriate field role if they choose to conduct observation or ethnographic research. Researchers carrying out ethnographic research as more established academics have highlighted numerous challenges that come with their position, not least managing to find a field role.[56] It is frequently said that the researcher must be unthreatening and find a role somewhere between stranger and friend. The research student has the advantage of being relatively unthreatening and also can probably ask probing questions with the guise of naivety which might not otherwise be credible. It is submitted that magistrates are likely to feel relatively comfortable with being observed and questioned by a research student, perhaps less so by a team of academics sponsored by a government department. Guarantees of anonymity and confidentiality may be a sufficient cushion to reassure respondents, but they might not. On the other hand, if the researcher is observing a group such as magistrates for a long time, it is pretty hard for them to pretend to behave in a way that they otherwise would not and usually the business of the moment is more important than the fact of observation, even if known.[57]

---

55 Denzin refers to different types of triangulation, including triangulation of methods which can provide confirmatory data (see N. Denzin, *The Research Act in Sociology*, London: Butterworths, 1970).

56 P. Rock, 'Participant Observation', in A. Bryman and R. Burgess (eds), *Qualitative Research*, Vol. II, London: Sage, 1989; P. Rock, *The Social World of an English Crown Court*, Oxford: Clarendon, 1993.

57 On observation and ethnography, see the relevant chapters in Gilbert, *Researching Social Life* and Burgess, *Field Research*.

Decision-making of jurors in rape cases

In England and Wales, jurors are not required to give reasons for their decisions. Furthermore, section 20 of the Juries Act 1974, as amended by the Criminal Justice and Courts Act 2015, makes it a criminal offence to obtain, solicit or disclose opinions expressed, arguments advanced or votes cast by members of the jury during deliberations. This prohibition means that empirical research into the decision-making of juries based on direct observation is not possible. Sometimes, jurors have published accounts of their experiences, and these can be illuminating, but of course are anecdotal. Socio-legal scholars interested in jury deliberations have come up with a variety of different approaches to getting around the prohibition on direct observation.[58] One approach has been to compare jury verdicts with professional opinions, although this has been criticised as disagreement between lay jurors and legally trained professionals does not necessarily mean that the jury reached the 'wrong' decision.[59] An alternative approach is direct observation of shadow or mock juries. 'Shadow' juries listen to a real case in tandem with a real jury; as such, they have realistic stimuli, but whether they approach the deliberations in the same way as the real jury is a matter for debate. While there is a high degree of correspondence between the real and shadow jurors in many such studies, obviously the defendant's fate does not lie in the hands of the shadow jury. However, an approach which relies on mock jurors' deliberations might be regarded as even more artificial, as this involves groups of people observing mock trials rather than real cases. Nevertheless, the mock juror approach has considerable advantages methodologically, not least the ability to manipulate variables in order to explore the influence of particular factors in jury deliberations.[60] Mock jurors have been used very successfully in recent research by Finch and Munro,[61] and Ellison and Munro,[62] to explore the decision-making of jurors in rape cases.

58 Sanders et al., *Criminal Justice*, pp. 593–602 provides an overview of the research evaluating the jury's performance with reference to the variety of methodologies used. Vidmar, 'Lay Decision Making in the Legal Process', also summarises some of this research.
59 *Ibid.*
60 See E. Finch and V. Munro, 'Lifting the Veil: The Use of Focus Groups and Trial Simulations in Legal Research', *Journal of Law and Society* 35, 2008, 30.
61 E. Finch and V. Munro, 'Breaking the Boundaries? Sexual Consent in the Jury Room' *Legal Studies* 26(3), 2006, 303; and E. Finch and V. Munro, 'The Demon Drink and the Demonized Woman: Socio-Sexual Stereotypes and Responsibility Attribution in Rape Trials Involving Intoxicants', *Social and Legal Studies* 16(4), 2007, 591.
62 L. Ellison and V. Munro, 'Reacting to Rape: Exploring MockJuror's Assessments of Complainant Credibility', *British Journal of Criminology* 49(2), 2009, 202;

Finch and Munro used mock juries to investigate the impact of complainant intoxication on jurors' deliberations in rape cases. Ellison and Munro also used mock juries in a study which explored the influence of jurors' prejudices and stereotypes about such factors as lack of physical injury in a rape complainant, calm demeanour at trial and delay in reporting. Both of these studies have in common a refreshing open and full account of the methods and an assessment of the strengths and weaknesses of the approach taken. As such, the research is valuable methodologically and not just for its substantive findings.

Finch and Munro have written in detail about the problems of empirical research involving mock jurors.[63] One of the issues is inadequate sampling; typically, academics have relied on students, who are easy to recruit, but not representative of the wider community. Even when the net is cast wider, self-selecting members of the public might be different from conscripted real jurors. Another issue is the adequacy of the stimuli; mock jurors might be given written vignettes which are far removed from the visual stimuli of a real trial. Vidmar concurs, arguing the 'ecological validity' of mock jury research is often questionable; stimulus materials are often very limited compared with the weeks of evidence that may be sat through by real jurors.[64] Even when videos or acted live mini-trials are used, the stimuli are more limited than a real trial. Furthermore, the mock trials are designed to explore the impact of specific variables and as such more prominence might be given to them than in a real trial, perhaps exaggerating the effect they have on the deliberation process. Despite these limitations, it has been argued that mock jurors offer better insights into the deliberative process than alternative approaches, such as focus groups. Finch and Munro used both focus groups and mock jurors. They argued that the mock jurors enabled them to gain insights into the deliberative process which would not have been possible via other methods. Despite some limitations with their approach, which involved self-selected members of the public viewing 75-minute mini-trials using actors in a university teaching room rather than a courtroom, they argue that

L. Ellison and V. Munro, 'Of "Normal Sex" and "Real Rape"; Exploring the Use of Socio-Sexual Scripts in (Mock) Jury Deliberation', *Social and Legal Studies* 18(3), 2009, 291; and L. Ellison and V. Munro, 'Getting to (Not) Guilty: Examining Jurors' Deliberative Processes in, and beyond, the Context of a Mock Rape Trial', *Legal Studies* 30(1), 2010, 74.

63 Finch and Munro, 'Lifting the Veil'.
64 Vidmar, 'Lay Decision Making in the Legal Process', 637. He argues that the fact that mock juries comprising students do not differ significantly in their results to juries made up of wider sections of the community does not give greater confidence in the validity of the findings where the stimulus for both is so limited.

the sampling was more adequate and the stimuli more realistic than many mock juror studies. Furthermore, unlike many mock jury studies, they were focusing on group deliberation rather than the views of individual jurors.

Finch and Munro illustrate how the method selected is often a compromise between what is desirable and practical/ethical. In England and Wales, the standard jury is twelve members of the public randomly selected from the electoral register. In their trial simulations, Finch and Munro used eight mock jurors; even then they had to recruit 168 self-selecting members of the public to observe their mini-trials. They note that the self-selected jurors may have been different in some way from real jurors, but contend that their personal characteristics might not be relevant to their verdicts, and in any event self-selection was the most practical and ethical approach for the study.[65] Of course, the mock jurors knew that they were not observing a real trial; that would have been obvious from the venue and stimuli, but even if not, the researchers contend ethical treatment of the participants would require disclosure of the mock nature of their task. Finch and Munro were encouraged by their analysis of mock deliberations that the participants undertook their task seriously and were willing to suspend their disbelief and engage in the process as if it were a real trial with real consequences. This seemed to be evident from the comments made by mock jurors which indicated that they were treating the case as if it were real and had consequences for the parties.[66] They note the difference between the participants in focus groups carried out before the mock trials and the mock juror group; the latter being more prepared to take into account contextual factors, despite the relatively limited nature of the stimuli compared with a real trial.

From a methodological point of view, Finch and Munro conclude that jury simulation has a great deal to offer socio-legal researchers, and is the best alternative given the lack of access to the real jury room. It is hard to disagree with this conclusion, and Ellison and Munro have used the approach to shed further light on deliberations in rape cases, making similar comments about the methodological strengths and limitations of jury simulation. They found

---

65 On the relevance of personal factors, such as race, see Thomas, *Are Juries Fair?*. See also the survey of international research carried out by Darbyshire et al. for the Auld review into Criminal Courts in England and Wales (P. Darbyshire with research by A. Maughan and A. Stewart, 'What Can We Learn from the Published Jury Research? Findings for the Criminal Courts Review', *Criminal Law Review*, 2001, 970). Much of the research in this area is inconclusive about the importance of factors such as the gender, ethnicity and professional background of jurors.

66 This was also the case with the research carried out by Ellison and Munro, 'Reacting to Rape' and 'Of "Normal Sex" and "Real Rape"'.

that jurors rely on stereotypes about the level of injury that would be suffered by a 'real' rape victim; in some instances, expecting unrealistically high levels of injury to verify a complaint. They also discovered that delay in reporting could undermine the credibility of a compliant in the eyes of mock jurors, as could a flat demeanour when giving evidence.[67] It should perhaps be noted that the studies by Finch, Munro and Ellison, including a forthcoming study by Ellison and Munro examining the impact of special measures on mock juror deliberations in rape trials, have all been funded by the ESRC. Such research is undoubtedly resource-intensive and not the type that could be readily undertaken by a lone PhD researcher. However, that a major research council should fund a series of interrelated research in this area is encouraging. Otherwise, the bulk of recent research in this area, in England and Wales at least, is government commissioned. While this brings its own advantages in terms of access to contextual data, it affords no distinct advantage in terms of access to juries being subject to the same legal prohibitions on direct observation of real juries.[68] There are many other examples of jury research which could have been explored here, but the studies selected here demonstrate some of the main methodological issues of this type of research.

Conclusion

This chapter contains a brief overview of selected studies of empirical research into lay decision-making. As such, it is a far from complete account of the empirical work that exists in this area. For decades, socio-legal scholars have

---

67   In this respect, rape complainants seem to be in a no-win situation; if they appear too emotional they might be thought to be putting on a show, yet if emotionally flat suspicions are also raised. See Ellison and Munro, 'Reacting to Rape' and 'Of "Normal Sex" and "Real Rape"'.

68   Lloyd-Bostock was able to interview jurors in a real fraud trial (the 'Jubilee line' case), but only because the jury did not reach a verdict and was discharged. Interviews took place several months after the case was concluded, which perhaps raises some concerns about recall (see S. Lloyd Bostock, 'The Jubilee Line Jurors; Does Their Experience Strengthen the Argument for Judge Only Trials in Long and Complex Fraud Cases?', *Criminal Law Review*, 2007, 225). However, Lloyd-Bostock's approach arguably had much more to commend it than Honess et al., who had a very similar research question, examining the competency of jurors in complex and lengthy fraud cases, but in their research used a method of case simulation with mock jurors which was considerably more limited than the stimuli available to the real jurors in the Maxwell case (T. Honess, M. Levi and E. Charman, 'Juror Competence in Processing Complex Information from a Simulation of the Maxwell Trial', *Criminal Law Review*, 1988, 763). See Vidmar, 'Lay Decision Making in the Legal Process', for a discussion of these two studies.

been using a variety of research techniques to try to better understand the gap between the law in books and the law in action. It is well understood that there are many extra-legal factors which may explain how discretion is exercised in practice and that studying the legal rules alone will provide limited insights into decision-making in practice. Empirical work is therefore not so much a choice as a necessity for some research questions, such as how lay decision-makers approach their cases. It can be an uncomfortable necessity in that it involves practical and ethical choices which represent real challenges for the researcher. If possible, it is best to remain as free as one can in negotiating access to the research subjects, while at the same time giving appropriate weight to their interests and concerns. Some subjects will be harder to research than others. As the jury deliberation example highlights, there may be legal as well as practical obstacles in the way. Collecting the data is just one step in the research process; data analysis and generation of theory are large components. It is wise, therefore, always to be mindful of the resources available for the project. Resources, as well as theory, will input into the research design. Empirical research is often a marriage between what is desirable and practical, with that all-important element of chance thrown in. In an ideal world, the empirical researcher will adopt a multi-method approach which will do much to strengthen their claims to have produced reliable and valid research; however, some questions lend themselves more readily to one technique than to another and data triangulation may not be possible. Honesty about the limitations of any given methodology provides the reader with the information and reassurance they need to evaluate the substantive findings of the research. Finch and Munro's research on juries, followed by that of Ellison and Munro, provides a model of good practice in this respect. Despite the challenges of empirical research, more often than not, the results outweigh the costs. It is hard to describe the thrill of uncovering data and, from that data, developing theories about an area of legal process previously neglected by empirical scholarship.

Recommended reading

Bryman, A., *Social Research Methods*, 4th edn, Oxford: Oxford University Press, 2012.

Cane, P. and Kritzer, H. (eds), *The Oxford Handbook of Empirical Legal Research*, Oxford: Oxford University Press, 2010.

Gilbert, N. (ed.), *Researching Social Life*, 3rd edn, London: Sage, 2008.

Silverman, D. (ed.), *Qualitative Research: Issues in Theory, Method and Practice*, 3rd edn, London: Sage, 2011.

4   Legal research in the humanities

Steven Cammiss and Dawn Watkins

'Herald, read the accusation!' said the King. On this the White Rabbit blew three blasts on the trumpet, and then unrolled the parchment scroll and read as follows:

'The Queen of Hearts she made some tarts,
All on a summer day:
The knave of hearts, he stole those tarts
And took them quite away!'

'Consider your verdict,' the King said to the jury. 'Not yet! Not yet!' the Rabbit hastily interrupted. 'There's a great deal to come before that!'[1]

Introduction

The appearance of an extract from *Alice's Adventures in Wonderland* in the context of a legal research methods book is seemingly incongruous. How might children's literary fiction bear any relevance to the pursuit of serious, academic legal research? This chapter will seek to answer this question within a broad-ranging consideration of a law and humanities approach to legal research, as well as considering, more specifically, some ways in which the topic of lay decision-making in the legal system might be addressed within a law and humanities remit.

What is 'law and humanities'?

'Law and humanities' is an all-encompassing term that has become used relatively recently to refer to a variety of interdisciplinary approaches to law, legal education and legal research. The *Oxford English Dictionary* defines 'the

---

1 The extract is from Lewis Carroll's *Alice's Adventures in Wonderland*, first published by Macmillan & Co. in 1866. This particular extract is taken from a full colour edition published by Macmillan Children's Books in 1995.

humanities' as the 'branch of learning concerned with human culture' and it lists history, literature, ancient and modern languages, law, philosophy and art as 'the academic subjects collectively comprising this branch of learning'.[2] This is a useful definition for our purposes, since it not only identifies law itself as a humanities discipline, but also describes all of the humanities disciplines as being interested in 'culture'. This 'cultural turn' is a perspective that has been incorporated increasingly within legal analysis[3] and it is the theme that unites all of the approaches that fall within the remit of 'law and humanities'.[4]

The first comprehensive text in the field was published as recently as 2010, and from the outset its editors concede that 'scholars in [the] field are supported by a well-developed infrastructure of professional associations and scholarly journals, but the precise contours of this field are anything but clear'.[5] Philosophical, historical, literary and artistic methods have all been applied to legal processes, but there is no clearly defined area of work that forms a law and humanities 'corpus'. However, what can be said with some certainty is that some of these approaches are more firmly established than others. For example, legal history[6] and the interface between law and philosophy[7] both have a long tradition within legal scholarship, while literary and artistic methods, or other examples of the 'cultural turn' in law, are relatively

---

2 "humanity, n.", OED Online, September 2012, Oxford University Press, http://www.oed.com/view/Entry/89280 (accessed 15 September 2016).

3 L. J. Moran, 'Legal Studies after the Cultural Turn: A Case Study of Judicial Research', in S. Roseneil and S. Frosh (eds), *Social Research after the Cultural Turn*, Basingstoke: Palgrave Macmillan, 2012.

4 This is arguably most apparent when we observe the practice of placing academic law schools within wider faculties (or colleges) of either social sciences or the humanities.

5 A. Sarat, M. Anderson and C. O. Frank (eds), *Law and the Humanities: An Introduction*, New York: Cambridge University Press, 2010, p. 1. The professional associations referred to are located in the United States of America. Similarly, two of the leading journals in the field are American: namely, the *Yale Journal of Law and Humanities* and *Law, Culture and the Humanities*. The leading UK journal, *Law and Humanities*, was launched in 2007.

6 English legal history is a particularly long-standing and well-established specialism, supported by associations such as the Selden Society, established as long ago as 1887, and respected journals such as the *Journal of Legal History*. It is a discrete specialism that is considered by Philip Handler in Chapter 5 of this book.

7 Philosophical analysis of law, whether this be based on analytical philosophy, moral philosophy, continental philosophy or any other branch, has a rich tradition in legal studies, both within the broad field of jurisprudence and more specific subject areas.

new perspectives within the legal academy. These more recent approaches are the concern of this chapter, with law and literature (by far the most prominent in this group) receiving particularly close attention.

As discussed elsewhere in this book, legal research can of course be identified both as a social science and a humanities discipline.[8] The law and humanities approach does not seek to displace legal research entirely from the remit of the social sciences; there is no such agenda. Rather, scholars working in this field seek to fully embrace the notion of law as a humanities discipline, being 'principally concerned to engage with those aspects of human experience which are not empirically quantifiable or scientifically predictable'[9] and thereby to challenge the primacy of approaches to legal research that are founded upon methods traditionally associated with the social sciences. Research carried out in a law and humanities remit is then very obviously at odds with a doctrinal, positivist approach to legal research, but is not belligerently so.

In his defence of the value of law as a humanities discipline, Gary Watt acknowledges this point. He states: 'It cannot be denied that a great deal of legal scholarship employs empirical and statistical research methodologies of the sort that one associates with the social sciences', but he goes on to emphasise that 'a major component of legal research . . . is research into the meaning of texts and, related to it, research into the meaning of texts in practical performance'.[10] When Watt refers to 'text' here, we might tend to envisage this as meaning 'words on a page' in the form of a statute or law report, or perhaps in the form of a legal instrument such as a contract or a will. Yet it is also possible to conceive the meaning of 'text' more broadly and within a wider tradition of, for instance, semiotic analysis or conversation analysis that looks to many other forms of human expression as a 'text'.[11]

It is this broad sense that illuminates the distinction between doctrinal legal methods and law and the humanities. Doctrinal legal scholarship is engaged in a search for meaning within the text; and much ink is spilled by legal scholars on the 'correct' interpretation of statutes, cases and other legal

---

8　See further Fiona Cownie and Anthony Bradney's 'Socio-Legal Studies: A Challenge to the Doctrinal Approach', in Chapter 2 of this book.

9　As stated in the description of the aims and scope of the *Law and Humanities* journal. Available at http://www.tandfonline.com/action/journalInformation?sho w=aimsScope& journalCode=rlah20 (accessed 13 March 2017).

10　G. Watt, 'Hard Cases, Hard Times and the Humanity of Law', in J. Bate (ed.), *The Public Value of the Humanities*, London: Bloomsbury Academic, 2012, 197.

11　M. Valverde, *Law and Order: Images, Meanings, Myths*, Abingdon: Routledge-Cavendish, 2006; and M. Rosner, 'Emotions and Interaction Ritual: A Micro Analysis of Restorative Justice', *British Journal of Criminology* 51(1), 2011, 95–119.

instruments. The doctrinal scholar may well look to a wider context so as to enable the interpretation of legal texts, such as the social conditions at the time the text was produced, perhaps to find the 'mischief' that the text aims to address, but doctrinal scholarship will always return to the text and its primacy. Of course, this is inevitably a caricature of doctrinal scholarship, but it serves as a useful point of departure for describing an approach within law and humanities. Following doctrinal scholarship, work within 'law and humanities' is also involved in the interpretation of texts, but the choice of text may well be different, as are the means of interpreting and engaging with such texts.

Law and literature

Law and humanities scholarship has at its core the so-called 'law and literature' movement,[12] and this remains the mainstay of the discipline. There has developed within this field of scholarship two distinctive approaches; namely law *in* literature and law *as* literature. A strict definition of disciplinary boundaries is, of course, fraught with danger, and not necessarily useful.[13] However, for our purposes, this distinction is a useful heuristic device.

Law *in* literature is, as the term suggests, concerned with the identification and analysis of law within literary texts. Scholars working in this field seek to utilise the fictional legal scenarios that literature provides as a means to discovering and investigating the cultural aspects of the law. These are the aspects that inform the creation and application of the law, but which will not be made apparent by a study of legal texts alone.[14] Dickens' *Bleak House*,

12 Sarat et al., *Law and the Humanities*, 2: 'the first blush of humanistic study of law in the modern era occurred with the exploration of the conjunction of law and literature'.
13 J. B. Baron, 'Law, Literature, and the Problems of Interdisciplinarity', *Yale Law Journal* 108, 1999, 1059–85.
14 Scholars pursuing research in this field have been described as follows: 'We share the belief that key legal issues can not only be brought to life in literary texts but explored there in ways that orthodox legal materials cannot rival. Notions of justice or injustice, the social creation and policing of concepts of difference and deviance or even standards of ethical lawyering are not ideas that can be fully explored by looking only at statutes, law reports, official crime figures or even Bar Council reports on standards. The proper mission of the Law and Literature movement is to read literature, not as ("wannabe") literary critics but as lawyers seeking to pursue the legal themes of power, authority, order, adjudication, penalty, justice and so on which occupy us all' (J. Morison and C. Bell (eds), *Tall Stories? Reading Law and Literature*, Aldershot: Dartmouth Publishing, 1996, 1).

Kafka's *The Trial* and many of Shakespeare's plays represent rich sources for scholars working in this field,[15] but this is by no means a fixed canon. As Richard Posner has pointed out, 'a surprising number of literary works – some immensely distinguished, some much less so – are "about" legal proceedings in the sense that such a proceeding, usually a trial of some sort, plays a central or climatic role in the work'.[16] Posner lists a significant number of works, many of which would be relevant to the chosen topic of this book.[17] Notably, he makes reference to the mock trial scene in *Alice's Adventures in Wonderland*, identifying this as being 'notable for a depiction of the jury system that critics of the system should find apt'.[18] This text receives attention also in Ian Ward's consideration of children's literature and legal ideology. Ward makes reference to Carroll's use of metaphor and satire to highlight aspects of the trial process, most notably 'the pomposity of the occasion: the judge's wig, the length of the trial, the fact that the King is also the judge and above all the ineptitude of both judge and jury'.[19]

There are then a number of specific texts that offer this opportunity for a 'cultural investigation' of law and legal practices. However, we do not wish to create the impression that the scope of law in literature scholarship is limited to the critical analysis of 'lawyerly aspects' of a given text, so as to provide insight into the cultural aspects of law in a particular context. The approach adopted by many law and literature scholars is much broader and seeks to make more general claims about the place of law in society. Literature can be said to be a reflection of wider culture, and so understanding conceptions of law within a literary context can provide a valuable insight into our

15 See, e.g., P. Raffield and G. Watt (eds), *Shakespeare and the Law*, Oxford: Hart, 2008; D. Manderson, '"As If" – the Court of Shakespeare and the Relationships of Law and Literature', *Law, Culture and the Humanities* 4, 2008, 3–19; A. G. Harmon, '"Slender Knowledge": Sovereignty, Madness, and the Self in Shakespeare's King Lear', *Law, Culture and the Humanities* 4, 2008, 403–23; R. Banakar, 'In Search of Heimat: A Note on Franz Kafka's Concept of Law', *Law & Literature* 22(3), 2010, 463–90; and K. Dolin, 'Law, Literature and Symbolic Revolution: Bleak House', *Australasian Journal of Victorian Studies*, 12(1) (2007), 10–18.

16 R. Posner, *Law and Literature: A Misunderstood Relation*, London: Harvard University Press, 1988, 6.

17 Texts such as J. L. Breen, *Novel Verdicts: A Guide to Courtroom Fiction*, London: Scarecrow Press, 1984, offer a useful starting point for a researcher in this area. Posner refers also to J. F. Cooper's novel, *The Ways of the Hour*, London: George Routledge & Sons, 1889, as 'another notable literary criticism of the jury system' (*ibid.*, 8).

18 Posner, *Law and Literature*, 8.

19 I. Ward, *Law and Literature Possibilities and Perspectives*, Cambridge: Cambridge University Press, 1995, 103.

understandings of law and legal processes. Aristodemou, for instance, explores
literature so as to understand the nature of law and to deconstruct law.[20] She
sees law as a discourse that 'tends to abstract and detach itself from everyday
experience'[21] in a manner that hides the ideologically constructed nature of
the legal subject. Legal subjects, in short, are constructed in the image of the
law and the political aspect of this constructing is made to appear natural.
So, within the criminal law, defendants are just that – defendants – with
much of their character and life reduced to a single category; the law simply
wants to know, 'Did you do it?' For Aristodemou, a turn to literature is
important because it allows one to understand the ambiguities inherent in
discourse, and to deconstruct legal literature allows one to then deconstruct
law itself. For instance, in her seventh chapter, she explores Carter's *The
Bloody Chamber*,[22] a work that is regarded as a feminist reworking of classic
fairy tales, in order to explore how feminist concerns can be reworked into
the law. For Aristodemou, 'fairy tales operate in the realm of ideology'[23] and
Carter exposes this ideology and subverts it in her retellings:

> By exposing gender roles and categories as the *effects* of laws and power
> rather than their cause or origin, Carter enables us to rethink them for a
> new, feminist imaginary and a feminist symbolic order.[24]

The aim, then, is to reconstruct the story in an image that contests the political
nature of constructions of the subject. Specifically, Aristodemou deconstructs
the patriarchy inherent in legal stories (and in law) so as to rewrite law in a
feminist image.

There has been some considerable debate as to the advantages and disadvantages that the law and literature approach offers, and to its political
tendencies. The comments cited above from Richard Posner's work are made
within the context of his early, influential text that sought to limit some of the
claims of the law and literature movement, arguing that literary works are
concerned primarily with 'the eternal problems of the human condition'
rather than with our current legal or political problems.[25] Notably, however,

---

20 M. Aristodemou, *Law and Literature: Journeys from Her to Eternity*, Oxford: Oxford
    University Press, 2000.
21 *Ibid.*, 24.
22 A. Carter, *The Bloody Chamber*, Harmondsworth: Penguin, 1979.
23 Aristodemou, *Law and Literature*, 157.
24 *Ibid.*, 171, emphasis in original.
25 Posner, *Law and Literature*, p. 357. See in response R. L. West, 'Law, Literature,
    and the Celebration of Authority', *Northwestern University Law Review* 83(4),
    1989, 977–1011. See also R. Weisberg, 'Literature's Twenty-Year Crossing into

Posner has remained broadly supportive of the educational benefits that the study of law and literature may bring. Ward, too, favours strongly the 'educative ambition'[26] of law and literature, referring back to one of the foundational law and literature texts, James Boyd White's *The Legal Imagination*,[27] which was written not as an abstract monograph, but as a means for developing a new way of reflective learning for law students. This debate over the political agenda of some law and literature scholarship will be returned to later in the final part of this chapter, within a broader consideration of the justifications and acknowledged limitations of law and humanities research.

Law *as* literature has been described simply as a 'literary approach to legal writing'.[28] Historically, it has involved the close and formal examination of a legal text, 'the way that a literary text might be examined, sometimes with the help of tools provided by literary theory and literary criticism'.[29] However, increasingly scholars have been willing to adopt a wider definition of 'text' (as outlined above) and have applied various literary methods to the interpretation of that text. This might involve, for example, an examination of 'law as narrative and rhetoric',[30] an approach that has involved both the consideration of specific judgments as narratives[31] and a broader examination of the construction (and exclusion) of narratives in a courtroom setting. Alternatively, it may be a 'law as language' approach[32] that seeks to deconstruct the legal text, whether following the work of literary theorists such as Derrida or other post-structuralist or postmodern theorists.[33] Notably, the influence of

the Domain of Law: Continuing Trespass or Right by Adverse Possession?' in M. Freeman and A. Lewis (eds), *Law and Literature, Current Legal Issues*, Vol. 2, Oxford: Oxford University Press, 1999.

26 Ward, *Law and Literature Possibilities and Perspectives*, 23.

27 J. B. White, *The Legal Imagination: Abridged Edition*, London: University of Chicago Press, 1985.

28 K. Dolin, *A Critical Introduction to Law and Literature*, Cambridge: Cambridge University Press, 2007, 26.

29 P. Gerwitz, 'Narrative and Rhetoric in the Law', in P. Brooks and P. Gewirtz (eds), *Law's Stories: Narrative and Rhetoric in the Law*, London: Yale University Press, 1996, 4.

30 *Ibid.*, 2.

31 See, e.g., A. G. Amsterdam and J. Bruner, *Minding the Law: How Courts Rely on Storytelling, and How their Stories Change the Ways we Understand the Law – and Ourselves*, London: Harvard University Press, 2000.

32 G. Binder, 'The Law-as-Literature Trope', in M. Freeman and A. Lewis (eds), *Law and Literature, Current Legal Issues*, Vol. 2, Oxford: Oxford University Press, 1999, 80.

33 See Aristodemou, *Law and Literature*; and P. Goodrich, 'Jani Anglorum: Signs, Symptoms, Slips and Interpretation in Law', in C. Douzinas, P. Goodrich and

linguistic analysis (a recognised sociological discipline) is evident in both of these broad approaches. As Dolin states:

> {L]inguistic analysis is one of the tools of a critical sociology of law. The language of law is an important key in the understanding of how the institution operates. How a *universalising attitude* necessary for legal interpretation and judgment is inculcated. Thus, legal language is not studied for its own sake, but for the light it sheds on legal practices.[34]

This concern for the construction of meaning, rather than the discernment of meaning, as we shall see later, is important in our understanding of what we mean by 'the humanities' in the context of law and humanities research.

Researching lay participation in the legal system

As stated previously, one means by which the production of texts in the legal system has been studied is through the consideration of narratives within law. Legal processes, in the construction of narratives, focus upon 'the trouble'.[35] So, within the criminal justice process, narratives are constructed around the central element of the relevant legal offence. Preceding and subsequent events are of secondary importance to the narrative. For instance, while the events leading up to an assault, and the reactions of the parties subsequently, are part of the legal story, in that they may help to explain motive, culpability or be important to the question of the credibility of the parties,[36] the main business of the criminal law is focused upon the assault. The stories that law tells, therefore, are partial.[37] However, as narratives are after-the-event reconstructions, one cannot expect them to be faithful to an 'external reality'.[38] Law's stories, therefore, in focusing upon the trouble, are different from the sorts of stories that we may tell in everyday conversation. To call them incomplete is to fail to fully recognise that this is the status of all stories,

Y. Hachamovitch (eds), *Politics, Postmodernity and Critical Legal Studies: The Legality of the Contingent*, London: Routledge, 1993.
34 Dolin, *A Critical Introduction to Law and Literature*, 28–29, emphasis in the original.
35 K. L. Scheppele, 'Foreword: Telling Stories', *Michigan Law Review* 87, 1989, 2073–98, 2073.
36 A. Kjus, *Stories at Trial*, Liverpool: Deborah Charles, 2011.
37 S. Cammiss, '"He Goes Off and I Think He Took the Child": Narrative (Re)Production in the Courtroom', *Kings College Law Journal* 17, 2006, 71–95.
38 G. Mungham and Z. Bankowski, 'The Jury in the Legal System', in P. Carlen (ed.), *The Sociology of Law*, Keele: University of Keele, 1979.

as reconstructions. Nevertheless, their difference is important, particularly for how stories are told within law and for the way in which everyday stories are received within legal processes.

There is a growing literature on the way in which narrative construction is important for lay adjudicators within the criminal justice process. Within England and Wales, decisions as to guilt or innocence are made, after trial, by lay adjudicators, be they magistrates or jurors. Narratives delivered within the criminal courtroom, therefore, are interpreted not by lawyers, but by lay members of the court, and we have already noted how these narratives are 'different' from 'everyday' narratives. Nevertheless, as lay adjudicators are, in effect, deciding upon the veracity of each party's story, the construction of that story is said to be important for how it will be received. Stories that are internally consistent and appear to correspond to the adjudicator's world view are more likely to be believed. This is a finding that has been repeated in a number of research studies that have explored the reception of stories within the courtroom.

Bennett and Feldman, in *Reconstructing Reality in the Courtroom*, claim that trial discourse is centred upon the construction of alternative narratives.[39] Advocates within the trial courtroom are mainly concerned with the construction of narratives that aim to explain 'what happened', and the success, or otherwise, of the case depends upon whether this narrative is accepted. Whether a narrative is regarded as believable is a function of two elements of the presented story; whether it is internally coherent and whether it corresponds to the adjudicator's world view. Adjudicators do not, therefore, listen to individual pieces of testimony and decide, in isolation, if this or that witness is credible or reliable. Rather, the evidence is interpreted as a totality, as a narrative construction. The skilful advocate, therefore, engages in the questioning of each witness so as to build this narrative, one that is internally consistent and plausible. For Bennett and Feldman, jurors decide cases on these two criteria, and they even go so far as to suggest that bias within the criminal justice process is a result of the rejection of the narratives of the marginalised because they are regarded as implausible. This view of narrative reproduction in the courtroom is firmly linked to psychological approaches that seek to understand how we interpret the world around us. Frames, scripts and schema are all said to be influential in the construction and interpretation of social reality; narratives told within the court are reconstructions of events within the courtroom and when we interpret these reconstructions, we make use of

---

39 W. S. Bennett and M. S. Feldman, *Reconstructing Reality in the Courtroom: Justice and Judgment in American Culture*, London: Tavistock, 1981.

mental schema so as to interpret these raw data.[40] Narrative construction and interpretation therefore involves a creative 'flattening', 'sharpening' and 'rationalisations' whereby events are shaped into narrative form.[41] To borrow from Van Roermund, the interpretations that we access to make sense of the world are also influential in the way in which we select events so as to construct narratives that fit with these interpretations.[42]

Others have also adopted a narrative framework so as to explore how lay adjudicators make sense of the evidence within a trial. Pennington and Hastie have adopted more overt psychological perspectives in their exploration of how jurors interpret evidence, also calling for an understanding of adjudication as being based on the interpretation of narratives.[43] Kjus has used the model outside of the common law system, and looked at how judges also use a narrative model so as to make sense of the evidence.[44] Bernard Jackson's work, *Fact, Law and Narrative Coherence*,[45] is widely quoted in the literature on narrative within the courtroom. Jackson, commenting on Bennett and Feldman, drew a distinction between the narrative *in* the trial and the narrative *of* the trial;[46] Bennett and Feldman were describing the narrative *in* the trial, but lost sight of the narrative *of* the trial and its importance in the adjudicatory process. In short, the trial itself is a drama, an unfolding story with characters, events and a climax (the verdict, and sentence, if appropriate). Jackson pointed out that the parts that each of these different characters play could influence the outcome. So, for instance, while Kjus does reference Jackson, he says little on the drama of the trial, taking, for instance, the construction of narratives at face value and saying little on how the narratives within the court were constructed

40 M. Cortazzi, *Narrative Analysis*, London: Falmer, 1993; F. Ungerer and H. J. Schmid, *An Introduction to Cognitive Linguistics*, Harlow: Longman, 1996; and S. L. Winter, 'The Cognitive Dimension of the Agon between Legal Power and Narrative Meaning', *Michigan Law Review* 87, 1989, 2225–79.
41 Cortazzi, *Narrative Analysis*, 61.
42 B. van Roermund, *Law, Narrative and Reality: An Essay in Intercepting Politics*, London: Kluwer, 1997.
43 N. Pennington and R. Hastie, 'The Story Model for Juror Decision Making', in R. Hastie (ed.), *Inside the Juror: The Psychology of Juror Decision Making*, Cambridge: Cambridge University Press, 1993.
44 Kjus, *Stories at Trial*.
45 B. S. Jackson, *Fact, Law and Narrative Coherence*, Liverpool: Deborah Charles, 1988.
46 This can be expressed as calling for an understanding of 'the relationship between the narrativisation of semantics and the narrativisation of pragmatics' (B. S. Jackson, *Making Sense in Law: Linguistic, Psychological and Semiotic Perspectives*, Liverpool: Deborah Charles, 1995, 16).

in situ.[47] This is important in two respects. A simple elucidation of the point concerns an understanding of advocates as being influential (or not) in the process due to their inherent charisma (or lack of it).

A more complex point here concerns the manner in which the narrative within the courtroom is constructed; they are produced, as are nearly all court-room utterances, within the question and answer adjacency pair.[48] Atkinson and Drew apply conversation analysis to courtroom interaction and show that courtrooms differ from more everyday settings in that the vast majority of discourse is effected through a question and answer sequence.[49] Advocates, therefore, in constructing the narrative of the case, have to do so by asking questions of witnesses. Importantly, the type of question asked, and the extent to which the question is 'controlling', is largely a function of the stage in the proceedings at which the question is asked.[50] In short, advocates are more likely to ask closed questions in cross-examination and open-ended questions within examination in chief. This accords with the well-known adage that a lawyer should not ask a question in court to which she/he does not know the answer. Witnesses, therefore, are rarely given free rein to tell their story to the court. This is important, as there is a degree of evidence to suggest that narrative testimony, as opposed to fragmented testimony, is more influential within the courtroom.[51] Advocates, therefore, have to balance eliciting the story from the witness in a controlled manner, and over-controlling the witness so that the evidence appears to be fragmented.[52] In short, the process of narrative construction in situ – the story *of* the trial – can be just as important as the story in the trial *in* influencing the outcome.

What are the implications of this brief literature review for the researcher who wants to adopt a law and humanities approach to lay adjudication within law? We can see that, given the importance of lay involvement in adjudication in the criminal justice system, there is a developing tradition of research that can be used as a starting point to refine an appropriate research topic.

47 S. Cammiss, 'Law and Narrative: Telling Stories in Court', *Law and Humanities* 6(1), 2012, 130–43.
48 For more on adjacency pairs, see I. Hutchby and R. Wooffitt, *Conversation Analysis*, 2nd edn, Cambridge: Polity Press, 2008.
49 J. M. Atkinson and P. Drew, *Order in Court: The Organisation of Verbal Interaction in Judicial Settings*, London: Macmillan, 1979.
50 S. Harris, 'Fragmented Narratives and Multiple Tellers: Witness and Defendant Account in Trials', *Discourse Studies* 3(1), 2001, 53–74.
51 W. M. O'Barr, *Linguistic Evidence: Language, Power and Strategy in the Courtroom*, London: Academic Press, 1982.
52 As Anthony Good explains in Chapter 10, this 'usual' story can itself be disrupted by the inclusion of an interpreter.

Furthermore, in considering the selection of methods that are appropriate, there is similarly a rich tradition upon which the student can draw. Given the largely qualitative nature of the exercise, most work within the field relies upon small samples (frequently the single case)[53] so as to explore the use of language in depth. How to capture the data (recording, be it audio or video) and the method of transcription raises some choices, but again others have developed the basic techniques that are applicable to work in this field so that any new work does not have to 'reinvent the wheel'.[54] However, work in this tradition can use much larger samples or a 'corpus' that can be subject to analysis. The work of Heffer, for instance, which explores narrative construction in the courtroom, is based upon a large corpus of data.[55] Echoing the range of methods appropriate to research in this field, there are similar choices that have to be made in the development of a theoretical framework for research. As explained above, work in this tradition draws upon a range of theoretical perspectives that are available to understand the use of language within the law. Each of these perspectives has a well-developed theoretical literature that can be drawn upon so as to place one's findings within an appropriate context.

53 G. M. Matoesian, *Law and the Language of Identity: Discourse in the William Smith Rape Trial*, Oxford: Oxford University Press, 2001; and J. Cotterill, *Language and Power in Court: A Linguistic Analysis of the O J Simpson Trial*, Basingstoke: Palgrave Macmillan, 2003.

54 For instance, choosing how to transcribe one's data may, at first glance, appear to be a simple matter. But there are numerous pitfalls. For instance, does one transcribe speech as it is said, or does one 'clean up' a transcript so that the spoken word appears to be similar to the written word? This has long been a feature of socio-legal studies, where research subjects appear to speak with unfeasibly correct grammar and sentence construction. Such orthographic transcription conventions lose much of the nuances of the spoken word; inflections, delays, hedges (ums), repeats and self-corrections are all lost in the transcription process. If we accept that these are important for understanding, and conversation analysts state that they are, then a transcription process that does not account for such paralinguistic features will inevitably result in a loss of content. As a result, Gail Jefferson, in particular, has developed a 'standard' transcription notation that is designed to capture these aspects of the spoken word: see J. M. Atkinson and J. Heritage, 'Jefferson's Transcript Notation', in A. Jaworski and N. Coupland (eds), *The Discourse Reader*, 2nd edn, London: Routledge, 2006.

55 C. Heffer, *The Language of Jury Trial: A Corpus-Aided Analysis of Legal-Lay Discourse*, Basingstoke: Palgrave Macmillan, 2005. Calvalieri uses more than the single case, but a somewhat smaller corpus: see S. Calvalieri, 'The Role of Metadiscourse in Counsels' Questions', in A. Wagner and Le Cheng (eds), *Exploring Courtroom Discourse: The Language of Power and Control*, Farnham: Ashgate, 2011.

Endless possibilities

We have provided in this chapter some discrete examples of how a researcher working on the topic of lay participation on the legal system might pursue his or her research within a law and humanities remit. Yet in light of the broad and undefined scope of the field, it is clear that the possibilities and potential for research are endless. Indeed, given the plurality of approaches that fall within the broad umbrella of law and humanities scholarship, it would be impossible to provide a comprehensive survey of all methods and theories that might be relevant to research on this topic. Certainly, we have demonstrated that work that focuses on law *as* literature is particularly relevant, but if only through our very brief consideration of *Alice's Adventures in Wonderland*, we have demonstrated that there is also potential for a law *in* literature approach. And these traditional categories of law and literature research are not, of course, closed. It is possible, for example, to consider the role of trial experts in the regulation of literature or visual art and law, both present and historic, as being pertinent to this topic.[56] Going beyond law and literature, Sharon Krause's consideration of the impartial deliberation of jurors and her proposal for a revised approach that both allows and calls for an empathetic angle offers a completely different but equally relevant body of research that is firmly within the scope of 'law and humanities' research.[57]

We have also demonstrated that for researchers working in the field of law and humanities, the possibilities and potential for research are not only endless but boundless. We mean this in the literal sense, in that there is no insistence upon a 'pure' humanities approach in this discipline. Strict boundary policing could, for example, result in Atkinson and Drew's work,[58] based on conversation analysis, being conceived or categorised as 'socio-legal' analysis. This, however, would be to underplay the importance of the humanities in such work and the role of linguistics within the tradition. Similarly, much of the work we have explored on the importance of narrative in the work of lay adjudicators within the legal system cannot be easily slotted into a pre-existing 'school'. The focus upon narrative and storytelling calls for a literary approach, particularly narrative theory, so as to understand the construction of narratives within the courtroom and within law more generally. However, this work also draws

---

56 For a discussion of the historical approach, see D. Watkins, 'The Influence of the Art for Art's Sake Movement upon English Law, 1780–1959', *Journal of Legal History* 28(2), 2007, 233–56.

57 S. Krause, 'Empathy, Democratic Politics, and the Impartial Juror', *Law, Culture and the Humanities* 7, 2001, 81–100.

58 Atkinson and Drew, *Order in Court*.

upon methods from the social sciences, particularly psychology. Frames, scripts and schema are said to be important in the construction and reception of narratives;[59] the literary and the social sciences intersect in this work. Indeed, when exploring law as literature, much of the work we draw upon is empirical, socio-legal and yet within 'the humanities'.

The question that inevitably arises at the end of this chapter is: What is the benefit of conceiving of such a school or approach? If law and humanities incorporates so many different perspectives, which, on the face of it, have so little in common, except for some non-exclusive affinity with 'the humanities', why should we be concerned with this as a common approach? And what, in any event, are the advantages of pursuing this sprawling relationship between law and humanities in the context of legal research? The challenge of defining the scope of law and humanities with any precision was acknowledged at the outset of this chapter. It is acknowledged by the editors of the first comprehensive overview of the field, *Law and the Humanities: An Introduction*, echoing the concerns expressed in 1988 by the editors of the first academic journal in the field, the *Yale Journal of Law and the Humanities*, that the law and humanities remit was so wide as to defy any adequate definition.[60] Nevertheless, in both of these contexts it is agreed that 'the field could still be *described*'.[61] Drawing on a variety of examples that are relevant to a particular topic, this chapter has sought to demonstrate that the acknowledgement and development of research in this field creates an opportunity for a distinctive 'manner of engagement' with law and legal processes that is concerned to discover, or to investigate, the *cultural* aspects of law; the word 'cultural' here being broadly conceived as the physical, emotional, philosophical, social, ethical and even spiritual environment or context which both gives rise to law and legal processes, and which profoundly influences their progress. It allows the researcher to step beyond the 'usual' modes of enquiry, thereby leading to 'new' research questions and 'new' research findings of a type that could not have been discovered through more traditional means. The work of Atkinson and Drew, for instance, provides an explanation for many features of courtroom discourse that have traditionally been regarded as alienating.[62] The distance, for instance, between speakers in court may well lead to difficulties when witnesses have to describe sensitive events.[63] However, this distance is

---

59 See n. 40 and associated texts.
60 See Sarat et al., *Law and the Humanities*, Introduction.
61 *Ibid.*, 9. Emphasis added.
62 Atkinson and Drew, *Order in Court*.
63 P. Carlen, 'The Staging of Magistrates Justice', *British Journal of Criminology* 16(1), 1975, 48–55.

effective for shared attentiveness in that it results in speakers being sufficiently audible so that all members of the single conversation are able to hear
the utterance.

The above discussion goes some way in explaining the potential benefits of
this 'cultural turn' in legal research, but what of its explicit affiliation with 'the
humanities'? We began this chapter with a definition of 'the humanities' as
the 'branch of learning concerned with human culture' that comprises a broad
range of academic disciplines, including law.[64] In light of the quantifiable
benefits of scientific research, the value of qualitative research (and especially
funding for research) in these disciplines has to be positively demonstrated,
and particularly so in times of austerity. In the context of a broad-ranging
consideration of *The Public Value of the Humanities*, Watt argues convincingly
that '[l]egal research as a humanities discipline, as a search for meaning, exerts
a significant influence on our laws, lawyers and lawmakers' and that 'more
humane laws, a more humane legal system and a more humane legal profession
will flow from legal research that is nourished from the founts of other humanities disciplines'.[65] It is this concern for the 'cultivation of humanity' that has
been a central feature of scholarship in the law and humanities field.

James Boyd White and Martha Nussbaum have been particularly influential
in arguing for the 'cultivation of humanity' through the development of a
relationship between law and literature in the context of legal education.[66]
This allegiance to the positive benefits of engagement with literature is not
new. In the late nineteenth and early twentieth centuries, literary critics such
as Arnold, Richards and Leavis argued that engagement with certain forms of
poetry, and subsequently the novel, represented the only means to redeeming
(in their view) a culturally impoverished society. As Culler states '[i]t would
at once teach disinterested appreciation, provide a sense of moral greatness,
create fellow-feeling among the classes, and ultimately, function as a replace-
ment for religion, which seemed no longer to be able to hold society together'.[67]

64 See p. 87 of this chapter.
65 Watt, 'Hard Cases, Hard Times and the Humanity of Law', 198–99.
66 See, e.g., M. Nussbaum, *Cultivating Humanity: A Classical Defense of Reform in Liberal
Education*, Cambridge, MA: Harvard University Press, 1997. For White, the
teaching of literature offers 'the stimulation of our capacity to imagine other people,
not only as they suffer or enjoy what we do, but more deeply as they inhabit different
universes of meaning, different spheres of language' (J. B. White, 'What Can a
Lawyer Learn from Literature?', *Harvard Law Review* 102(8), 1989, 2014–47, 2036).
For a useful overview of this area, see C. Douziinas, 'A Humanities of Resistance:
Fragments for a Legal History of Humanity', in Sarat et al., *Law and the Humanities*.
67 J. Culler, *Literary Theory: A Very Short Introduction*, Oxford: Oxford University Press,
1997, 36.

By the end of the twentieth century, this view had been wholly discredited, Easthope arguing that '[s]tudying literature was supposed to make you a better person, to develop your "imagination" so you could enter imaginatively into the experiences of others, thus learning to respect truth and value justice for all. If this is its moral aim literary study simply does not work.' He concludes that 'this humanist project' was 'an ineluctable failure'.[68] Neither White nor Nussbaum possess such an elitist agenda, but their claims have been both developed and disputed, as have the claims of law and literature more generally. The debate between Posner and West is a good example of this.[69] However, the outcome of this debate has not resulted in the discrediting of the law and literature approach; rather it has served to establish more firmly the field of law and humanities research as a respectable discipline. Indeed, Sarat et al. maintain that 'to claim that an understanding of law needs the humanities hardly seems polemical to us these days, so far have the arguments of White and West (and many others) spread'.[70]

Consequently, the influence of law and humanities research has become increasingly acknowledged, as has its *potential* to influence. Watt's consideration of the public value of law as a humanities discipline incorporates, inter alia, a consideration of the invasion of Iraq and the credit crunch.[71] In a similar vein, a leading scholarly journal in the field, namely *Law, Culture, and the Humanities*, introduced recently a new feature called 'Heeding the Call of Justice: Humanistic Perspectives on Contemporary Affairs'. It is the editors' aim to publish on a regular basis papers written by law and humanities scholars, commenting on a matter of pressing public urgency. The editors' hope is that 'these pieces would illuminate ways in which the humanities contribute to public debate'.[72] The field of law and humanities offers then a credible means to adopting a qualitative approach to legal research, which attaches importance to human concerns and values, rather than focusing on the more quantifiable principles that derive from a more scientific, positivist approach. At the same time, it falls short of the theoretical abstraction of critical legal studies, offering a means to considering the cultural aspects of law for the development of a deeper understanding of its nature. This understanding not only contributes to knowledge in general terms, but also provides insights into current legal, political and social issues.

68 A. Easthope, *Literacy into Cultural Studies*, London: Routledge, 1991, 9.
69 See n. 25 and associated texts.
70 See Sarat et al., *Law and the Humanities*, 8.
71 Watt, 'Hard Cases, Hard Times and the Humanity of Law', 197–207.
72 A. Sarat, 'Editorial', *Law, Culture and the Humanities* 7(2), 2011, 169.

Recommended reading

Boyd White, J., *The Legal Imagination: Abridged Edition*, London: University of Chicago Press, 1985.

Brooks, P. and Gewirtz, P. (eds), *Law's Stories: Narrative and Rhetoric in the Law*, London: Yale University Press, 1996.

Dolin, K., *A Critical Introduction to Law and Literature*, Cambridge: Cambridge University Press, 2007.

Sarat, A., Anderson, M. and Frank, C. O. (eds), *Law and the Humanities: An Introduction*, New York: Cambridge University Press, 2010.

Ward, I., *Law and Literature Possibilities and Perspectives*, Cambridge: Cambridge University Press, 1995.

5 Legal history
Philip Handler

> The largest difficulty in legal history is precisely that we look at past evidence in the light of later assumptions about the nature and workings of law itself.
> S. F. C. Milsom[1]

Students and practitioners of English law have regular recourse to history. They look to the past as a source of authority and, in a system that has medieval origins, this may involve looking back through centuries to excavate a particular case or statute for current use. This method requires no investigation of the historical context in which a case was decided or the circumstances that brought a statute about, only in the point of law that it established. Lawyers routinely ignore or suppress evidence that does not assist their case or which is not deemed relevant according to the conventions of legal argument. This approach may serve the practising lawyer, but it is inimical to the writing of legal history. It produces 'lawyers' history', in which universal legal ideas and concepts are traced through historic seams of authority in unbroken lineage and the past is enlisted to serve present ends. The lawyer perceives history as 'the law read backwards, the inevitable unfolding of things as they came to be; and the thinking is seen as a fumbling for a result eventually reached'.[2]

The risk of projecting current understandings and conceptions of law and its institutions onto the past is particularly high for those trained as lawyers, who may have had only very limited exposure to the study of legal history. The subject does not occupy a central place in the English law school curriculum. It may feature in the introduction to a course or perhaps as an elective.

1 S. F. C. Milsom, *A Natural History of the Common Law*, New York: Columbia University Press, 2001, xvi.
2 S. F. C. Milsom, *Historical Foundations of the Common Law*, London: Butterworths, 1969, ix, quoted in K. Smith and J. McLaren, 'History's Living Legacy: An Outline of the "Modern" Historiography of the Common Law', *Legal Studies* 21, 2001, 251–324, 311.

Assiduous students may read some legal history in introductory chapters of textbooks, but will seldom be prompted to delve any deeper. The subject is not an essential part of the modern law degree and there was only a brief window, when university legal education was being revived in the nineteenth century, when it seemed as if it might become one.[3] If it is not widely taught in English law schools, it is studied and researched extensively by scholars who have deployed a range of methodologies in its pursuit. This chapter provides an introduction to some of these methodologies as they have been applied to English legal history, before examining how they might be applied to a study of the criminal trial jury. The focus on England keeps the discussion within manageable bounds, although the methodologies discussed may be more widely applicable.[4] The final part of the chapter makes some brief observations on the possibilities for research and on the uses to which a study of legal history might be put.

Internal and external legal history

> What is Legal History a History of? Law. That at any rate is the easy answer. Unfortunately, it is not obviously correct; and insofar as it may be correct it begs rather difficult questions in its turn.[5]

The distinction commonly drawn between internal and external legal history makes a convenient starting point. Internal legal history is the study of legal doctrine and of its processes. It is usually practised within law schools and focuses on the foundations and development of the English common law. John Baker's *An Introduction to English Legal History* exemplifies this tradition of writing legal history.[6] It has tended to focus on the medieval and early modern periods, although some leading works analyse legal change over the whole life of the common law.[7] External legal history examines the law in context. The second half of the twentieth century witnessed a considerable growth in the study of the relationship between law, legal institutions and society,

---

3 M. Lobban, 'Introduction: The Tools and Tasks of the Legal Historian', in M. Lobban and A. Lewis, *Law and Legal History*, Oxford: Oxford University Press, 2004, 1.

4 On comparative legal history, see: D. Ibbetson, 'Comparative Legal History: A Methodology', in A. Musson and C. Stebbings, *Making Legal History: Approaches and Methodologies*, Cambridge: Cambridge University Press, 2012, 131–45.

5 D. Ibbetson, 'What Is Legal History a History of?', in Lobban and Lewis, *Law and Legal History*, 33–40, 33.

6 4th edn, London: Butterworths, 2002.

7 See, e.g., Milsom, *Historical Foundations*; and D. Ibbetson, *A Historical Introduction to the Law of Obligations*, Oxford: Oxford University Press, 1999.

especially in the modern period. This diversification, which drew in scholarship from a range of academic disciplines, has been enriching, but has also made it more difficult to discern clear boundaries of the field. Internal legal history may be described as the history of law, but external legal history encroaches onto the political, intellectual and social realm in ways that make it difficult to distinguish from general historiography.

The starting point for most legal historical methodologies is the source material. Traditional common law history is based on close scrutiny of the primary materials produced by the legal process. These records have been preserved, from almost the beginning of the system, to form a remarkably rich record of the life of the English common law. Writing at the end of the nineteenth century, the most revered of all English legal historians, Frederic Maitland, drew attention to the value and scope of these archival sources and was the first to produce a history of English law that was firmly grounded in them.[8] The legal history that Maitland practised demanded that the historian eschew present-mindedness and harvest the available primary sources to reconstruct the law as it was understood in its historical context. His work and method provided the foundations for modern professional standards of legal historiography.

Common law historians have to grapple with two key sources: the legal record and the law reports. The abundant official records, to which Maitland drew attention, are preserved in miles of plea rolls which record the formal procedural steps and outcomes in cases decided by the Royal Courts of Justice from the 1190s in an almost unbroken account.[9] They are an essential resource for the student of English legal history before the modern period, but they do not tell us why courts did what they did. For that, we need law reports. The earliest of these date from about the middle of the thirteenth century in what are now called year books. These anonymous notes of cases, whose authorship is uncertain, did not record all the details of the case. By the Tudor period, these were being printed and from this period we also see the emergence of reports compiled by individuals. These nominate reports varied greatly in reliability and it was only in 1865 that the system of law reporting was formalised and fully professionalised. As with any historical source, the law reports cannot be accepted at face value. It is not clear how cases were selected to be reported and it is far from clear that they were reported

---

8 F. Pollock and F. Maitland, *The History of English Law*, Cambridge: Cambridge University Press, 1895. The work was almost entirely Maitland's.
9 It has been estimated that more than a million sheep over a period of six centuries gave their skins to the record. See J. Baker, 'Why the History of English Law Has Not Been Finished', *Cambridge Law Journal* 59, 2000, 70.

accurately. Those that were may have been notable for their unusual or untypical nature.[10]

Early English legal sources present considerable methodological challenges. Knowledge of Latin and medieval French, and familiarity with the multiple and technical procedures of the common law are minimum requirements, but ones which relatively few scholars possess. One important task for legal historians is therefore to edit and translate early English records and reports to render them more widely usable.[11] Valuable work has been conducted to produce selections of cases on particular themes from the plea rolls, although this represents only a small fraction of the available records.[12] Some of the year books and early modern law reports, particularly those that were printed, are more accessible.[13] Even this lays a trap for the unwary scholar. There was little system in deciding which reports were printed and many available only in manuscript for the medieval and early modern period are more reliable or informative.[14]

Studying and interpreting these legal records and reports requires much more than technical and linguistic expertise. Modern lawyers are used to seeking substantive rules in statutes, cases and other legal literature. Using such modern legal questions to guide a search of the archival sources will be unavailing. Medieval and early modern lawyers were primarily concerned with procedure and seldom addressed issues of substantive law directly. The few statutes that were passed focused upon specific issues in property law or criminal law. In the absence of an overarching statutory framework, much change had to be effected through litigation, but there was little elaboration of common law principles in judgments. Judges expressed opinions on law at the pleading stage (before the case went to trial) and often took pains to avoid setting down law on difficult points.[15] The legal historian therefore has to beware seeking answers that the sources will not reveal. The task is to understand and perceive the limitations on what could be asked then in order to grasp the questions that can be addressed now.[16]

---

10 See Baker, 'Why the History of English Law', 73–78.
11 See P. Brand, 'Editing Law Reports and Doing Legal History: Compatible or Incompatible Projects?' in Musson and Stebbings, *Making Legal History*, 18–29.
12 Since its foundation by Maitland in 1887, the Selden Society has been the principal publisher of original legal historical sources.
13 In addition to the Selden Society publications, see the online database: 'An index and paraphrase of printed year book reports, 1268–1535' compiled by David J. Seipp, http://www.bu.edu/law/seipp/ (accessed 6 March 2017).
14 See Baker, 'Why the History of English Law', 73–78.
15 *Ibid.*, 73.
16 J. Baker, 'Reflections on Doing Legal History', in Musson and Stebbings, *Making Legal History*, 9.

The challenge of recovering the basic assumptions of past periods and, indeed, the whole conceptual framework within which lawyers functioned is difficult to underestimate.[17] These assumptions and the framework were not anywhere set out or made explicit and historians have had to attempt to learn the law without the guide of the medieval or early modern equivalent of a textbook. Indeed, it is one of the most striking features of the history of English law that, until the nineteenth century, and with the exception of land law, there were almost no books which performed the work of digest and synthesis that is so central to our understanding of law today.[18] This absence increases the temptation for the legal historian to project existing legal categories backwards anachronistically. For example, the classification of contract as a separate legal category was not known in English law until the nineteenth century. There were cases that a modern lawyer might recognise as containing contractual elements, but these were not viewed as part of a whole law of contract.[19] Focusing upon what the evidence can tell us about the law in its historical context requires a methodology that attends as much to those parts of legal doctrine which did not persist into the modern era as those that did. Legal historians strive, insofar as the available evidence permits, 'to make the interpretation which best reflects what contemporary agents understood the law to be'.[20]

If internal legal history focuses on that understanding as it manifested itself in a legal professional context, external legal history looks at the law in action, as it was applied and understood in its social context. Much, although by no means all, of this type of legal history has focused on the modern period (from the eighteenth century onwards), when the available source material expands dramatically and the law infiltrated increasingly diverse fields of social activity. The range of such scholarship defies brief summary.[21] The legal realist movement in the early twentieth century provided much of the impetus for the search for new methods and suggested new ways of viewing

17 'It is what was assumed that we need to know, not what was said.' S. F. C. Milsom, 'Introduction' to Pollock and Maitland, *The History of English Law Before the Time of Edward I*, Cambridge: Cambridge University Press, 1968, xxvi.
18 See S. F. C. Milsom, 'The Nature of Blackstone's Achievement', *Oxford Journal of Legal Studies* 1, 1981, 1–12.
19 For a discussion of the relationship between conceptual and historical analysis in relation to private law, see S. Waddams, 'Classification of Private Law in Relation to Historical Evidence: Description, PPrescription and Conceptual Analysis', in Lewis and Lobban, *Law and History*, 265–84.
20 Lobban, 'Introduction', 1.
21 For a historiographical survey, see Smith and McLaren, 'History's Living Legacy', 273–81.

the relationship between law and society. It undermined formalist claims and the premise of internal legal history that the law and its institutions were largely autonomous and self-contained.

The common law historical methodology continued to dominate the practice of much legal history until the 1970s, when the critical legal studies movement produced new and provocative legal histories. For example, Horwitz's study of American law in the modern period presented an interpretation in which doctrine was inextricably bound up with contemporary movements in political and economic ideology.[22] Atiyah's work on English contract law in the nineteenth century adopted a similar methodology.[23] Both focused on the decisions of higher courts and related them to the prevailing ideology of the period. Atiyah suggested that nineteenth-century English judges reformulated contract law doctrine to facilitate the growth of the economy in an age of laissez-faire ideology. Critical legal histories emphasised the contingent nature of law, the influence of external factors upon it and, importantly, the possible outward effects of law on social, economic and cultural developments. Some drew criticism from those who have argued that interpretations of the evidence were strained to fit the identified ideologies. Critics of Horwitz and Atiyah, for example, have argued that they present too tidy a picture of what were multi-faceted, complex and non-lineal legal developments.[24]

The consequent, highly productive debates have broadened the scope and appeal of legal history. Historians have been prompted to investigate the myriad relations between law and society from diverse perspectives. They have asked how law affected social relations, including class and gender, how it related to political and economic development and how cultural attitudes were manifested in legal processes. Studies of rates of litigation in different eras have provided insights into who used the law and why. Historians have been prompted to look beyond the superior common law courts to the activities of local and specialist courts. The history of law has been investigated from the perspectives of previously neglected groups such as women, workers, juveniles, criminals and lunatics.[25]

Historians working from these different perspectives do not necessarily deploy radically different methodologies to those deployed within traditional

---

22 M. Horwitz, *The Transformation of American Law 1780–1860*, Cambridge, MA: Harvard University Press, 1977.

23 P. Atiyah, *The Rise and Fall of Freedom of Contract*, Oxford: Clarendon Press, 1979.

24 See A. W. B. Simpson, 'The Horwitz Thesis and the History of Contracts', *University of Chicago Law Review* 46, 1979, 533. On Atiyah's thesis, see the review by J. Baker, *Modern Law Review* 43, 1980, 467.

25 For a discussion of the historiography, see Lobban, 'Introduction', 10–11, 25.

common law historiography. Fidelity to the primary sources and detailed empirical and archival research are common features. The emphasis in critical legal scholarship on historicism has much in common with the insistence of legal historians such as Baker and Milsom that the law is interpreted in terms that reflect the needs and purposes of contemporaries. The key differences relate to questions regarding the extent to which it is possible to study law and legal institutions in isolation from other forces that were shaping society. Legal histories, which might loosely be labelled 'external', bring these questions into sharper focus and make demands on all legal historians to examine their working methods and assumptions. Postmodernist scholars have questioned the very basis of these methods, rejecting the possibility of the researcher escaping contemporary preconceptions to recover any sort of historical truth. This has produced some provocative work on past legal texts, but it is questionable whether it can be characterised as historical.[26] Few legal historians claim to recover a single objective meaning of past events, but in their constant and critical engagement with the historical sources, most claim to present perspectives on those events in a form which is distinguishable from general literature.

The criminal trial jury

What might these legal historical methodologies contribute to an understanding of the role played by laypersons in the legal system? It is one of the most distinctive features of the English common law that it functioned for so long with so few professional judges.[27] This was only possible because of the participation of laypersons, the most significant of which were jurors and the justices of the peace in the counties and boroughs. The field of legal history therefore provides very wide scope to study ways in which lay persons have contributed to legal development and legal processes. Many of these areas are little explored, but this chapter focuses on one that has been, the criminal trial jury.

The institution of the jury is central to common law historiography. The emergence of trial by jury in the thirteenth century displaced older methods of proof, most notably the ordeal. From then up until the early twentieth

---

26 For an excellent summary of the contribution and limitations of the postmodernist critique of legal history and the work that it has produced, see Lobban, 'Introduction', 8–13. See also Smith and McLaren, 'History's Living Legacy', 321–22.

27 Even at the beginning of the nineteenth century, there were only 12 common law judges, together with the Lord Chancellor and Master of the Rolls in the Court of Chancery.

century, most civil and criminal cases in the common-law courts were tried using juries. The effect on the shape and form of legal development was profound because, unlike the ordeal, which reflected God's judgment, jury trial involved fallible human judgment.[28] Jurors required guidance before their verdict and, if they did fall into error, some means were needed to review and correct decisions. In the medieval period, the legal action took place at the pleading stage at the Royal Courts in Westminster Hall, when the issue or question to be put to the jury was settled. These steps and their outcomes can be charted using the plea rolls and law reports. In the early modern period, new procedures allowed for points of law to be considered after the jury's verdict and the legal action gradually moved to processes that took place after the jury's verdict and findings of fact.

In much common-law historiography, the institution of the jury is the key mechanism for legal change, but the activities and verdicts of juries are not of interest in themselves because they did not make law. They are inscrutable because the jury usually returned a blank verdict and inaccessible because the trials that took place locally were not reported. Common-law historians have focused on what lawyers and judges did before and after the trial, at the pleading and post-trial stages. In Milsom's highly influential view, much of the common law was driven forward by lawyers' attempts to adapt and manipulate existing forms to gain new remedies for clients.[29] This dynamic shaped the law of obligations, for example, but it was absent from the criminal law because the plea (guilty or not guilty) did not vary and the formal means of reviewing points of law after the verdict were very limited until the modern period. The result, for Milsom at least, is that until the nineteenth century: 'The miserable history of crime in England can be shortly told. Nothing worthwhile was created.'[30] There is no development for historians of law to trace because the legal questions that interest them 'were asked and answered in the jury room'.[31]

---

28 J. Baker, *An Introduction to English Legal History*, 71–96. The one highly significant exception was the development of equity in the Court of Chancery.

29 'The life of the common law has been in the unceasing abuse of its elementary ideas. If the rules of property give what now seems an unjust answer, try obligation . . . If the rules of contract give what now seems an unjust answer, try tort' (Milsom, *Historical Foundations*, xi).

30 S. F. C. Milsom, *Historical Foundations of the Common Law*, 2nd edn, London: Butterworths, 1981, 403.

31 Milsom, *A Natural History*, 8. For an internal account of the means by which the criminal law did develop, see J. Baker, 'The Refinement of English Criminal Jurisprudence, 1500–1848', in Baker, *The Legal Profession and the Common Law*, London: Hambledon Press, 1986, 303–24.

This view of common law development suggests that a study of the history of the jury will not be revealing of the criminal law's substantive content. Yet even in the earliest periods of the common law, historians have found ways of using contextual evidence to interpret jury verdicts to suggest ways in which they affected legal change. For example, Groot's study of larceny in the thirteenth century reconstructs how the jury's finding of fact, namely the value of stolen goods, could determine the outcome of a trial.[32] He argues that there was a working practice that certain minor thefts would not be punished capitally and that juries undervalued stolen goods in the knowledge that this would have the effect of mitigating the punishment. This 'rule', which distinguished between capital and non-capital felonies, pre-dated by some 50 years the Statute of Westminster I in 1275 which is supposed to have created the distinction between grand and petit larceny. Groot's method demands close scrutiny of limited evidence in the legal texts and an evaluation of other contextual evidence, in this case concerning the value of the goods stolen.

Green's masterful study of the criminal trial jury in the period 1200 to 1800 is premised on the view that the history of legal doctrine is intricately bound up with social processes in which jurors played a critical mediating role.[33] One of the key themes in his work is the role played by jury nullification, defined as the 'exercise of jury discretion in favor of a defendant whom the jury nonetheless believes to have committed the act with which he is charged'.[34] In the medieval period, a comparison of the plea rolls and the coroners' rolls allows him to identify various ways in which jury activity had a direct effect on shaping the law and establishing boundaries between different degrees of homicide. He deploys different methodologies to trace shifts in jury function and behaviour in the early modern and modern period. As well as mining the court records, he analyses key cases or crisis points, such as the seditious libel cases in the 1790s, or explores the views of contemporary commentators on the jury. In linking themes in the history of the jury across such a long period, Green's pioneering study opened up new fields for research.

32 R. Groot, 'Petit Larceny, Jury Lenity and Parliament', in J. Cairns and G. McLeod (eds), *The Dearest Birth Right of the People of England: The Jury in the History of the Common Law*, Oxford: Hart, 2002, 47–62.

33 'The evolution of the substantive criminal law cannot be understood apart from the social processes; yet the social processes were so complicated that we may never be able to sort out fully the strands of that relationship.' T. Green, *Verdict According to Conscience Perspectives on the English Criminal Trial Jury 1200–1800*, Chicago, IL: University of Chicago Press, 1985, 380.

34 Green, *Verdict According to Conscience*, xiii.

Much of this research has focused on the eighteenth century when jury nullification and mitigation reached a high point. The functioning of a criminal justice system that contained over 200 capital statutes gave wide scope for juries to mitigate the law. The jury practice of reaching verdicts against the evidence to mitigate the harshness of the capital laws is clear enough on the record and attracted considerable contemporary commentary. Blackstone called it 'pious perjury' and, by the end of the eighteenth century, penal reformers condemned the sanguinary laws that, they maintained, placed the jurors in such an invidious position.[35] Whig historians, such as Radzinowicz, have echoed these views of jurors and their motivations and argued that, at least by the end of the eighteenth century, the criminal law and its administration was out of touch with public opinion.[36] An influential group of historians based in Warwick in the 1970s took a less sanguine view. The focus of their research and much of what has followed has been on what the operation of the criminal justice system can tell us about social relations in eighteenth-century England. In a seminal essay in 1975, Hay argued trenchantly that the ruling classes used the eighteenth-century criminal law as an ideological tool to secure their own authority and maintain existing property relations.[37] The focus in the 1970s and 1980s on the class interests served by the criminal justice system has given way, in the last two decades, to other themes, as historians have focused on areas such as juvenile crime or asked what the criminal justice process reveals about attitudes to gender and race.[38]

The history of the jury provides a good illustration of the sort of purchase that the legal records, in combination with other sources, can offer on these issues. Historians have been able to construct a detailed picture of the social background of jurors using a variety of sources, including court records, jury lists, tax returns and freeholder books.[39] They have charted how often jurors

---

35 W. Blackstone, *Commentaries on the Laws of England*, facsimile of the first edition of 1765–69, Chicago: University of Chicago Press, 1979, 239.

36 L. Radzinowicz, *A History of English Criminal Law from 1750*, Vol. 1: *The Movement for Reform*, London: Stevens, 1948, 329–30.

37 D. Hay, 'Property, Authority and the Criminal Law in England', in D. Hay, P. Linebaugh and E. P. Thompson, *Albion's Fatal Tree Crime and Society in Eighteenth-Century England*, London: Allen Lane, 1975, 17–63.

38 See J. Innes and J. Styles, 'The Crime Wave: Recent Writing on Crime and Criminal Justice in Eighteenth Century England', *Journal of British Studies* 25, 1986, 380–435; and P. King, *Crime and Law in England 1750–1840: Remaking Justice from the Margins*, Cambridge: Cambridge University Press, 2006, 1–72.

39 Parish constables were obliged to return yearly lists of inhabitants eligible for jury service. See the following essays in J. S. Cockburn and T. Green (eds), *Twelve Good Men and True: The Criminal Trial Jury in England 1200–1800*, Princeton, NJ: Princeton

served and which were most likely to serve as foremen. For example, in London in the 1690s, Beattie found that many jurors were experienced as jurors and in local governance. They were likely to be relatively prosperous traders drawn from the top third of the rate-paying population.[40] King's study of late eighteenth-century Essex found that jurors had often served numerous times previously, were usually literate and also had experience of serving on other local decision-making bodies.[41] This type of evidence may help to explain certain features of the criminal justice system, such as the apparent haste with which trials, often involving capital crimes, were conducted in the eighteenth century. Experienced jurors would have needed less instruction and less time in which to deliberate. Empirical studies of the patterns of verdicts are revealing of the sorts of factors, such as character, youth, gender and social class, that could influence juries in exercising their discretion to mitigate the law.[42]

The social composition of a jury, its experience and the patterns of its verdicts can only tell us so much about its role. As Green puts it, we also need to know 'the constraints within which juries acted, even when they were not cognizant of those constraints'.[43] One of the most important constraints, although not one that has received much direct attention from social historians, was law. Langbein's work on the eighteenth-century trial and its processes offers a more legalistic perspective on the jury's role. It charts the emerging presence of lawyers in felony trials and consequent establishment of adversary process.[44] One consequence of this development was that lay participants in the trial were marginalised. Jurors slowly ceded their active, questioning role in trials and assumed a passive position as silent adjudicators. Langbein traces these developments within the legal process and attributes the development to the growth of professional adversarial culture which followed the judicial decision to admit defence counsel to felony trials in the 1730s. This internal perspective begins with the sources. Langbein was the first historian

University Press, 2014: J. Beattie, 'London Juries in the 1690s', 214–53; P. King, '"Illiterate Plebeians, Easily Misled": Jury Composition, Experience and Behavior in Essex, 1735–1815', 254–304; and D. Hay, 'The Class Composition of the Palladium of Liberty: Trial Jurors in the Eighteenth Century', 305–57. See also J. Beattie, *Crime and the Courts in England, 1660–1800*, Oxford: Clarendon Press, 1986, 378–89.

40 Beattie, 'London Juries', 237–48.

41 King, 'Illiterate Plebeians', 274–89.

42 See Beattie, *Crime and the Courts*, 410–29; and P. King, *Crime, Justice and Discretion in England, 1740–1820*, Oxford: Oxford University Press, 2000, 221–58.

43 T. Green, 'A Retrospective on the Criminal Trial Jury, 1200–1800', in Cockburn and Green, *Twelve Good Men and True*, 358–400, 386.

44 See J. Langbein, *The Origins of the Adversary Criminal Trial*, Oxford: Oxford University Press, 2003.

to recognise the importance of a collection of trial reports from the Old Bailey, which began in the late seventeenth century and continued into the twentieth. For the eighteenth century in particular, these reports are invaluable because they provide more detail than any other source on routine trial proceedings. Previous histories had relied on the untypical state trials.[45]

This illustrates the need to find and to exploit the best available primary sources, rather than to rely exclusively upon law reports or other orthodox legal texts. The Old Bailey reports were not aimed at or used by lawyers in the eighteenth century; they were produced for popular consumption. Legal developments have to be traced obliquely in them, but they provide inform-ation for the historian of law and legal process that is not available anywhere else. They do not resemble modern law reports and seldom contain detail on questions of substantive law or clear statements of law on evidence or pro-cedure. Indeed, they routinely omitted legal detail, including the arguments of lawyers and the judicial directions to juries, as uninteresting or for fear of making public successful defence strategies.[46] The legal historian has to be keenly conscious of these limitations, to seek corroboration in other sources and, where appropriate, to draw inferences based on omissions.

Langbein's work could be viewed as a typical example of internal legal history, in contrast to the external, critical legal history practised by social historians such as Hay, Beattie and King. Langbein certainly offers a strident critique of Hay's thesis based on a close study of the trial notes of a judge and the Old Bailey reports. Langbein finds Hay's account of the jury 'baffling': 'If I were going to organise a ruling-class conspiracy to use the criminal law to terrorize the lower orders, I would not interpose autonomous bodies of non-conspirators like the petty juries.'[47] The Hay–Langbein debate has become a classic illustration of the clash between the internal (conservative) approach of legal historians and that adopted by social historians of crime.[48] Langbein's

---

45 Most notably J. Stephen, *A History of the Criminal Law* (3 vols), London: Macmillan, 1883.
46 Between 1790 and 1792, the City of London prohibited the publication of cases resulting in acquittals, for this reason. For the value of the reports as a historical source, see: J. Langbein, 'The Criminal Trial before the Lawyers', *University of Chicago Law Review* 45, 1978, 267–72; Clive Emsley, Tim Hitchcock and Robert Shoemaker, 'The Proceedings – the Value of the Proceedings as a Historical Source', *Old Bailey Proceedings Online*, http://www.oldbaileyonline.org (accessed 6 March 2017), version 7.0, 19 July 2012.
47 J. Langbein, 'Albion's Fatal Flaws', *Past and Present* 98, 1983, 96–120, 107.
48 For a highly critical riposte to Langbein's critique of Hay, see P. Linebaugh, '(Marxist) Social History and (Conservative) Legal History: A Reply to Professor Langbein', *New York University Law Review* 60, 1985, 212.

work is insensitive to social context in places and underestimates the subtlety and power of Hay's thesis, but the detailed perspective it offers on the law and legal process qualifies some of the claims about the ideological functions of the system.[49] Moreover, the detailed work of other social historians, notably Beattie and King, which is based on a very close reading of the court records, provides an empirical basis for challenging Hay's characterisation of the system and supports many of Langbein's criticisms. The social composition of juries and the pattern of verdicts have been analysed to draw conclusions concerning the extent to which juries exercised independent power and acted on interests that were distinct from those of the elite.[50]

The eighteenth-century criminal trial and the role of the jury within it has attracted much more scholarly attention than its nineteenth-century counterpart. This is not due to a lack of source material; on the contrary, nineteenth-century newspaper trial reports recorded much of the legal detail omitted in the eighteenth-century Old Bailey trial reports and covered trials from across the country.[51] That this rich source material has not been fully explored may be explained by the view that the collapse of England's 'bloody code' in the early nineteenth century also signified the end of the species of discretionary justice in which jurors played such a central role.[52] The attempts to produce a statutory criminal law framework, the increasingly reliable and comprehensive law reports and the growth in legal literature, including criminal law treatises, in the nineteenth century have drawn doctrinal and procedural historians' focus away from trials. The triumph of lawyers and establishment of adversarial culture are assumed to have made the criminal law, finally, the business of legal professionals, not lay people.

Wiener's work on Victorian homicide trials provides cause to question this assumption and provides an illuminating contrast in methodology to the social and legal historical approaches discussed above. His detailed study suggests that newspaper reports of trials can be as revealing of legal change as the law reports. He argues that judge–jury relations provide the key to the

---

49 One aspect of Langbein's misreading of Hay's thesis is evident from the quote above (n. 47). Hay does not suggest a conscious, organised conspiracy of the type implied in Langbein's criticism.

50 Contrast the conclusions of Beattie, King and Hay in the essays cited above in n. 39.

51 The Old Bailey reports also became more detailed and were marketed increasingly at professional lawyers.

52 For an example of jury nullification on the eve of the collapse of the 'bloody code', see P. Handler, 'The Limits of Discretion: Forgery and the Jury at the Old Bailey, 1818–21', in Cairns and McLeod, *The Dearest Birthright*, 155–72.

shifting boundary between murder and manslaughter in the period. Victorian judges, on a 'civilising' mission to inculcate habits of self-discipline and sobriety among an apparently unruly and violent populace, sought to restrict the scope for excuses such as provocation and intoxication to reduce murder to manslaughter. Jurors were generally more sympathetic to such excuses. Wiener evaluates judge–jury negotiations, focusing on judicial directions (which were reported in the newspapers), jury verdicts and other indicators such as jury recommendations to mercy. Using these means, he suggests that the meanings of key legal terms such as intention and the scope of certain defences were refined in ways that were not reflected in contemporary law reports.[53]

In seeking to bring the history of legal doctrine into closer contact with the history of criminal justice policy, Wiener attempts to chart how judges and juries reflected and acted upon broader currents of opinion about violence and criminal responsibility. This is an explanation of legal change that depends upon an interpretation of the cultural meaning of courtroom interactions. Doctrine appears as a dimension of legal policy that was, to a large extent, determined by judicial attempts to use criminal law as a means of prosecuting the Victorian 'civilising offensive'. This instrumentalist view of the criminal law is vulnerable to the criticism that it takes insufficient account of internal professional legal culture. Little attempt is made to integrate the technical details of criminal law doctrine into the analysis, not all of which fitted these broader patterns of cultural and policy development.[54] The method of close analysis of judge–jury interaction in routine trials is nonetheless suggestive of new ways of thinking about legal change. As Simpson points out, legal scholars are very reluctant to engage in the empirical study of cases.[55] The available evidence for the nineteenth century provides a valuable opportunity to study trials and the role of the jury in influencing the content of the substantive law.

This may suggest new ways of thinking about the relationship between legal process and legal doctrine in the nineteenth century.[56] It certainly

53 M. Wiener, 'Judges v. Jurors: Courtroom Tensions in Murder Trials and the Law of Criminal Responsibility in Nineteenth-Century England', *Law and History Review* 17, 1999, 467–506.

54 See P. Handler, 'The Law of Felonious Assault in England, 1803–61', *Journal of Legal History* 28, 2007, 183–206.

55 A. W. B. Simpson, *Leading Cases in the Common Law*, Oxford: Clarendon Press, 1996, 8–9.

56 See P. Handler, 'Legal Development in Victorian Criminal Trials', in M. Dyson and D. Ibbetson (eds), *Law and Legal Process Substantive Law and Procedure in English Legal History*, Cambridge: Cambridge University Press, 2013.

provides cause to check assumptions that the remarkably rapid construction of much of the modern framework for criminal law and justice in the first half of the nineteenth century was accompanied by a similarly rapid shift in mentalities and understandings. It is tempting, once the sources become familiar and the law-making apparatus of the criminal justice system assumes a recognisably modern form, to deploy the methodological tools of the modern doctrinal scholar, but this risks making anachronistic assessments. Baker's argument that the legal historian must look beyond the canonical sources of authority to recover the actual state of juristic understanding at any given time is as applicable to the nineteenth century, when those canonical sources expand and become more accessible, as it is to earlier periods.[57] Nineteenth-century criminal law judges viewed codifying legislation and the prospect of a court of criminal appeal with great distrust.[58] Close study of trials may illuminate aspects of professional and lay understandings of criminal law that do not appear elsewhere.

Possibilities and uses

This survey of methods suggests that it is not always easy to categorise work as internal or external legal history. Indeed, a pure form of either would not make for very good history.[59] In the Victorian period, it has been suggested that the type and wealth of source material available make it difficult for the historian to confine attention to legal doctrine without any reference to legal outcomes or of law's effects in society more generally.[60] In the twelfth and thirteenth centuries, English land law cannot be described or analysed without some understanding of the structure of the society and economy within which it operated. Conversely, if some historians maintain that law and legal institutions always conform to more general patterns of historical development, most recognise that they lead complex lives of their own and that the inter-relationship between legal, social, economic, political and cultural influences

---

57 J. Baker, *The Law's Two Bodies: Some Evidential Problems in English Legal History*, Oxford: Oxford University Press, 2001, 2 and *passim*.
58 See P. Handler, 'Judges and the Criminal Law', in P. Brand and J. Getzler (eds), *Judges and Judging in the History of the Common Law and Civil Law*, Cambridge: Cambridge University Press, 2012, 138–56.
59 For an argument that the internal/external dichotomy is a false one, see C. Donahue, 'Whither Legal History', in D. Hamilton and A. Brophy (eds), *Transformations in American Legal History: Essays in Honor of Professor Morton J. Horwitz*, Cambridge, MA: Harvard University Press, 2009, 327–43, 339.
60 C. Stebbings, 'Benefits and Barriers: The Making of Victorian Legal History', in Musson and Stebbings, *Making Legal History*, 72–87, 86–87.

is multifaceted and demands sensitive interpretation. In 1989, Cornish and Clark's groundbreaking textbook, *Law and Society in England, 1750–1950*, signified the extent to which this had become accepted as an orthodox current in English legal historical scholarship.[61] Written from within the legal academy, it presents the law in its social and economic context and engages directly with general historical themes of the period.

The possibilities for pursuing all kinds of legal historical enquiry have grown considerably in recent years. Much more accessible source materials have accompanied the expanding range of methods. Already, the digitisation of large volumes of material has rendered a vast range of sources almost instantly accessible. These databases and digitised records may be a more inviting prospect to the researcher in search of a project than that of handling large, dusty rolls describing obsolete procedures in abbreviated Latin. It may facilitate interdisciplinary work. For example, historians of all kinds have made extensive use of the online database of Old Bailey trial reports and associated records.[62] The wide range of search facilities that it offers and the increasingly sophisticated links to other online resources have opened up new avenues for research. There are, however, associated pitfalls. Online sources may distract attention from other less accessible records that contain more valuable information. The plea rolls provide the most striking, but not the only, example. The Old Bailey online database may deter research into court records elsewhere; London was not representative.[63] Current concerns and preconceptions are easily entered into the search box. Starting with the available evidence in order to get a sense of what questions were being asked by contemporaries is more likely to generate research questions that lead to meaningful results.

How might these methods be deployed to make a contribution to legal and historical scholarship? The relatively marginal position of legal history in the English law school curriculum makes the question pressing. As one leading scholar puts it: 'legal historians remain in danger of being regarded as erudite court jesters in the law faculty, full of curious information, but marginal to the practical and current needs of the law student'.[64] One function of legal history is to challenge the assumptions that inform and underpin modern legal scholarship. It is a commonplace of legal argument to refer to the historical pedigree of a particular rule or institution as an indicator of its strength

---

61 W. Cornish and G. de N Clark, *Law and Society in England, 1750–1950*, London: Sweet & Maxwell, 1989.

62 See http://www.oldbaileyonline.org (accessed 6 March 2017).

63 See Beattie, 'London Juries', 252 and passim.

64 Lobban, 'Tools and Tasks', 1.

and value. The history of the jury provides a striking example. Debates over the role played by the jury in the current system are littered with claims of its age-old role as a bulwark of liberty against oppression, often supported by vague references to the Magna Carta.[65] Testing the validity of claims using historical evidence may serve a useful myth-dispelling function.

This is not to say that the legal historian's role is to establish a single and authoritative interpretation of the legal past and its meaning, but legal history may have an unsettling effect on current understandings. It can certainly provide cause to challenge the lineal view of doctrinal development that characterises 'lawyers' history'. Scrutiny of past law in its historical context and the study of seams of doctrine that did not survive to the current day may expose errors in current thinking about law or provide cause to question analytical models.[66] A historical perspective on law can give a sense of the contingency and indeterminacy of law and provide a valuable check on assumptions about the universality or permanency of current institutional and doctrinal arrangements. To take just one example, recent research has demonstrated the relatively recent origins of the lawyer-dominated adversarial criminal trial and the passive trial jury.[67]

A core aim of legal history is to provide insight into the mechanisms and dynamics of legal change. Some accounts focus on the interaction of factors within the legal system in order to explain change and it is one of the distinctive features of common law historiography that it offers accounts of legal development over long periods of time. The most successful of these studies are sensitive to the undetermined nature of such change and to the fact that the law is often in a state of flux. This is true not only of the changing rules, but also of the surrounding intellectual framework which, as we have seen, is one of the most difficult dimensions of the past for the historian of legal doctrine to reconstruct. As Ibbetson points out, the legal historian has to be sensitive to ambiguities and the fact that at any given point in time there may have been competing intellectual frameworks and no settled understanding of a particular issue.[68] One benefit of a historical perspective is that some attempt can be made to chart these shifts and to offer explanations, however tentative, of underlying causes of legal development. Much of the

---

65 'It has always been bad history to trace the system back to Magna Carta' (W. Cornish, *The Jury*, London: Allen Lane, 1968, 12).
66 For some difficulties with the Hartian model of law that are suggested by a historical perspective, see Ibbetson, 'What Is Legal History', 34–35.
67 See Langbein, *The Origins of the Adversary Criminal Trial*.
68 Ibbetson, 'What Is Legal History', 36–37.

practice of legal history has eschewed theory or generalisation in favour of close study of primary materials. Nonetheless, such study may prompt some basic questions such as what law is for the purposes of legal history, which may in turn lead to insights and hypotheses as to how and why certain types of legal development occur.[69]

The production of a contextualised account of law in past societies serves an important function for historical scholarship generally. The histories of law, legal institutions and processes are an essential part of social, political, economic and cultural histories. Investigating the place of law in this broader context seldom, if ever, yields a clear picture of cause and effect, but it does illustrate how important a role law played in regulating diverse areas of social activity. This has long been recognised for the medieval period, but law has assumed a more prominent role in early modern and modern English history.[70] The territory of the law is a specialised one and the work of legal historians can ensure that general history is served by a nuanced interpretation of law and its institutions. If historians sometimes complain that lawyers show insensitivity to social and political contexts, lawyers sometimes have just cause to complain that general histories gloss over or disregard the detail of legal history.

The legal historian has to be able to employ historical methodologies at the same time as showing a lawyer's sensitivity to doctrine and legal processes. If this presents difficulties to scholars trained in one discipline only, one solution is to pursue training in both. Joint programmes exist, mostly in the United States, but it is an expensive route and, in many instances, impractical.[71] It may not be necessary. Legal scholars can adopt some historical methods without acquiring a history degree and should be prepared to engage in meaningful dialogue with experts in different fields. The study of legal history has not always been distinguished by such dialogue, but the engagement between the two disciplines has been mutually beneficial. Few legal scholars now fail to heed Maitland's example and consciously adopt whiggish and present-minded perspectives on the past. They are mindful of the ever-present, if not entirely avoidable, risk of being 'enticed into carrying concepts and even social frameworks back into periods to which they do not belong'.[72]

Those who wish to engage in legal historical study will not want for subject matter. The diversification of legal historical scholarship in the last few

69 See, e.g., Milsom, *A Natural History*.
70 See Lobban, 'Introduction', 1.
71 See Donahue, 'Whither Legal History', 339–43.
72 Milsom, *Historical Foundations*, vi.

decades has opened up many new avenues for enquiry. Many of the sources of early English legal history to which Maitland drew attention remain uninvestigated over a century after his death. Few areas offer such opportunities 'to delve into unbroken ground and recover lost worlds' and studying the history of law and legal change is more relevant than ever in an era when the legal landscape is shifting with unprecedented speed.[73]

Recommended reading

Baker, J., 'Why the History of English Law Has Not Been Finished', *Cambridge Law Journal*, 59, 2000, 62–84.

Lobban, M., 'Introduction: The Tools and Tasks of the Legal Historian', in M. Lobban and A. Lewis, *Law and Legal History*, Oxford: Oxford University Press, 2004, pp. 1–32.

Musson, A. and Stebbings, C., *Making Legal History: Approaches and Methodologies*, Cambridge: Cambridge University Press, 2012.

Smith, K. and McLaren, J., 'History's Living Legacy: An Outline of the "Modern" Historiography of the Common Law', *Legal Studies* 21, 2001, 251–324.

73 Baker, 'Why the History of English Law', 84.

6 Comparative law and its methodology
Geoffrey Samuel

The question that this chapter will consider is easy enough to state. How does – or, perhaps one ought to say, how should – a comparative lawyer approach the question of lay participation in law? If for reasons of space and convenience one narrows the subject matter of comparison, namely lay participation, down to the single institution of the jury in English and French law, the framework would seemingly be straightforward. How should the research student conduct her investigation into this institution in both countries? Yet, as we shall see, the question of research methods in comparative legal studies is by no means as straightforward as it might seem. There are serious methodological issues behind which lie important epistemological questions and difficulties.[1] Consequently, while the jury itself will not be ignored, the emphasis will be primarily focused on comparative law method.

Introduction: preliminary questions

Otto Kahn-Freund once wrote that comparative law 'is not a topic, but a method'. Comparative law, he continued, 'is the common name for a variety of methods of looking at law, and especially of looking at one's own law'.[2] Thirty years later, Pierre Legrand retorted that to represent comparative law as simply a method 'is to take a formalist view of comparative legal studies' and to 'take it to its logical conclusion is to deny, in sum, any substantive content to comparative work about law and to ensure that it ultimately loses its status as a discrete, autonomous intellectual domain'. In Legrand's view, comparative law 'presents a new *perspective*, allowing one critically to illuminate a legal system – another or one's own – much in the same way as, say, critical legal studies, feminist legal

1 See generally G. Samuel, *An Introduction to Comparative Law Theory and Method*, Oxford: Hart Publishing, 2014.
2 O. Kahn-Freund, 'Comparative Law as an Academic Subject', *Law Quarterly Review* 82, 1966, 40, at 41.

studies, legal semiotics or economic analysis of law can do'. And nobody 'would think of reducing feminist legal theory, for instance, to a mere method'.[3] Professor Legrand has also asserted two other characteristics that ought to be central to comparative legal studies, namely that there should be a commitment to theory and a commitment to interdisciplinarity.[4]

One preliminary question that emerges from these two positions is whether or not they can be reconciled.[5] Is there a fundamental dichotomy between 'method' and 'perspective'? One purpose of this present chapter is to show that method is in fact central to comparative law, but that in understanding what is meant by 'method' in this domain one must have a commitment both to theory and to interdisciplinarity. It is through methodology that comparative legal studies is able to present a new, or at least different, perspective in respect of the discipline of law.[6] In fact, as this chapter will hopefully indicate, work in social science theory, in particular epistemology, reveals that to make rigid distinctions between 'theory', 'method' and 'substance' is intellectually misleading. The way a scientific subject or mind (*intellectus*) interacts with the object of a science (*res*) is a matter not just of actual reasoning methods such as induction, deduction, analysis, synthesis, analogy and so on; it is equally a matter of schemes of intelligibility and paradigm orientations.[7] And these schemes and paradigms are just as much issues of methodology as are reasoning techniques. What comparative legal studies is bringing to law research, then, is possibly more than just a different perspective. It is a domain of study that is establishing, and advancing,[8] legal epistemology as a new direction in the area of legal theory.

This first question immediately provokes another. Surely the comparison of a relatively straightforward institution like the jury is hardly going to raise deep epistemological and theory issues? Of course, much depends on why

3 P. Legrand, 'Comparative Legal Studies and Commitment to Theory', *Modern Law Review* 58, 1995, 262, at 264 (emphasis in the original).
4 See P. Legrand, 'How to Compare Now', *Legal Studies* 16, 1996, 232; and P. Legrand, *Le droit comparé* 5th edn, Paris: Presses Universitaires de France, 2015.
5 cf. S. Glanert, 'Method?' in P. G. Monateri (ed), *Methods of Comparative Law*, Cheltenham: Edward Elgar, 2012, 61.
6 G. Samuel, 'Does One Need an Understanding of Methodology in Law Before One Can Understand Methodology in Comparative Law?' in M. Van Hoecke (ed.), *Methodologies of Legal Research: Which Kind of Method for Which Kind of Discipline?* Oxford: Hart, 2011, 177.
7 See generally Samuel, *An Introduction to Comparative Law Theory and Method*.
8 The pioneering work of Professor Christian Atias must be fully acknowledged: C. Atias, *Épistémologie juridique*, Paris: Presses Universitaires de France, 1985; and C. Atias, *Épistémologie du droit*, Paris: Presses Universitaires de France, 1994.

someone might want to compare the jury in one system with the jury in another. If one wishes to obtain only a certain amount of technical information – say because an English lawyer is involved with helping defend a client facing a trial in France – then it is a question just of accessing descriptive data available in the various data sources. However, this kind of technical exercise is not comparative law.[9] If one looks outside the discipline of law, in particular to comparative approaches in literature, Yves Chevrel, in his introductory book, says that to compare is indispensable to the progress of knowledge. It is, he says, to put together (*cum*) several objects or several elements of one or more objects in order to examine the degrees of similarity (*par*) so as to be able to draw conclusions from them that the analysis of each of them alone would not necessarily have allowed one to draw.[10] If one returns to law and applies this test to lay participation, or more precisely to the jury, the overriding epistemological aim is to draw out of the process of comparison knowledge that could not be obtained from examining separately the jury in England and in France. The overriding issue facing the postgraduate researcher, particularly when formulating his or her research question, is this: Why compare?[11] What new knowledge is likely to emerge from *comparing* the jury (to use the example adopted in this chapter) in England with the jury in France?

Paradigm orientations: cultural otherness

Chevrel says that the 'scientific' aspect of the comparative process is to be found in the way comparatists construct a space with frontiers that deliberately mark off a body, or bodies, of literature that come from 'other' cultures. The key notion is the idea of the 'foreign' or the 'other'.[12] This approach, however, is conducted very much within what might be described as a paradigm dichotomy, that between a 'natural' and a 'cultural' approach.

The 'nature' paradigm is one that starts out from the assumption that the social sciences are no different from the natural sciences. 'The pole that we propose to call "naturalist" is', wrote a leading social science epistemologist, 'one that considers social phenomena as being an extension of natural phenomena and not giving rise to a specific explanation'. And thus it 'is enough, in

---

9 M. Van Hoecke, 'Deep Level Comparative Law', in M. Van Hoecke (ed.), *Epistemology and Methodology of Comparative Law*, Oxford: Hart, 2004, 165, at 172.
10 Y. Chevrel, *La littérature comparée*, 5th edn, Paris: Presses Universitaires de France, 2006, 3.
11 J. Husa, *A New Introduction to Comparative Law*, Oxford: Hart Publishing, 2015, 58–95.
12 *Ibid.*, 5.

order to analyse such phenomena, to determine the mechanisms upon which they depend'.[13] The comparative lawyer who operates within this paradigm (or pole) would consider the jury as an objective phenomenon in itself and thus one that transcends any particular state. In turn, as will be seen, such a paradigm assumption brings with it a number of methodological approaches and attitudes.

The cultural paradigm, in contrast, is one in which 'it is the cultural norms and values of the group or society which, through the medium of socialisation, enculturation or inculcation define the meaning of behaviour or, according to some, the practices'.[14] The cultural paradigm is, in other words, one in which the phenomenon being considered is regarded as being the product uniquely of its cultural context. Consequently, when Chevrel states that 'comparatists construct spaces which quite deliberately set themselves apart from works coming from other practices and cultures', and that therefore the notion of 'the foreigner is the touchstone' of comparative studies,[15] he is functioning within this cultural pole or paradigm. It is a question of confrontation with the 'other'.

One can see at once the implications of this paradigm dichotomy. Is the researcher to treat the jury as an institution that rises above any particular legal tradition or is each national jury to be regarded as a cultural phenomenon in itself? There is no right or wrong answer, as such, that can be asserted with regard to this paradigm question.[16] However, the methodologies and assumptions associated with each paradigm orientation – and the nature versus culture is not the only paradigm dichotomy of importance to the comparatist – can be examined in themselves and such examinations might point a way, if not to a resolution of the paradigm question itself, at least to the avoidance of a number of methodological pitfalls that the competent comparatist should be at pains to avoid.

This said, there is no denying that the movement within comparative law has been progressively towards a cultural approach. As Roger Cotterrell has put it:

---

13 J.-M. Berthelot, 'Programmes, paradigmes, disciplines: pluralité et unité des sciences sociales', in J.-M. Berthelot (ed.), *Épistémologie des sciences sociales*, Paris: Presses Universitaires de France, 2001, 457, at 498.
14 J.-M. Berthelot, 'Les sciences du social', in Berthelot, *Épistémologie des sciences sociales*, 203, at 247.
15 Chevrel, *La littérature comparée*, 5.
16 cf. B. Du Laing, 'Promises and Pitfalls of Interdisciplinary Legal Research: The Case of Evolutionary Analysis in Law', in Van Hoecke, *Methodologies of Legal Research*, 241, at 249–52.

An interest in understanding law in its various cultural settings might be thought to underlie all imaginative comparative law scholarship. In the past this has often been merely implicit. However, since the early 1990s, an explicit concern with law's relation to culture, and especially with the concept of legal culture, has become much more prominent in comparative legal scholarship. In particular, the idea of legal culture has had an important place in major recent debates about the nature and aims of comparative law. Indeed, it has been taken up by some comparatists as a tool to try to reorient the entire field of comparative legal studies.[17]

And he goes on to explain that the 'idea of legal culture entails that law (as rules, practices, institutions, doctrine, etc.) should be treated as embedded in a broader culture of some kind'.[18] Cotterrell concludes that culture therefore 'appears fundamental – a kind of lens through which all aspects of law must be perceived, or a gateway of understanding through which every comparatist must pass so as to have any genuine access to the meaning of foreign law'.[19]

One of the leading contemporary comparatists to stress this cultural approach is Pierre Legrand.[20] There would be no question, for Legrand, of studying the jury as some kind of institution that transcends France and England. Quite the opposite: French and English law belong to quite different traditions[21] and any aspect of any legal system – concept, category, rule, institution or whatever – must be understood within its particular legal culture itself, situated within the wider culture of the relevant society. *Extra culturam nihil datur.*[22]

Legrand insists therefore on several fundamental requirements. The first is that comparative legal studies is dedicated to understanding the 'other'.[23] Consequently, although a comparison of the jury in France and in England would appear to be an exercise in micro-comparison – one is comparing a particular object within each system rather than comparing two legal systems

---

17 R. Cotterrell, 'Comparative Law and Legal Culture', in M. Reimann and R. Zimmermann (eds), *The Oxford Handbook of Comparative Law*, Oxford: Oxford University Press, 2006, 709, at 710. See also D. Nelken, 'Legal Culture', in J. M. Smits (ed.), *Elgar Encyclopedia of Comparative Law*, Cheltenham: Edward Elgar, 2006, 372.
18 Cotterrell, 'Comparative Law and Legal Culture', 710.
19 *Ibid.*, 711.
20 See generally Legrand, *Le droit comparé.*
21 On which see P. Legrand and G. Samuel, *Introduction au common law*, Paris: La Découverte, 2008.
22 Legrand, *Le droit comparé*, 82.
23 *Ibid.*, 73–109.

(French and English) at a general level[24] – the researcher cannot escape from the macro because one must understand the jury not just within one's home legal culture, but equally within the legal culture of the 'other'. One must strive to comprehend French legal culture and of course the wider legal tradition within which it is situated, namely the Civil Law. How does one do this? According to Legrand:

> The essential key for an appreciation of a legal culture lies in an unravelling of the cognitive structure that characterises that culture. The aim must be to try to define the frame of perception and understanding of a legal community so as to explicate how a community thinks about the law and why it thinks about the law in the way it does. The comparatist must, therefore, focus on the cognitive structure of a given legal culture and, more specifically, on the epistemological foundations of that cognitive structure.

What one is seeking to understand is the legal *mentalité* within which an institution like the jury is situated. 'It is this epistemological substratum', he says, 'which best epitomises . . . the legal *mentalité* (the collective mental programme), or the interiorised legal culture, within a given legal culture.'[25]

Secondly, the methodology – or more precisely the scheme of intelligibility[26] – employed in this *mentalité* search is hermeneutics.[27] Legal texts are not to be treated as objects in themselves – things capable, for example, of being transplanted from one system to another[28] – but as signifiers of something culturally more profound about the 'other'. One might compare this method

24 K. Zweigert and H. Kötz, *An Introduction to Comparative Law*, trans. T. Weir, 3rd edn, Oxford: Oxford University Press, 1998, 4–5.
25 P. Legrand, 'European Legal Systems Are Not Converging', *International and Comparative Law Quarterly* 45, 1996, 52, at 60.
26 '*The hermeneutical scheme* . . . [is] a very ancient scheme of intelligibility, probably one of the first developed by humanity in its attempt to explain reality. It consists of developing systematically a vertical logic of the beyond of appearance or surface of things: B is not only B . . . B is simultaneously something else, a force, a spirit, a power which is recognisable by this form. In this case however B and A combine in an animistic ontology where B is both A and B . . . Used in science, the hermeneutical scheme does not go in for such pre-scientific thinking. It involves B being seen only as a sign, and thus divided into a signifier (what it is) and a signified (what it expresses) . . .': J.-M. Berthelot, *L'intelligence du social*, Paris: Presses Universitaires de France, 1990, 72, 73 (emphasis in the original).
27 Legrand, *Le droit comparé*, 49–71.
28 On which see Husa, *A New Introduction to Comparative Law*, 105–08.

with a causal scheme.[29] Take, for example, a notion such as 'contract'. The late Professor Birks, discussing the Roman law of obligations, saw this category of contract as a scientific response to a 'causative event' and as such it was a category that transcended any particular legal system.[30] The law of obligations, whether in Roman, French or English law, concerned different kinds of claim, each having different causative events; and a claim in contract was a response to a claim arising out of the non-performance, or defective performance, of an obligation which in turn had as its causative event an agreement. Accordingly, this kind of analysis sees contract as a universalist concept; that is, a concept not confined to any particular society in that it is a rational and scientific response to a common causative event no matter where and when the event takes place.

A hermeneutical approach operating within the context of the cultural paradigm would, in contrast, regard 'contract' as a sign whose cultural meaning must be deciphered by the comparatist. 'For the interpretation is', says Legrand, 'a reading which wants to give an account not only of the directly visible aspects of legal phenomena but also their sense.'[31] And this sense is to be obtained only by deconstructing the law 'object' (contract, jury or whatever) as an object in itself and reconstructing it an interdisciplinary context which will reveal its cultural complexity.[32] Such a deep hermeneutical approach is impossible if one considers the legal phenomenon – that is the notion of contract, the jury or whatever – as a universal. 'Since,' says Legrand, 'the law can exist only in a language and since a language always constitutes only a significant articulation that is singular and contingent it is impossible – and one must insist on this – to create a legal universal object.'[33]

---

29 *'The causal scheme* . . . means that B depends on A according to a relation such that, in the absolute, that is to say in a situation where A would be the unique cause of B, you cannot have B without A and that in any variation of A there corresponds a variation in B (reciprocal implication). It follows that A and B are distinct either in reality (different objects or realities) or analytically (different levels of a global reality) and that the element A is conceived as being necessarily prior, chronologically or logically, to the element B': Berthelot, *L'intelligence du social*, 62–63 (emphasis in the original).

30 See, e.g., P. Birks, 'Definition and Division: A Meditation on *Institutes* 3.13', in P. Birks (ed.), *The Classification of Obligations*, Oxford: Oxford University Press, 1997, 1.

31 Legrand, *Le droit comparé*, 15.

32 *Ibid.*, 33–47.

33 *Ibid.*, 99.

Differential comparison

One might observe in this comment a third requirement insisted upon by Legrand, that of interdisciplinarity.[34] Simply looking at the jury from what might be called a traditional 'black-letter' framework is not an option for the comparatist because many of the methodological and epistemological issues underpinning the comparison question are located at a social science level rather than at the level of a single discipline.

One such issue, as we have seen, is the problem of 'universalisation'. In comparative literature, it has been said that the 'recognition of differences between facts or objects to be compared is often neglected or omitted in favour of a too hasty focussing on what appears *similar* and, by extension, *universal*'.[35] This search for universal themes can be problematic in the area of literary myths because it can eclipse objects of comparison through the relating of 'cultural facts to an abstract construction (the constitution of a prototype or of a list of myth-themes (*mythèmes*) . . .)'.[36] Accordingly, Ute Heidmann has proposed what is called differential comparison which, as the name suggests, consists in putting the emphasis on distinguishing cultural facts which at first sight might seem similar. 'In other words,' says Heidmann, 'if we take the differential option, we are engaged in the construction of a comparison axis sufficiently relevant and complex to take account both of the common perceived trait and of the fundamental differences of the phenomena being compared.'[37]

This idea of differential comparison has given rise to a debate within comparative law. In one of the leading textbooks on the subject, the authors, Zweigert and Kötz, make the assertion that 'as a general rule developed nations answer the needs of legal business in the same way or in a very similar way' and indeed 'it almost amounts to a "*praesumptio similitudinis*", a presumption that the practical results are similar'. The authors explain the importance of this presumption of similarity as follows:

> As a working rule this is very useful, and useful in two ways. At the outset of a comparative study it serves as a heuristic principle – it tells us where to look in the law and legal life of the foreign system in order to discover similarities and substitutes.

34 See generally Legrand, 'How to Compare Now'.
35 Ute Heidmann, 'Épistémologie et pratique de la comparaison différentielle', in M. Burger and C. Calme (eds), *Comparer les comparatismes: Perspectives sur l'histoire et les sciences des religions*, Paris: Edidit/Arehè, 2006, 141, at 144 (emphasis in the original).
36 *Ibid.*, 145.
37 *Ibid.*, 145–46.

They then go on to say:

> And at the end of the study the same presumption acts as a means of
> checking our results: the comparatist can rest content if his researches
> through all the relevant material lead to the conclusion that the systems
> he has compared reach the same or similar practical results, but if he finds
> that there are great differences or indeed diametrically opposite results,
> he should be warned and go back to check again whether the terms in
> which he posed his original question were indeed purely functional, and
> whether he has spread the net of his researches quite wide enough.[38]

If one applies this presumption to comparative legal research on the jury, the
'working rule' would appear, then, to be one where the researcher starts out
from the assumption that the functions of the jury in the two systems (England
and France) are more or less the same.

One might note here the importance of another methodological scheme of
intelligibility, that of functionalism. This is a scheme that puts the emphasis
not on an analysis of the institution itself, but on its function.[39] This scheme
achieved such prominence during the last century that Zweigert and Kötz
assert that it is the 'basic methodological principle of all comparative law'
since 'in law the only things which are comparable are those which fulfil
the same function'.[40] One should not, of course, be surprised by this methodological assertion from authors, who have equally proposed that the working
presumption for the comparatist should be that of similarity. Accordingly, for
these authors, the comparatist working on the institution of the jury will need
to research carefully exactly what the jury does in each country and to be aware
of the difficulties and dangers, as well as of course the benefits, of a functional
approach. However, it has to be recognised at the outset that the whole issue
of function can prove more difficult than it might seem.[41] For example, in
assuming a clear distinction between 'law' and 'function', the researcher may
well be unconsciously applying a theory, or epistemology, of law which might
work well enough for the researcher's own system, but could well be a form of

---

38 Zweigert and Kötz, *An Introduction to Comparative Law*, 40.
39 '[T]he *functional* scheme (S→X→S, [is one] where one phenomenon X is analysed
     from the position of its function – X→S – in a given system)': J.-M. Berthelot,
     'Programmes, paradigmes, disciplines: pluralité et unité des sciences sociales', in
     J.-M. Berthelot (ed.), *Épistémologie des sciences sociales*, Paris: Presses Universitaires
     de France, 2001, 457, at 484 (emphasis in the original).
40 Zweigert and Kötz, *An Introduction to Comparative Law*, 34.
41 Samuel, *An Introduction to Comparative Law Theory and Method*, 79–81.

epistemological imperialism with regard to the other foreign system. Does a legal system that approaches legal knowledge from a realist perspective assume that a clear frontier exists between positive legal rules ('law') and the social and institutional operation of these rules ('function')? An example of this problem has been discussed in more detail elsewhere.[42]

However, whatever the strengths of the functional approach,[43] the comparatist will need to be aware that both the assertions of Zweigert and Kötz have been severely criticised on grounds, inter alia, not dissimilar to those articulated by Heidmann. Leading the attack is, once again, Professor Legrand, who argues that Zweigert and Kötz are simply wrong in their assertion. Comparison, he says, involves quite the opposite presumption – a presumption of difference – because it is about identifying diversity in law. Comparative law itself is rooted *dans la différence.*[44] The presumption of similarity has, then, to be abandoned for a rigorous experience of distance and difference and, in 'this sense, a respect for alterity is not so much the result of a quest for difference as it is its pre-requisite'.[45]

Faced with this debate, what is the comparative law research student to do? Does she presume that juries in England and France are similar in their functions or does she presume difference? In one sense, there is no easy answer to this question since it involves what might be called a 'scientific' choice whose basis cannot be epistemologically tested by reference to some kind of Karl Popper test.[46] However, it is at this point that the researcher must be conscious of another methodological dichotomy, that between genealogical and analogical comparison. A genealogical comparison aims to establish a filial relationship between the objects that are being compared and thus it 'is a matter of explaining similarities between . . . systems in terms of *real* historical connections: any resemblance is interpreted as the sign of a genealogical connection'.[47] An analogical comparison is one which puts the emphasis on a similarity of form and structure between two objects or elements not descend-

42 G. Samuel, 'Dépasser le fonctionnalisme', in P. Legrand (ed.), *Comparer les droits, résolument*, Paris: Presses Universitaires de France, 2009, 405.

43 See Husa, *A New Introduction to Comparative Law*, 151–54.

44 Legrand, *Le droit comparé*, 99.

45 P. Legrand, 'The Same and the Different', in P. Legrand and R. Munday (eds), *Comparative Legal Studies: Traditions and Transitions*, Cambridge: Cambridge University Press, 2003, 240, at 272.

46 On which see Samuel, *An Introduction to Comparative Law Theory and Method*, 91.

47 Y. Bubloz, 'Augustine et Porphyre sur le salut: Pour une comparaison analogique et non apologétique du Christianisme et du Néoplatonisme', in M. Burger and C. Calme (eds), *Comparer les comparatismes: Perspectives sur l'histoire et les sciences des religions*, Paris: Edidit/Arehè, 2006, 113, at 115 (emphasis in the original).

ing from a common ancestor. In 'a comparison between religious systems having been in no direct contact with each other neither in space nor in time', the 'object of the comparison is not ... the bringing to light of some real properties in the objects of comparison'. Instead, the 'comparison is purely an *intellectual exercise* on the part of the person doing the comparing' in that one is comparing the *relations and aspects* between the objects and not the objects themselves.[48]

In the light of this distinction, the comparatist will be required to research the historical roots of the jury in France in comparison with its history in England. Are there filial links between the two institutions? And, if so, how close are such links in reality? However, great care must be taken when undertaking such historical research because, even if a clear genealogical link can be established, the object of comparison cannot be assumed to be a similar object in the context of either system. Thus, it may be that 'the origins of the jury [in France], of the kind established following the Revolution, must in reality be researched on the other side of the Channel, in England'.[49] But if one merely 'transplants' such an institution from one system to another, this raises further methodological and epistemological questions. Are such transplants really possible? Can one take an institution such as the jury and establish it in another legal culture in such a way that it retains the essential characteristics of the home institution; or, once transplanted, does it become something different?

This is a very complex question for several reasons. First, it is complex because the history of law in continental Europe could be said to be a history of one legal system formed within one social system, Roman law, being transplanted into the environment of a completely different social and legal system, namely eleventh-century Europe.[50] Some civil lawyers even like to insist that there were Roman transplantations into England whose feudal model is often seen as having been resistant to such importations.[51] Second, it is complex because there seem to be endless examples of transfers from one

---

48 *Ibid.*, 116–17. See also Jonathan Z. Smith, *Drudgery Divine: On the Comparison of Early Christianities and the Religions of Late Antiquity*, Chicago: University of Chicago Press, 1994, 36–53 (emphasis in the original).

49 W. Roumier, *L'avenir du jury criminel*, Paris: LGDJ, 2003, 3.

50 See, e.g., P. Stein, *Roman Law in European History*, Cambridge: Cambridge University Press, 1999.

51 M. Graziadei, 'Comparative Law as the Study of Transplants and Receptions', in Reimann and Zimmermann, *The Oxford Handbook of Comparative Law*, 441, at 446–47. See also R. Zimmermann, 'Comparative Law and the Europeanization of Private Law', in Reimann and Zimmermann, *The Oxford Handbook of Comparative Law*, 539.

legal system to another. Different societies seemingly borrow and export a variety of legal concepts, institutions and rules.[52] Third, it is complex because it is not always easy to distinguish between institutions, concepts and rules which form part of what might be termed the notion of law in general and institutions, concepts and rules that belong to some specific legal system. Is the idea of legal personality or enforceable agreements an idea that has been formed within one particular legal system and transplanted into a range of others or is it simply a result of legal thought in general?[53] Accordingly one can ask whether the jury should be seen as a specific institution belonging to a specific legal culture or whether it should be seen as nothing more than some kind of universal example of lay participation in the legal process.

Nevertheless, even if one accepts that there have been legal transplants from one system to another, Pierre Legrand has posed an important question. What, exactly, gets transplanted? In his view what at best 'can be displaced from one jurisdiction to another is, literally, a *meaningless* form of words' and to 'claim more is to claim too much'. And he continues:

> In any *meaning-ful* sense of the term, 'legal transplants', therefore, cannot happen. No rule in the borrowing jurisdiction can have any significance as regards the rule in the jurisdiction from which it is borrowed. This is because, as it crosses boundaries, the original rule necessarily undergoes a change that affects it *qua* rule. The disjunction between the bare propositional statement and its meaning thus prevents the displacement of the *rule* itself.[54]

Legrand is working, as we have seen, within the cultural paradigm and so the idea that some institution such as the 'jury' can have any meaning over and above, or divorced from, any particular legal culture is unthinkable. Others take a different view. Michele Graziadei, for example, asserts that 'it is far from clear that the transfer of law from one community to another is impossible'.[55] For the question is this: how does one view culture? It is arguable that culture

52 See generally Graziadei, 'Comparative Law as the Study of Transplants and Receptions'.

53 This question becomes even more difficult once one appreciates that much general legal theory is founded on Roman legal thought: see, e.g., J. W. Jones, *Historical Introduction to the Theory of Law*, Oxford: Oxford University Press, 1940; P. Stein, *Legal Evolution: The Story of an Idea*, Cambridge: Cambridge University Press, 1980.

54 P. Legrand, 'The Impossibility of "Legal Transplants"', *Maastricht Journal of European and Comparative Law* 4, 1997, 111, at 120.

55 Graziadei, 'Comparative Law as the Study of Transplants and Receptions', 468.

'is the outcome of mishmash, borrowings, mixtures that have occurred, though at different rates, ever since the beginning of time'.[56] Graziadei does not, for all that, dismiss Legrand's claim. What he argues is that transplants are not just 'a meaningless form of words'. It is more complex.

Whatever the situation, if one returns to the jury itself the transplant issue is a sensitive one. In England, the jury played a central role in the early development of the common law. Indeed, so central was this role that before the sixteenth century the formulation of pleadings and the reduction of litigation to a series of questions to be decided by the jury was nothing less than the common law itself; the judge was a mere umpire and advisor whose judgment automatically followed from the jury's verdict.[57] On the continent, where Romano-Canonical procedure has dominated since the fourteenth century, the canon lawyers who helped formulate the *ius commune* procedure 'rejected the idea of the jury, which left the decisive verdict in a law case in the power of a dozen illiterate rustics, as utterly ridiculous and absurd'.[58] Now it may be that the continental view changed to some extent in the eighteenth and nineteenth centuries and that the jury as an institution was imported into criminal procedure. However, the very different institutional roles played by the jury in the histories of common law and the civil law traditions mean that the comparatist must remain very alert to the cultural and mentality contexts in which the jury in each system has functioned and continues to function. In the common law tradition, the jury has undoubtedly had a considerable impact on the development of the substantive law.[59] In contrast, one might not so easily be able to say this of France, whose substantive law has been fashioned by professors working and re-working the concepts, categories and rules of Roman and canon law.[60]

Analytical comparison

This is not to say that the institution of the jury in each system cannot be examined and analysed as an object in itself. In fact, such an analytical

---

56 *Ibid.*, 469.
57 J. H. Baker, *An Introduction to English Legal History*, 4th edn, London: Butterworths, 2002, 79.
58 R. Van Caenegem, *Judges, Legislators and Professors: Chapters in European Legal History*, Cambridge: Cambridge University Press, 1987, 119.
59 See, e.g., Baker, *An Introduction to English Legal History*, 76; and S. Milsom, *Historical Foundations of the Common Law*, 2nd edn, London: Butterworths, 1981, 79–81.
60 See generally Van Caenegem, *Judges, Legislators and Professors*; and Stein, *Roman Law in European History*.

examination is an essential part of the comparatist's research. Being analytical, the methodology in play takes as its starting point a causal scheme of intelligibility; that is to say the researcher will, for example, take apart the judicial process in order to determine how the relationships between the members of the jury as an institution and the witnesses, lawyers, judge and other judicial players causally affect the decision of the jury and how this causal relationship will in turn impact upon any appeal procedure. Evidently, the comparatist will adopt such an approach with regard to each system that forms part of the research project. And at this level of analysis what will be striking are of course the differences and the similarities.

Thus, when discussing the cross-examination of witnesses before the jury in France and in England, there are clearly some points of similarity. For example, the examination of witnesses in both systems is conducted in an oral hearing through an oral cross-examination (that is, by responses to questions rather than by narration) under the control of a judge whose role is primarily to guarantee the proper progress of the questioning (*bon déroulement des débats*) by the parties' lawyers.[61] As for the members of the jury themselves, who as individuals are listening to this oral cross-examination, another similarity between the two systems is the requirement of impartiality on the part of each individual juror. Indeed, as a result of this requirement, both systems have built up bodies of case law that are themselves capable of acting as an object of comparison.[62] Equally, there are major points of difference. There are technical differences such as the number of jurors, but a more notable one is the fact that in England the jurors deliberate independently of the presiding judge, while in France they do not.[63] In France, the President of the court takes part in the deliberation and this of course impacts in a major way on the more general question of lay participation in the legal process. The comparatist will need to investigate analytically how this judicial participation might affect the deliberation and reasoning processes and the reaching of a verdict. An even more general difference between the two systems is of course to be found at the level of the procedural models themselves: the English jury functions within the procedural context of an accusatorial (or adversarial) process, while the French jury has been inserted into an essentially inquisitorial system. Again, the comparatist will need to analyse the technicalities of these different models.

61 Roumier, *L'avenir du jury criminel*, 309.
62 *Ibid.*, 391–425.
63 Code de Procédure Pénale art. 355. However, this is a relatively recent development.

This kind of analytical process is of itself quite capable of producing useful technical knowledge. Noting the apparent fact that on both sides of the Channel the presiding judges are highly respected with regard to their conduct of the legal proceedings before a jury, one thesis writer analyses this respect in rather different ways. In England, the respect attaches to the Crown Court judge as an individual who usually fulfils his or her duty in a calm and attentive way, motivated by a sense of justice, while in France the respect attaches not to the individual, but to the section of the corps of judges in the *Cour d'assises*.[64] The explanation for this difference, the writer points out, is to be found in the way in which judges are appointed in the two systems. In England, the judges are (or at least were) appointed from practising barristers and thus have their roots in a community of practitioners who have respect for the interests of either party in any litigation dispute. This encourages an attitude of neutrality when weighing the evidence. In France, the presiding judge has his or her roots in the criminal investigation and (or) prosecution service and might thus once have been a *juge d'instruction* or *ancien parquetier*, with the result that the mentality of the judge is orientated towards the bringing of charges rather than towards weighing the evidence and assessing the weaknesses of the accusing party's case. The conclusion to be drawn from this comparison is that in France there might be a certain tendency to favour the prosecuting case.[65] Having made this observation, the thesis writer is able then to go on to make a number of suggestions with regard to the role of the presiding judge in France when overseeing the oral debate before the jury. One major argument advanced by the writer is that France should develop a more adversarial framework with regard to the oral debate and that one way of doing this is to import into the criminal procedure the common law model of a more passive judge, thus putting greater emphasis on the parties' cross-examination.[66] The writer makes it clear that he is not advocating a change from the inquisitorial process to an adversarial trial; he is simply arguing that in making the oral debate more accusatory in nature, the rights of the defendant will be enhanced.[67]

There are, of course, positive and negative aspects to this kind of comparative analysis. The positive aspect is that the writer is going beyond the figure of the presiding judge in each system and attempting to place this object of comparison within a professional, cultural context that goes some way in

64 Roumier, *L'avenir du jury criminel*, 299–300.
65 *Ibid.*, 300.
66 *Ibid.*, 309–13.
67 *Ibid.*, 313.

revealing the mentalities in play. The different ways in which judges are recruited in France and in England is of major importance and should certainly not be ignored by the comparatist. Nevertheless, there are some negative aspects. The description of the Crown Court judge may well have some basis in social fact, but to paint a picture of a calm and serene judge is to indulge in simplicities – perhaps to create a universal myth – since more detailed research would quickly reveal a rather complicated picture not just of the judge, but of the jury process as well. There are, for example, serious problems with regard to the summing up of the law and the facts by the judge to juries[68] and there is a major constitutional debate about the role and function of the jury within the English legal system as a result of a leading judge, Lord Justice Auld, asserting in his review of the criminal courts that 'juries have no right to acquit defendants in defiance of the law or in disregard of the evidence'.[69] Professor Zander, a noted expert on English judicial institutions, certainly did not regard Auld LJ's comment as one to be associated with a calm and serene judge; for him, it was a comment displaying 'an authoritarian attitude that disregards history and reveals a grievously misjudged sense of the proper balance of the criminal justice system'.[70] In addition to these points, historical research indicates that the traditional view of the English jury trial must be treated with caution; and so, for instance, in the seventeenth century, the judge had great power in controlling juries mainly because neither of the parties were represented by lawyers.[71] Any contemporary English lawyer who is minded to criticise the French *Cour d'assise* process should reflect upon Professor Zander's observation that in the seventeenth century 'the accused ... lacked the safeguards both of the inquisitorial and of the adversarial systems'.[72]

Models, programmes and schemes

No doubt many comparatists from the common-law world are equally capable of painting simplistic pictures of aspects of the French judicial system and, in fairness to the thesis writer, he was using comparative law as a means of promoting his own perfectly proper legal agenda rather than as a vehicle for the discovery of new knowledge about law itself. One major danger, therefore, that is to be found in comparative legal studies is that of superficiality, in

68 See M. Zander, *Cases and Materials on the English Legal System*, 10th edn, Cambridge: Cambridge University Press, 2007, 521–23.
69 *Ibid.*, 527–28.
70 *Ibid.*, 527.
71 *Ibid.*, 550–54.
72 *Ibid.*, 553.

the sense that the researcher undertakes neither a proper analysis nor strives to engender a real understanding of the other. Comparison is used only as a means of advancing a domestic agenda. Methodology in comparative law cannot therefore be divorced from methodology in the social sciences in general.[73] Accordingly, the researcher who is embarking on comparative work must first be very clear about his or her research question, for it is this question that will largely determine what might be called the models and programme to be adopted.[74] Models, says one French social science theorist, 'are schematic representations of the world made up of dimensions put into relation and constituting the privileged vehicle of knowledge'. They are an 'analytical structure' consisting of propositions forming part of a language which itself is to a greater or lesser extent formal – for example, graphic schemes, equations and the like – and possessing an 'empirical sphere' defined both by the structural system and the context in which it is employed and recognised as valid.[75] A programme sets out the 'investigative methodologies' defining the strategies through which reality will be apprehended by specific data collection and treatment tools.[76]

These definitions have, of course, been fashioned in relation to an empirical investigation of social reality, but they are relevant to comparative law research inasmuch as choices must be made about the actual object that is going to form the focal point of investigation. Thus, to respond to this point by stating merely that the focal point will be 'lay participation' in the legal process or the 'jury' would be methodologically meaningless. Is one going to take as the object of comparison the jury as an institution or individual jurors (for example, a series of interviews with ex-jurors in England and France), or the legal texts establishing and defining the role, powers and responsibility of jurors or the courts in which juries form part of the process or whatever? Each object chosen – or perhaps one might say the level of observation (text, court, jury or jurors) at which the programme is to function – will result in rather different types of knowledge.[77]

---

73 This is a particularly important point. Comparative methodology cannot be divorced from research methods in general and thus all the chapters in this present work are, or may be (depending on the type of research), of relevance to the comparatist.

74 See Samuel, *An Introduction to Comparative Law Theory and Method*, 25–44.

75 B. Walliser, 'Avant-propos', in B. Walliser (ed.), *La cumulativité dv savoir en sciences sociales*, Paris: Éditions de L'Ecole des Hautes Études en Sciences Sociales, 2009, 8–9.

76 *Ibid.*

77 See generally D. Desjeux, *Les sciences sociales*, Paris: Presses Universitaires de France, 2004.

In addition to, and closely interwoven with, this programme question is the issue of schemes of intelligibility. As we have seen, the researcher can quite legitimately construct a *tertium comparationis* in which technical and analytical similarity and differences of the jury in two (or more) systems can be noted and discussed.[78] One can then attempt to explain these similarities and differences with regard, for example, to an institutional history of court procedures in both systems, noting in particular the elements that have given rise to the points of convergence and divergence. However, such causal explanations do not necessarily permit an understanding, as opposed to an explanation, of the jury in each system, nor does such an approach necessarily give rise to new knowledge. Understanding and knowledge require recourse to other schemes of intelligibility such as structuralism, functionalism and hermeneutics.[79]

A causal approach, as we have suggested, is founded on the idea that one phenomenon (A) is dependent upon another phenomenon (B). Thus, the existence and characteristics of the French jury (A) can be explained by reference to another phenomenon – for example, the importation of the notion of a jury from the common law (B) – which in turn can be explained by a political phenomenon (C), itself explained by a social movement (D) and so on. A structural approach, however, envisages the jury as an interrelating model of elements more circular than linear in its pattern. Thus, a jury is envisaged as consisting of a range of elements such as a number of lay persons (A) sitting together in a court process involving a professional judge or President (B) listening to oral submissions of professional lawyers representing each party (C), after which they sit together in deliberation (D) in order to produce a verdict (E). These various elements are not causal as such, but operate as a system whose interaction will provide of itself relevant knowledge. A functional model will, as we have seen, provide an understanding of the institution of the jury (A) by reference to its social role (B). What does the jury do in each system and to what extent does the function of it in each system provide a basis for understanding it as an item of knowledge?

A further important scheme is (again, as we have seen) the hermeneutical method. This would be particularly relevant if the researcher was focusing on the legal texts which define, describe and prescribe the function of the jury. A hermeneutical method is one where a phenomenon (A) is regarded as a signifier of a deeper phenomenon (B), the signified. This kind of scheme is associated with what might be called a deep textual analysis, although there is no reason why a hermeneutical scheme need be confined to a text. One

---

78 Husa, *A New Introduction to Comparative Law*, 151–54.
79 See generally on schemes of intelligibility Berthelot, *L'intelligence du social*, 62–83.

might examine the notion of a jury (A) in terms of what the institution reveals about the legal mentalities (B) in France and in England. Is the jury simply a convenient method of fact-finding within the court process, or does it represent something deeper; for example, does it signify the expression of the *populus* as the ultimate source of law making?

Another approach is an 'actional' one whereby a social phenomenon (A) is regarded in terms of its individual actors or agents (B). The tendency here is to focus on the behaviour of the individual, and the scheme has attracted the name methodological individualism which is contrasted with a holistic approach.[80] An actional approach in history would thus be one that focuses on individuals such as Napoleon, Stalin or Hitler, whereas a holistic methodology would be concerned with, say, particular classes or group interests. An actional approach to juries in France and in England would, for instance, be one that concentrates not on the jury as an existing object so to speak, but on individual actors, that is to say on the jurors and their experiences and opinions with regard to the jury process. It would be an approach that would probably be largely based on interviews with jurors or on questionnaires completed by them. An actional approach might also engender particular concepts such as the 'reasonable juror' or the 'typical juror', these notions perhaps acting as comparative reference points.

A final scheme identified by the late Professor Berthelot was the dialectical method whereby a phenomenon (A) is to be understood as resulting from an internal contradiction within a second phenomenon (B and not B). The scheme is 'a system basically defined by the existence of two terms at one and the same time indissociable and opposed constituting what can be called a contradiction' and thus 'explaining [the phenomenon A] from a dialectical point of view is to consider it as a *moment in a future stage*'.[81] A researcher may well adopt this scheme when examining the controversies and debates surrounding the use of juries in England and in France. In France, in particular, there is a body of opinion that sees the jury as an aberration. Does not jury trial infringe the idea that the criminal law should be applied in an equal manner to all citizens, and cannot this equal application be assured only by a professional body of judges?[82] If juries are to be seen as representing the *populus*, ought they not to be elected?[83] A further problem is the question of an appeal against the jury verdict. How can the absence of such an appeal be

---

80 *Ibid.*, 80–81.
81 *Ibid.*, 82 (emphasis in the original).
82 Roumier, *L'avenir du jury criminel*, 117–19.
83 *Ibid.*, 151.

justified, yet how can such an appeal procedure be instituted which does not invade the sovereignty of the jury? In England, there are also those who dissent, but the criticisms are usually aimed at what might be described as various practical shortcomings. For example, it has been argued that juries acquit too many defendants;[84] that they are unsuitable for long and complex trials;[85] or that they are too expensive. This is not to suggest that these practical criticisms do not arise in France, but criticism of juries in England as a constitutional aberration are arguably rare. The supporters of jury trials tend, in contrast, to adopt an argument that functions on the constitutional level; the lay participation in the legal process is to be considered as part of England's unwritten constitution and represents a bargain between the law and the *populus*.[86] A dialectical approach between the French and the English debates would, therefore, surely reveal that the jury is more than just a procedural institution fulfilling similar functions in both systems. It goes to the core of a debate about what is meant by 'law' itself.

In France, it is not impossible to insert the jury into a constitutional framework, for the jury can be seen as a means of directly giving expression to the power of the people as the ultimate source of legal authority. However, given the history of law as a science of rules (or norms) within the civilian tradition, the jury sits very uneasily within the idea of *le procès* as a highly professionalised procedure applying legal norms.[87] In England, where the absence of university law faculties before the nineteenth century has been one of the common law's characteristics, the view that trials should be highly professionalised institutions under the control of judges trained in legal science is much less engrained, and when this is combined with the jury's long heritage, it becomes easy to see why its existence causes fewer constitutional problems. Law in England is, as a result of its history and of the influence of American Realism, as much a procedure founded on the determination of facts as a body of abstract rules. Nevertheless, the role of legal theory still remains central, even in the United Kingdom; for Lord Justice Auld's view of 'law' is markedly different from Professor Zander's. Auld sees a distinction between the 'law' and the 'jury' process, whereas Zander seems to see the jury as part of the common law itself. The dialectical contradictions are not, then, just between the English and French systems; they occur within single systems at various different levels and this adds to the complexity of

---

84 Zander, *Cases and Materials on the English Legal System*, 537–40.
85 *Ibid.*, 543–44.
86 *Ibid.*, 527.
87 As to the role of the judge in France (at least in civil cases), see *Code de Procédure Civile* art. 12.

approaching comparison purely in terms of a dialectical scheme between the home system and the other.[88]

In fact, it is not just the different schemes themselves which contribute to the methodological complexity in the social sciences. The complexity is intensified when one scheme is used in combination with another, which is often the case. The medieval jurists, for example, combined hermeneutics with dialectics, while, today, structuralism (systems) can be used with functionalism (the function of the system) or with a causal analysis (crime as a system is caused by, say, structural unemployment, caused in turn by variations in the economic system). Or perhaps crime is caused (causal scheme) by the motivations of individual actors (actional scheme) rather than from more holistic phenomena? Different combinations of schemes reveal different types of knowledge (or apparent knowledge). These complexities are, of course, well known to social science epistemologists, but they are of fundamental importance to comparative methodology in that there is no such 'comparative' methodology in itself other than the act of comparing. What one compares, the level at which one operates, the scheme(s) of intelligibility in play and the paradigm orientation in which the researcher's programme is situated are all an integral part of the 'how to compare' question. In addition, the comparatist cannot assume that the 'other' shares the same view of what amounts to law and legal knowledge. Is law just a model of rules or norms or does the phenomenon of law embrace (for example) its actors, its institutions and its mass of reasoning and taxonomical techniques? Indeed, does it embrace the psychological and ideological outlook of its actors?[89] The point to be stressed is that the comparatist is not a legal theorist as such; she is not there to impose a uniform understanding of law under the guise of a *tertium comparationis*. She is there to research difference as much as similarity, but both difference and similarity in turn depend upon the schemes, programmes, levels of operation and paradigm orientations in play. The comparatist needs to be ultra-sensitive to the epistemological significance of different methods.

Concluding remarks

This methodological and epistemological complexity no doubt gives an initial impression that comparison in law is 'so complicated that it may well

---

88 Some of these contradictions to be found in judging and legal reasoning are discussed in G. Samuel, *A Short Introduction to Judging and to Legal Reasoning*, Cheltenham: Edward Elgar, 2016.
89 G. Samuel, 'What Is Legal Knowledge?', paper delivered to the WG Hart Workshop: Valuing Expertise, Institute of Advanced Legal Studies, 20 September 2016.

discourage and deter scholars from becoming involved in the first place'.[90] One immediate response to this criticism is Legrand's rhetorical question: whoever said that the subject of comparative legal studies is easy?[91] This difference of outlook is partly rooted in the mentalities associated with the discipline of law on the one hand and a social science like sociology on the other.[92] Social scientists are not really able these days to retreat into a kind of rule-orientated positivism whose adherents are happy to rely on a few simplified methods imported from outside. Comparative law as a subject thus finds itself caught between two mentalities and it is only in more recent years that it has managed to free itself from the descriptive presentation of rules.[93] Many of today's comparative lawyers are now beginning to appreciate that their specialism is no longer just another rather positivistic subject (learning the rules of another system within the methodological context of a simplistic functionalism) in a law faculty list, but is an area located squarely within the social sciences in general.[94] It is a subject that is by its very nature interdisciplinary with all that this entails with regard to methodological and epistemological complexity.[95]

This complexity need not, however, defeat the research student. What such a student needs to do is to organise the methodological problems and debates within a framework that will continually remind her to be sensitive to and aware of the important link between the methods applied and the knowledge obtained.[96] Two fundamental questions associated with the subject 'comparative law' will help with this organisation.[97] The first question is this: what is meant by 'comparison'? This question should remind the research student of some of the fundamental dichotomies that have proved problematic, such as the ones between nature and culture, between a presumption of similarity and a presumption of difference, between a functional approach and its

90 B. Fauvarque-Cosson, 'Development of Comparative Law in France', in Reimann and Zimmermann, *The Oxford Handbook of Comparative Law*, 35, at 61.
91 The question was posed by Professor Legrand in his inaugural lecture delivered at Tilburg University on 20 October 1995.
92 J. Bell, 'Legal Research and the Distinctiveness of Comparative Law', in M. Van Hoecke (ed.), *Methodologies of Legal Research: Which Kind of Method for Which Kind of Discipline?* Oxford: Hart, 2011, 155.
93 *Ibid.*, 170.
94 See generally C. Vigour, *La comparaison dans les sciences sociales: Pratiques et méthodes*, Paris: Éditions La Découverte, 2005. See also Bell, 'Legal Research'.
95 See generally P. Legrand (ed.), *Comparer les droits, résolument*, Paris: Presses Universitaires de France, 2009.
96 See generally Desjeux, *Les sciences sociales*.
97 And see further Samuel, *An Introduction to Comparative Law Theory and Method*.

alternatives, between one paradigm orientation and another and so on and so forth. The second question concerns law. What is meant by 'law' in the context of 'comparative law'? This second question should remind the student of the great danger of legal imperialism; that is to say, it should remind her not to assume that the 'other' shares the same epistemological understanding of the term. Of course, this question is interwoven with the comparison question and so, for example, in approaching the expression 'law', the researcher should presume difference.[98] Yet the law question, taken separately, should help the researcher focus on the important issue of what will constitute the object of comparison and the theory implications involved in this issue. Is one to focus on rules, norms, cases, institutions, values, facts, reasoning methods or what?

In the context of the present work, the object of comparison has been lay participation in the form of the jury. However, as this chapter has attempted to indicate, merely focusing on the 'jury' as a legal institution, as some kind of 'thing' in itself, is insufficient since the object question is, in the end, bound up with the comparison question. Is one going to focus, say, on the jury in terms of its causal relations with legal verdicts and in turn legal sanctions and remedies, or is one going to focus on, say, the individual jurors and their experiences of participating in the legal process in England and France? Or perhaps the researcher will focus on something yet again different. What are the natures of the theoretical debates surrounding juries in the two systems and what do these debates reveal about the place and role of lay persons in the administration of justice? There are important debates surrounding the jury in England and in France, but, although they may overlap in part, these debates are not quite the same. They reveal different concerns and preoccupations which in turn should reveal differences in the nature of legal knowledge. Comparing the jury or jurors in each system ought not, then, to be an exercise in comparing things extracted from this knowledge context. The type of knowledge that emerges from a comparison will equally be dependent upon the programme and model in play, in turn informed by the scheme or schemes of intelligibility adopted. Is the researcher going to adopt, for example, a functional or a hermeneutical approach? No doubt some will argue that one programme, or one type of scheme of intelligibility (say a functional method), is preferable to another, just as jurists have long argued over legal theory (Hart's or Dworkin's model?). However, the existence of a plurality of methods, schemes and programmes is something that is inherent in social science research and it will always therefore be a matter of epistemological controversy. What is important for the research student is that she is able in her

98 But cf. Bell, 'Legal Research', 174–75.

thesis introduction clearly to articulate the programme, models and schemes – the methodology in other words – that will inform the research project. If she does this, she ought to be able to face any sceptical examiner with a combative confidence.

Recommended reading

Cotterrell, R., 'Comparative Law and Legal Culture', in M. Reimann and R. Zimmermann (eds), *The Oxford Handbook of Comparative Law*, Oxford: Oxford University Press, 2006, 709.

Glenn, H. P., 'Aims of Comparative Law', in J. M. Smits (ed.), *Elgar Encyclopedia of Comparative Law*, Cheltenham: Edward Elgar, 2006, 57.

Legrand, P., 'How to Compare Now', 16 *Legal Studies* 16, 1996, 232.

Monateri, P. G., 'Methods in Comparative Law: An Intellectual Overview', in P. G. Monateri (ed.), *Methods of Comparative Law*, Cheltenham: Edward Elgar, 2012, 7.

Riles, A., 'Comparative Law and Socio-Legal Studies', in M. Reimann and R. Zimmermann (eds), *The Oxford Handbook of Comparative Law*, Oxford: Oxford University Press, 2006, 775.

Samuel, G., *An Introduction to Comparative Law Theory and Method*, Oxford: Hart Publishing, 2014.

Samuel, G., 'Epistemology and Comparative Law: Contributions from the Sciences and Social Sciences', in M. van Hoecke (ed.), *Epistemology and Methodology of Comparative Law*, Oxford: Hart Publishing, 2004, 35.

7   Critical legal 'method' as attitude

Panu Minkkinen

On method

Writing about a 'critical legal method' with which to address the question of lay participation in law proves to be problematic for a number of different reasons.

What does 'critical' mean in this context? For one thing, 'critical judgment' is a generic intellectual skill that all researchers are supposed to be able to apply in relation to the object of their research. For example, the Bologna Process Qualifications Framework includes among the skills required at the third cycle (i.e. the doctoral level) the capacity for 'critical analysis, evaluation and synthesis of new and complex ideas'.[1] In this sense, all research at the doctoral level is expected to be 'critical'.

But 'critical analysis' as a generic research skill can hardly pass for what we mean by a 'critical method' in this instance. The latter implies a more radical and focused perspective to the matter at hand. We can, for example, imagine a researcher who rejects the internal perspective that, according to the legal positivist H. L. A. Hart, was the 'properly' legal perspective.[2] Internally viewed in Hart's sense, the legal system will always appear as a fundamentally legitimate way of regulating society. Like a participant in a game, we are required to acknowledge the rules if we want to play. And so the researcher will be stuck with tinkering with minor reforms that may or may not improve whatever political ends lay participation was intended to achieve. But adopting an external perspective, that is, an approach that is not 'properly' legal in Hart's

---

1 See, e.g., *A Framework for Qualifications of the European Higher Education Area. Bologna Working Group on Qualifications Frameworks*. Report published by the Danish Ministry of Science, Technology and Innovation. Copenhagen, 2005, 197.
2 H. L. A. Hart, *The Concept of Law*, 2nd edn, Oxford: Oxford University Press, 1997, 88–91. See also S. J. Shapiro, 'What Is the Internal Point of View?' *Fordham Law Review* 75, 2006, 1157–70.

sense, will emancipate the researcher from her obligations towards the law. It allows her to, for example, evaluate lay participation in relation to democratic ideals that are not extracted from the law itself. We could argue that the commitment to an internal perspective that Hart and his positivist followers demand of the legal researcher makes us blind to social and political practices that we as critics should become aware of. It is in this very sense that the German political philosopher Jürgen Habermas claimed that the motivation or 'knowledge interest' of all critical research is 'emancipatory':

> The methodological frame which settles the meaning of the validity of this category of critical statements can be explained in terms of the notion of self-reflection. This frees the subject from dependence on hypostatized forces. Self-reflection is influenced by an emancipatory concern with knowledge . . .[3]

Habermas' notion of critical research as self-reflection with an emancipatory objective comes already close to the political connotations with which we associate the word today. In common usage, 'critical' often refers to a practice of 'criticism', something that the German political philosopher Theodor Adorno somewhat pejoratively described as 'judging intellectual phenomena in a subsumptive, uninformed and administrative manner and assimilating them into the prevailing constellations of power which the intellect ought to expose'.[4] In other words, 'criticism' can be a rather simplistic albeit well-meaning attempt to rectify social wrongs that is motivated by the researcher's personal commitments rather than any academically informed encounter with society. In the eyes of the legal orthodoxy, this personal and 'subjective' commitment makes critical research suspect.

But if we understand the word 'critical' as something relating to 'critique' rather than 'criticism', then we seem to be back at square one. Would not all research need to be 'critical' as the etymology of the word already indicates?[5] Is not 'critiquing' the very definition of all legal research worth its name?

A further problem arises from the breadth of our critique. Is it enough to investigate 'critically' the object of our research, lay participation in law in our case? For if we are to adopt a truly critical position, then would not

3 J. Habermas, 'Knowledge and Interest', *Inquiry: An Interdisciplinary Journal of Philosophy* 9, 1966, 285–300, 294.

4 T. W. Adorno, 'Cultural Criticism and Society', in *Prisms*, trans. S. M. Weber and S. Weber, Cambridge, MA: MIT Press, 1984, 30.

5 The etymology of both 'critique' and 'criticism' is from the Greek verb *krinein*, 'to set apart', 'to discern', 'to judge'.

remaining consistently critical require us to also address the limitations of the various 'methods' or perspectives that are at our disposal? And would not this have to include any 'critical legal method' itself? Can a 'critical' perspective in the more substantive meaning alluded to by Adorno have a 'method' to begin with?

The somewhat illusory idea of a coherent 'critical legal method' is reinforced by the notion that there is a 'movement' behind it. Just like a socio-legal method presumes a corresponding movement, be it socio-legal or the sociology of law, a critical method seems to refer to some similar movement that is identifiably 'critical'. The modern story of critical research in law is often compressed into a Critical Legal Studies (CLS) movement that supposedly reflects what contemporary 'critiquing' is all about.[6] But one could also well claim that the CLS movement was never really a proper 'movement'. It was, rather, a community of loosely affiliated individuals who worked mainly in North American law schools from the late 1970s to the mid-1980s representing various non-doctrinal approaches. Although CLS researchers were politically all clearly left-of-centre, their political kinship was never enough to consolidate the various approaches into a 'method'. Instead, there were 'methods', ranging from Marxist[7] and feminist[8] to deconstruction,[9] that were often incompatible with each other. As two leading figures of the 'movement', Duncan Kennedy and Karl E. Klare, say in an early CLS bibliography (a valuable research tool in itself):

> CLS scholarship has been influenced by a variety of currents in contemporary radical social theory, but does not reflect any agreed upon set of political tenets or methodological approaches. Quite the contrary, there is sharp division within the CLS movement on such matters. CLS has sought to encourage the widest possible range of approaches and debate

---

6 Textbooks and readers will often include a section on the CLS. On CLS generally, see, e.g., R. Unger, 'The Critical Legal Studies Movement', *Harvard Law Review* 96, 1983, 561–675; M. Kelman, *A Guide to Critical Legal Studies*, Cambridge, MA: Harvard University Press, 1987; M. Tushnet, 'Critical Legal Studies: An Introduction to Its Origins and Underpinnings', *Journal of Legal Education* 36, 1986, 505–17; and M. Tushnet, 'Critical Legal Studies: A Political History', *Yale Law Journal* 100, 1991, 1515–44.

7 e.g. W. J. Chambliss, *Law, Order, and Power*, 2nd edn, Reading, MA: Addison-Wesley, 1982.

8 e.g. C. MacKinnon, 'Feminism, Marxism, Method, and the State: Toward Feminist Jurisprudence', *Signs* 8, 1983, 635–58.

9 e.g. J. Balkin, 'Deconstructive Practice and Legal Theory', *Yale Law Journal* 96, 1987, 743–86.

within a broad framework of a commitment to democratic and egalitarian values and a belief that scholars, students, and lawyers alike have some contribution to make in the creation of a more just society.[10]

The starting point of this chapter is the claim that all legal methods, be they conventional or allegedly 'critical', impose limitations into the ways in which the researcher produces legal knowledge. In scientific practice, a method is a mechanism with which, among other things, the personal and 'subjective' views of the researcher are supposedly filtered out, producing allegedly 'objective' knowledge. 'Methodologically' conducted research does not produce mere opinions, but, so the argument runs, scientifically valid knowledge. A 'critical legal method', if there is such a thing, would, then, be no different. Textbooks in the area[11] are cluttered with the nomenclature of acceptable frameworks for critical 'methods', and in its insistence on complying with them, critical legal research can often be just as orthodox in its approach as its more conformist cousins. It seems that it is, indeed, next to impossible to be 'critical' of the 'critical' without turning into a reactionary.

This chapter will try to argue that the essence of 'critique' makes the very idea of a 'legal method' problematic, and that a 'critical' perspective to law can only be more like an 'attitude' than a scientifically motivated methodic approach. Without reverting back to the 'anything goes' of Paul Feyerabend's methodological anarchism,[12] I will, however, try to show how the insistence on following methodological rules guides the production of legal knowledge towards the conformity of legal orthodoxy, and this would apply to a 'critical' method just as well as to any other. In this sense, the aim of this chapter is 'emancipatory'. And curiously enough, I will further argue that an awareness of tradition will provide one way of breaking away from that conformity.

10 D. Kennedy and K. Klare, 'A Bibliography of Critical Legal Studies', *Yale Law Journal* 94, 1984, 461–90, 461–62. A similar critical bibliography was compiled for at least international law. See D. Kennedy and C. Tennant, 'New Approaches to International Law: A Bibliography', *Harvard International Law Journal* 35, 1994, 417–60.

11 e.g. I. Ward, *Introduction to Critical Legal Theory*, 2nd edn, London: Cavendish Publishing, 2004; and C. Douzinas and A. Gearey, *Critical Jurisprudence: The Political Philosophy of Justice*, Oxford: Hart, 2005.

12 P. Feyerabend, *Against Method*, 4th edn, London and New York: Verso, 2010.

'Before you can break the rules, you have to know what the rules are'

My own doctoral thesis was criticised for the emphasis that it put on nineteenth- and early-twentieth-century German jurisprudence. At least to some extent, that emphasis has remained in my subsequent work. But the 'dead German men' are there for a reason. They are present in my work because they represent a tradition that I am trying to break away from. It is the 'baggage' of tradition that even a critic inevitably carries with her. Because to be critical is always to be critical *of* something, and as long as a given approach maintains a critical relationship with whatever it is a departure from, then the tradition will impose itself on the critical researcher in one way or another.

The possible benefit of such encounters with 'dead German men' is to better understand how that tradition imposes itself on the legal researcher in general and, in this case, on the critical legal researcher in particular. Understanding the tradition will not, perhaps, be able to immediately determine what a critical legal perspective to lay participation in law is or ought to be, but it will hopefully be able to point to possible ways of departing from an orthodoxy that dominates legal research and, at the same time, to also reduce the risk of being segregated into a critical ghetto reserved only for the like-minded. The critical legal researcher will always run the risk of being either 'defined in' or 'defined out', of being either absorbed and neutralised by her political adversaries or excluded into a meaningless and ineffectual existence outside of what is regarded as valuable academic work.[13] But an approach that will be able to address the legal tradition on its own terms will hopefully also identify avenues for critical departures that remain relevant.

Indeed, calls for critical departures in law are often explicitly spelled out with reference to tradition. This can be illustrated with the help of two hypothetical questions that, no doubt, most critically minded legal researchers have encountered in one form or another. Firstly, how do we overcome tradition? And, secondly, how can we change law?

The first question, now reformulated within the framework of this chapter – how can critical legal research overcome tradition? – is in fact rhetorical insofar as it also presents at least two claims. Firstly, it suggests that it is necessary to overcome tradition, if not in its entirety, then at least selectively. To be critical in legal research is often understood as being critical of a traditional way of doing things. But, secondly, the claim also implies that there is something in tradition that resists the necessary change. Even if the need for another

13 See T. Mathiesen, *Law, Society and Political Action: Towards a Strategy under Late Capitalism*, London: Academic Press, 1980, 224–26.

approach may well be recognised, tradition presents itself as an impediment, and it will want to have its say before the overenthusiastic critic causes any serious damage. In other words, the question 'How can critical legal research overcome tradition?' is articulated in the tension between the demands of the future and the obligations to yesteryear.

The second question, once again reformulated – how can critical legal research change law? – could perhaps be inferred from the first. Once the need for change and the possible obstacles have been recognised and identified, the critic would only need to find out how the required changes can come about. But if this second question was understood so literally, the reply would be much too tautological. For the critic could then simply answer: 'Law can be changed by researching it in a critical way.' However, even the second question is rhetorical. It also implies that something resists, that the researcher's 'traditional' way of doing things somehow obliges, and that it is not simply a matter of 'doing critical legal research', but, perhaps, of 'correcting previous mistakes', of moving forward from somewhere rather than uprooting oneself completely. Perhaps in a way that is similar to the judiciary's commitment to 'piecemeal reform', to use Joseph Raz's famous expression,[14] the legal researcher is expected to respect the democratic mandate of the legislator and to move forward with caution.

What the two questions have in common, however, is the notion that the tradition of law 'obliges', that it is, in a manner of speaking, a 'normative' tradition. A normative tradition requires adherence to, and anyone wishing to do critical research in law will sense this. And it is the normative nature of that tradition that this chapter will take up in more detail. How does the normative tradition of law display itself? What is the way in which it expresses its obligations to the legal researcher? How should the legal critic respond?

These questions will first be examined with an overview and interpretation of Hans Kelsen's (1881–1973) main contribution to law, namely the pure theory of law. Kelsen published two editions of the book on the theory: a short first edition in 1934[15] and a considerably enlarged second edition in 1960 on which this chapter will mainly draw.[16] In addition, many other works by Kelsen contribute towards the overall theory.[17] By emphasising the

14 J. Raz, *The Authority of Law: Essays on Law and Morality*, 2nd edn, Oxford: Oxford University Press, 2009, 196.

15 H. Kelsen, *Introduction to the Problems of Legal Theory* [1934], trans. B. L. Paulson and S. L. Paulson, Oxford: Clarendon Press, 1992.

16 H. Kelsen, *Pure Theory of Law*, trans. M. Knight, Berkeley, CA: University of California Press, 1967.

17 For example, the subtitle of Kelsen's book on sovereignty from 1920 is 'a contribution to a pure theory of law'. H. Kelsen, *Das Problem der Souveränität*

epistemological dimensions of Kelsen's theory, I will focus on the way in which the pure theory of law defines its 'logical' framework. My claim is that it is the particular way in which Kelsen understands logic that accounts for the normativity of the tradition that he both establishes and represents.

Why Kelsen? The pure theory of law and the legal positivism that claims to be its successor establish a tradition that we, as legal researchers, are expected to follow. It is the doctrinal or 'black letter' default position from which other approaches in legal research are regarded as deviations and departures. Methodological norms and, more generally, the very requirement to apply a method to legal research are typically at the heart of this normative tradition that we are supposed to honour. Finally, this chapter will suggest an alternative understanding of tradition, inspired by Hans-Georg Gadamer's (1900–2002) philosophical hermeneutics, which would enable critical departures from the tradition without having to fall back on the naivety of criticism to which Adorno was referring.

Law and knowledge

It would be difficult to overestimate the influence of neo-Kantian philosophy in the German tradition of legal positivism. Oversimplifying grossly, the neo-Kantians wanted to establish a scientifically valid way of investigating social and cultural phenomena such as law so that the resulting humanities and social sciences would not have to pale in comparison to their natural science counterparts. In many ways, neo-Kantianism in law was the final blow that ended the era of natural law that had been losing ground in legal thinking ever since the heyday of Hegel.[18] And Kelsen was the most prominent of the neo-Kantian lawyers, although his affiliations with the Marburg school of the movement are slightly more complicated than my argument here would imply.[19] Nevertheless, Kelsen's pure theory of law set the theoretical stage for the subsequent developments in modern law on the European mainland. Although Kelsen's immediate influence is, perhaps, more easily detectable in

und die Theorie des Völkerrechts. Beitrag zu einer reinen Rechtslehre [1920], Aalen: Scientia, 1981.

18 There was, however, a revival of natural law thinking in post-war Germany even if its effects were not lasting. This was, perhaps, most evident in the 'turn' of Gustav Radbruch, a neo-Kantian jurisprudent and contemporary of Kelsen. See, e.g., G. Radbruch, 'Statutory Lawlessness and Supra-Statutory Law (1946)', *Oxford Journal of Legal Studies* 26, 2006, 1–11.

19 See, e.g., S. L. Paulson, 'The Neo-Kantian Dimension of Kelsen's Pure Theory of Law', *Oxford Journal of Legal Studies* 12, 1992, 311–32.

continental European or South American legal cultures, Anglophone legal theorists have also presented their interpretations, although the local variant of legal positivism is quite different.[20]

How does the pure theory of law define itself? Although Kelsen rarely uses the term 'philosophy of law', instead speaking of either 'legal doctrine' or the 'science of law', the aims of the theory are clearly defined in a philosophical tone:

> As a theory, its exclusive aim is to know and to describe its object. The theory attempts to answer the question what and how law is, not how it ought to be. It is a science of law (jurisprudence), not legal politics.[21]

In order to be able to appreciate the full significance of Kelsen's undertaking, it is worth keeping in mind – and perhaps even emphasising – that the pure theory of law is essentially an epistemological project. Its aim is not primarily to provide judges or other legal actors with conceptual tools for their decisions or interpretations as the more doctrinal readings of Kelsen have often implied. In the long run, a more scientific and logical exposition of the law may well benefit both legislators and judges, but this is merely a happy consequence. *The sole purpose of the pure theory of law is to identify its objects of research, that is, legal norms, and to describe them in a scientifically valid way.* Within its overall neo-Kantian framework, one could even claim that the aim of the pure theory of law is not to address an ontological question ('What is law?') at all, as Kelsen's preamble quoted above seems to suggest, but to determine the epistemological preconditions of a science of law. Law, then, does not 'exist' as such, or, more precisely, the possible 'existence' of law is subordinate to the preconditions of knowing about it. So implicitly Kelsen rephrases his initial question about the 'what' of law thus: 'How must we conceptualize law in such a way that its scientific study would be possible?'

Kelsen is obviously captivated by the possibility of knowing about law in a scientific way. He seems to be well aware of the doubts and concerns that have been expressed about the scientific status of law, and he acknowledges that law has often been accused regarding its lack of methodological precision and consistency. The adversaries in Kelsen's dispute are defined in a neo-Kantian

---

20 See, e.g., Hart, *The Concept of Law*, 292–97, which are the footnotes to the central Chapter VI; and J. Raz, *The Concept of a Legal System: An Introduction to the Theory of Legal System*, 2nd edn, Oxford: Clarendon Press, 1980, 93–120.
21 Kelsen, *Pure Theory of Law*, 1. The original German text makes no reference to 'jurisprudence', which has been added by the translator.

manner as advocates of an impure 'methodological syncretism' which alludes to controversies in theology:

> The Pure Theory of Law undertakes to delimit the cognition of law against these [PM: other non-legal] disciplines, not because it ignores or denies the connection, but because it wishes to avoid the uncritical mixture of methodologically different disciplines (methodological syncretism) which obscures the essence of the science of law and obliterates the limits imposed upon it by the nature of its subject matter.[22]

Kelsen claims, then, that it is the 'subject matter' of the discipline – legal norms – that prescribes its method. In order to literally 'purify' law from alien influences, it must be 'liberated' from everything that does not belong to its object of study, that is, legal norms. This 'liberation' is curious in the sense that it implies a past and bygone era before law had entangled itself with the two main problems identified by Kelsen – namely, the causal explanatory models of the natural sciences and the 'ideological' framework of the social sciences.[23] It is, of course, clear that no such 'Golden Age' of law exists.

As mentioned, Kelsen's epistemological undertaking is essentially neo-Kantian. For Kant, the description of the legal norms of an organised society would not have constituted knowledge in the strict sense of the word at all because norms cannot be explained through causal relations. In Kantian terms, a legal norm belongs to the world of practical reason where an effect comes about autonomously because it is willed. For example, morality does not come about as the effect of a cause, but because man wills it autonomously and freely: I act in a morally significant – good or bad – way because I 'will' to do so, not because my environment compels me to do so. And one cannot 'know' about this domain of freedom, only 'think' it. This was the claim that the neo-Kantians wanted to refute by either expanding Kant's notion of theoretical reason and knowledge into a universal epistemology to cover even normative phenomena (the Marburg approach) or by developing the epistemological preconditions of a 'third approach' of cultural sciences somewhere between theoretical and practical reason (the Heidelberg or Baden approach).[24]

---

22 Kelsen, *Pure Theory of Law*, 1. See also D. Beyleveld and R. Brownsword, 'Methodological Syncretism in Kelsen's Pure Theory of Law', in S. L. Paulson and B. L. Paulson (eds), *Normativity and Norms: Critical Perspectives on Kelsenian Themes*, Oxford: Clarendon Press, 1998.
23 Kelsen, *Pure Theory of Law*, 75–76.
24 On the political and historical significance of neo-Kantianism, see C. Thornhill, *German Political Philosophy: The Metaphysics of Law*, Abingdon: Routledge, 2007, 239–60.

But for Kelsen, the normative structure of society seems to be much more than an isolated social phenomenon among others. Perhaps one could go so far as to claim that Kelsen regards legal norms significant because their normativity enables the scientific description of society as a whole:

> If it is said that a certain society is constituted by a normative order regulating the mutual behaviour of a multitude of men, one must remain aware that order and society are not two different things; that they are one and the same thing, that society consists in nothing but this order, and that, if society is designated as a community, then essentially that which these men have 'in common' is nothing else but the order regulating their mutual behaviour.[25]

In other words, the normative order is society and vice versa. But regardless of the claims that the pure theory of law makes about its aims at the outset, Kelsen then proceeds to reassess his task in ever more epistemological terms: in order to be able to describe that society in a scientifically valid way, society must be understood as a normative order.

The specificity of law can, Kelsen claims, be described using Kant's fundamental distinction between the 'is' and the 'ought', between what is factual and what is normative. The distinction also provides the criterion with which we can distinguish law as a discipline from the natural sciences. If Kant claimed that knowledge was possible only within the causal relations established by the laws of nature, Kelsen is a typical neo-Kantian in the sense that he is trying to extend the main claims of Kant's critical method to the study of normative phenomena. This is what makes the pure theory of law scientific. But in a legal science, social relations cannot be understood through the causes and effects of the natural sciences because they are exclusively normative phenomena.[26] For Kelsen, then, the normativity of law requires a specific form of knowledge.

The logic of science

But even if the object that the pure theory of law studies is normative, scientific knowledge is not. Nor can it be. For Kelsen, the requirement that scientific knowledge must be 'objective' precludes any normative commitment to the object of study even if the final results may call for reform and allow for conclusions

25 Kelsen, *Pure Theory of Law*, 86.
26 *Ibid.*, 76.

de lege ferenda. We can, for example, only commit ourselves to combatting climate change after 'objective' research has verified the phenomenon. Similarly, according to the same logic, we can commit ourselves to improving the participation of lay persons in legal decision-making only after 'objective' research has verified that lay persons are, indeed, excluded.

So how can one be objective about something that is in essence a norm?

Kelsen tries to resolve the issue by making a distinction between a legal norm and what has been translated as either the 'rule of law' or, more appropriately, the 'reconstructed legal norm' or 'legal proposition'.[27] A legal norm is a command or an imperative, and it is also the sole object of the pure theory of law. The legal proposition, on the other hand, is an objective description of the legal norm, and it commands nothing. The legal proposition merely associates a possible act with a possible sanction and prepares the legal norm for scientific description. Even if the legal norm is the pure theory's object of research, it cannot be identified with law as the theory understands it. The pure theory of law describes its objects, that is, legal norms, through legal propositions, but in the latter the normativity of the 'ought' serves merely a descriptive purpose. The legal proposition, on the other hand, can only describe the normative relationship of the 'ought' between act and sanction.

How would this work in practice?

The legal norm commands or entitles to associate a sanction with an act: 'If act x, then sanction y ought to follow.' For example, the crime of theft ought to be followed by the sanction that is prescribed by law. But as a descriptive science, the pure theory of law cannot 'endorse' the strong normativity of the legal norm ('If you steal, it is right and just that you ought to be punished in accordance with the law'), but can only describe the normative content of the legal norm through the legal proposition ('The law regarding theft that Parliament has passed states that if you steal, you ought to be punished in accordance with the law, but as a science that merely describes these norms the pure theory has no view as to whether you should or shouldn't'):

> The jurist who describes the law scientifically does not identify himself with the legal authority enacting the norm. The rule of law [PM: the legal proposition] remains objective description; it does not become prescription. The rule [PM: the legal proposition] does no more than state, like the law of nature, the link between two elements, a functional connection.[28]

27 On the problem of translating Kelsen's term *Rechtssatz*, see Kelsen, *Pure Theory of Law*, Introduction, 23, n. 20.
28 *Ibid.*, 79.

Legal norms do not come about 'naturally' as effects of a cause, but are 'willed' and are so created in an act. In other words, the existence of a will is always a precondition of law. But for Kelsen, such an act is always a factual pheno- menon, whereas the outcome of a legislative will, that is, the legal norm, must necessarily be normative. Because in Kelsen's neo-Kantian framework one cannot bridge the worlds of the 'is' and the 'ought', of factuality and norm- ativity, a legal norm cannot be inferred from the will that has created it.[29] Consequently, the validity of a legal norm cannot be inferred in a scientifically acceptable way from the legislative will that has enacted it ('The law of theft is valid law because Parliament has so decided'). Law can only exist if the legis- lator has willed it, but that is not the source of its validity. It is valid if and only if its legislator had the legal competence to do so:

> the norms, whose reason for validity is in question, originate from an authority, that is, from somebody competent to create valid norms; this norm bestows upon the norm-creating personality the 'authority' to create norms. The mere fact that somebody commands something is no reason to regard the command as a 'valid' norm, a norm binding the individual at whom it is directed. Only a competent authority can create valid norms; and such competence can only be based on a norm that authorises the issuing of norms.[30]

This is the point from which Kelsen constructs his infamous *Stufenbau*, the hierarchical and layered structure of higher and lower legal norms that accounts for the normativity of all legal norms. The validity of a lower norm can only be inferred from a competence to enact that norm that was author- ised by a higher norm. For example, local government is authorised to make by-laws concerning the prevention of nuisances only because the Local Government Act 1972, a law enacted by Parliament, authorises local govern- ment to do so. So, a by-law regulating the use of skateboards in public parks is valid as a legal norm because a higher law, the Local Government Act 1972, grants local government the legal authority to regulate such issues. Parliament, on the other hand, can give local government this delegated authorisation through the Local Government Act 1972 in a valid way only because a consti- tution establishes the legislative powers of Parliament. In this way, lower and higher norms are always in a logical relation to one another. In order to be normatively valid, a norm must always refer logically to a higher norm of competence. Hence: 'The law of theft is valid law because Parliament that enacted it had the constitutional competence to do so.'

29 *Ibid.*, 4–6.
30 *Ibid.*, 194.

But this logical hierarchy cannot be followed through *ad infinitum*. Indeed, the constitution provides the ultimate framework for legal norms from which the validity of lower norms can be logically inferred. As far as positive law is concerned, there cannot be anything above the constitution. But in order for the pure theory of law to meet the scientific criteria that Kelsen has set for it, even the highest positive norms must logically infer their validity from something higher.

So, what could possibly be above the constitution? Surely not God or natural law if we are to take scientific objectivity as a starting point.

In order to comply with the demands of his own theory and to avoid the abyss of eternal regression, Kelsen then makes a distinction between the constitution in its material or positive meaning and the constitution in its formal or logical meaning. The constitution in its logical meaning includes within itself a *basic norm* that the pure theory of law must presuppose in order to remain scientific. All normativity in law flows from it. The basic norm is the normative foundation of the act of positive legislation.[31]

Time and time again, Kelsen emphasises that the basic norm does not involve the recognition of any ethical standard that is transcendent in relation to positive law. So, it does not and cannot measure the acceptability of positive law. In other words, the basic norm cannot be a foundational norm of natural law as many of Kelsen's readers have attempted to either understand it or to criticise it. The basic norm is only an epistemological necessity. It is the 'transcendental-logical' precondition of the pure theory of law. The basic norm is not 'willed' in the same way as conventional legal norms, but it is required by the science of law. By presuming the existence of the basic norm, the pure theory of law establishes and fixes its own normative logic and its scientific validity.[32]

It is, however, problematic to insist on such a sharp distinction between 'willing' and 'presuming'. Could we not say that the pure theory of law legislates its own basic norm? In 1963, only three years after the publication of the enlarged second edition of his book, Kelsen had to revise his own position on the basic norm. Kelsen was originally uncomfortable with what the neo-Kantians called 'fictions'.[33] In neo-Kantian epistemology, a fiction is a heuristic conceptual tool that enables one to conceive of something as knowledge. It is the equivalent of Kant's 'as if' (*als ob*) postulate to which even Kelsen himself

---

31 *Ibid.*, 200.
32 *Ibid.*, 201–5.
33 *Ibid.*, 299–302.

makes a reference.[34] But now, in order to account for the 'non-willed' basic norm, Kelsen must resort to a 'double-fiction':

> The basic norm is a fictive norm, and it requires a fictive act of will that posits the norm. It is a fiction according to which some authority wills the norm to exist.[35]

In this case, the fictive nature of the basic norm itself as a 'transcendental-logical presumption' is fairly easy to fathom because it is not part of positive law itself. We must simply assume 'as if' the basic norm existed, for otherwise the normativity that the pure theory of law is trying to scientifically describe would be impossible. But in order to establish the scientific validity of the theory, Kelsen must now also postulate a fictive will 'as if' an authority enacted the basic norm. But clearly this authority is not fictitious at all. It can only be the pure theory itself. Through its own allegedly fictive authority, the theory establishes its own object of research by enacting the basic norm, and normativity, the supposedly constitutive element of all social life, cannot exist outside its realm.

How we 'ought' to do legal science

The critics of traditional legal approaches may not wish to engage with Kelsen's pure theory because, even if he was a socialist who openly sympathised with the women's rights movement and psychoanalysis in pre-war Vienna, his special brand of legal positivism apparently has preciously little to say about the social and political concerns that usually animate the critical research of law. And as a primarily epistemological project concerned with its own scientific status, it does not lend itself easily to any methodological diversions. Even more poignantly, legal critics may wish to deliberately avoid Kelsen because of the way in which the pure theory of law establishes a normative tradition that, in the guise of knowledge and science, tacitly delimits the possibilities of critical legal research. It serves as a model of the way in which the orthodoxy of the positivistic tradition in law in general regulates the production of legal knowledge.

34 H. Kelsen, *Reine Rechtslehre*, 2nd edn, Vienna: Verlag Österreich, 2000, 99. This is one of the many footnotes that have been omitted from the English translation. A typical legal fiction would be corporate personhood that enables legal thinking to conceive of the rights and obligations of corporations.
35 Kelsen, as quoted in F.-M. Schmöltz (ed.), *Das Naturrecht in der politischen Theorie*, Vienna: Springer, 1963 (my translation).

But conversely, legal critics may wish to deliberately engage with the pure theory of law – or any other tradition, for that matter – in order to be able to better understand how a given tradition imposes limits and regulates legal research. In Kelsen's case, it does not really concern an 'ideology', as tempting as it would be to discard him simply as a political reactionary. It has much more to do with the logical framework with which he validates his epistemology. In other words, it has more to do with the way in which he insists that we follow a certain positivistic method lest we end up with something deemed 'unscientific'. The strength and weakness of the pure theory of law is its obsessive belief in the emancipatory potential of scientific knowledge, and this belief seems to justify Kelsen's insistent claim that all legal research be 'pure'.

How does Kelsen, then, construct his 'normative tradition'?

In another instance, Kelsen claims that legal research must be 'normological'.[36] His thorny term brings together the two distinct claims that his pure theory of law makes. Firstly, he asserts that, unlike the main bulk of the social sciences that study factual social phenomena, law is a normative discipline. This meaning of the word 'normative' simply means that law's object of study is legal norms. For Kelsen, law as an academic discipline is normative in much a similar way as descriptive ethics that studies ethical norms without really telling us how we ought to act. We can, for example, study how changes in public morality relate to attitudes towards minorities without assessing the resulting attitudes normatively one way or another. Similarly, we can study the ideals of democracy that inform views on lay participation in law, but we need not necessarily take a stand as to whether we should endorse one or the other ideal. The object of study is a normative phenomenon even if the science that studies it can only describe it.

But, secondly, Kelsen also claims that legal norms, the object of the normative discipline, must be in logical relationships with one another. Primarily, Kelsen understands this 'logical' requirement to mean that every valid norm must by necessity be inferred from a higher norm. Because the factual is so categorically distinct from the normative – the 'is' from the 'ought' – Kelsen insists that a norm cannot be 'logically' inferred from factual circumstances. We cannot, for example, establish that a given legal norm is valid because it is either factually enacted by the legislative will of Parliament or factually observed in the so-called real world. As a legal norm, a statute can be valid only

---

36 I have dealt with this question from a slightly different perspective elsewhere. See P. Minkkinen, 'Why Is Law a Normative Discipline? On Hans Kelsen's "Normology"', *Res Publica* 11, 2005, 235–49.

if a higher norm has authorised the required legislative act. For Kelsen, such inter-normative relations are the 'logic' of law as a normative discipline.

This is where the allegedly descriptive pure theory becomes prescriptive.

Legal norms and their logical relationships make up law as a legal system, a layered or hierarchical structure that ascends from lower norms to ever higher norms until it reaches the hypothetical and presumed basic norm sitting at the summit of the structure. The logical character of the legal system does not necessarily refer to the so-called real world because statutes do not have to display the same 'logical' quality. The systematic logic is first and foremost a prerequisite of law as a science.

Notwithstanding the diverse social conventions that tend to acknowledge one approach to law as an 'authority' while disregarding others, legal doctrine – the 'dogmatic' tradition on the Continent, 'black letter' in the English-speaking world – often expresses its demands for such a systematic logic through conceptual, epistemological and methodological rules that the legal researcher must take into consideration if she wishes her work to be acknowledged as law. These rules are, then, normative to the extent that they 'ought' to be followed, and in Kelsen's scheme they constitute a second normative structure in addition to legal norms proper. So, there must accordingly be two normative structures: firstly, the legal norms that constitute the object of the pure theory of law and that are merely scientifically described, and, secondly, the systematic logic that the study of these norms requires and that the researcher is expected to follow. The requirement to observe and to follow a legal method belongs to this second normative structure.

Kelsen's pure theory of law is much richer and more complex than the preceding overview suggests. But for the sake of argument, allow me to condense the second normative structure, that is, all the different conceptual, epistemological and methodological rules that Kelsen formulates about law as a scientific discipline into a single normative claim: 'Legal research ought to be based on a pure theory of norms.' We can modify this claim into more familiar variations, as well: 'For the purposes of research, only positive law can be regarded as law.' Or: 'A PhD in law on lay participation should begin with an analysis of the relevant primary legislation.' Kelsen serves here merely as an example, for similar normative claims as to how legal research 'ought' to be done can be found regardless of what more or less conventional tradition one is talking about. A researcher with a socio-legal bent may well maintain that 'the study of law ought to be founded on verifiable social facts', and someone who finds Dworkin persuasive might claim that 'law ought to concern itself with legal interpretation emphasising liberal political values'. Even the more orthodox strains of critical legal research make similar normative claims, such as 'legal norms ought to be analyzed as part of an oppressive political economy'.

Regardless of what the contents of these claims are, they all convey a tradition in terms of norms. They express themselves as normative traditions that 'ought' to be recognised and upheld. And, as such, they also regulate and moderate any demands for departures into other directions.

The legal critic could, perhaps, reject or disregard a given tradition simply by referring to its conservative or conformist tendencies. But that would be the easy way out. If the pure theory of law imposes itself on the legal researcher as a normative tradition that 'ought' to be upheld by following certain conceptual, epistemological and methodological rules, then its normativity must lie in the way in which it constructs the logical framework through which these rules are established and communicated. In other words, the scientific logic of legal research that Kelsen elaborates and advocates makes law a normative and prescriptive discipline that tells the researcher what she 'ought' to do.

How, then, does the pure theory of law, with its conceptual, epistemological and methodological rules, address us? How does it capture us into a world where we are told what to do?

The phenomenologist philosopher Edmund Husserl (1859–1938) claims that the scientific logic of a discipline is always normative because its aim is to assess the extent to which the discipline in question – in our case law – measures up to its own 'idea'. In other words, it tells us what the 'legal' in 'legal research' is and sets this idea of the 'legal' as something that we should aspire to. Logic, then, both evaluates a discipline in relation to its ideal form and conducts it into that direction.[37] In, for example, Kelsen's case, the claim that 'legal research ought to be based on a pure theory of norms' presupposes that one approach in legal research may be 'purer' than another, and that there may even be approaches that do not live up to even the minimum requirements of a 'pure' theory. In addition, the measuring of different approaches in legal research implies that, to stick with our example, a 'purer' approach is in some way superior to an approach that is 'less pure': it is 'more legal', 'more accurate', 'more scientific', 'more useful' and so on. All in all, the evaluations and judgments are normative, for they all suggest how legal research 'ought' to be conducted.

For Husserl, these evaluations and judgments form together a normative hierarchy that ends up being very much like Kelsen's hierarchy of legal norms, where the validity of a lower norm was always inferred from a higher one. Evaluating, for example, the 'purity' of a particular approach in legal research is namely always done in a comparative mode, in relation to an approach

---

37 E. Husserl, *Logical Investigations*, Vol. 1: *Prolegomena to Pure Logic*, trans. J. N. Findlay, London: Routledge and Kegan Paul, 1970, 70–72.

that is either 'purer' or 'less pure' than the one being evaluated. Claiming, for example, that 'the level of purity in approach x is high' implies that there is an approach where the level is lower, for otherwise the assessment would have been impossible. And just like Kelsen, Husserl also claims that in making such comparisons one must presuppose a basic norm, a hypothetical and even fictive highest norm at the top of the hierarchy that is the origin and the source of all normative validity within the structure. Any claim about the level of purity presupposes the existence of something called 'purity' even if we cannot say exactly what it is. The basic norm is, then, not an 'existing' norm, but a presupposition required in any normative discipline.[38]

But unlike Kelsen, Husserl identifies two distinct functions in his basic norm. Firstly, the basic norm has what Husserl calls a 'regulative' function. In the case of logic, the basic norm establishes the validity with which the various normative evaluations and judgments within the hierarchy can perform their measuring function and direct a given approach towards the ideal form of the discipline. By doing so, the basic norm produces unity and cohesion within the discipline and, as such, it contributes to the development of a disciplinary tradition. So, for example, the 'logic' of the pure theory that includes all the different conceptual, epistemological and methodological rules that the legal researcher is supposed to take into account gradually directs law as a discipline in a particular direction.

But secondly and more importantly, Husserl's basic norm also includes within itself a 'constitutive content'. For if one claims that, to once again stick with our example, 'legal research ought to be based on a pure theory of norms', the claim simultaneously implies that such an approach, namely a 'pure theory of norms', has something unique about it. It must by necessity somehow stand out from all other approaches.[39] And for Husserl, this uniqueness, whatever it may substantially be, cannot be normatively determined through the regulative function of the basic norm, through claims, rules and propositions that tell us what we 'ought' to do if we wish our approach to be acknowledged as, for example, legal research. In order to say something significant about its normative object, law requires a theoretical elaboration of its own 'uniqueness', of its 'idea'. To paraphrase Husserl, all normative disciplines require knowledge about certain non-normative truths.

So, in Husserl's terms, Kelsen's 'normological' tradition of legal research with its emphasis on the necessity to follow prescribed methodological rules seems to only recognise the regulative function of the basic norm. Indeed, for Husserl, such a normative tradition could not even be scientific in any profound

38 *Ibid.*, 85–86.
39 *Ibid.*, 87–88.

meaning of the word. Legal research would, if that were the case, be reduced to a mere regulated practice the premises of which are determined elsewhere. The legal researcher would simply be blindly following her methodological rules without ever reflecting on what they are meant to achieve and why.

The challenge from tradition

So in the positivistic variants of legal research, Kelsen included, tradition is often understood as such a set of obliging rules that regulate the work of the researcher and direct it towards something that is itself seldom seriously questioned. In other words, the normative tradition of legal research will readily tell the researcher what she 'ought' to do, but it is less willing to engage in any 'navel-gazing' or reflections about its own uniqueness or its 'idea' even if the individual rules must by necessity be inferred from that uniqueness and not vice versa. The requirement to adopt and to elaborate a method of research to investigate, for example, lay participation in law, is typically such an obliging rule. By deviating from it, the researcher runs the risk of having her work excluded from the main body of legal research as 'impure', 'unscientific' or 'not law', or with a number of other pejorative condemnations. These are normative traditions of research, traditions that regulate the production of legal knowledge delimiting the options of critical departures and consequently also keeping a check on what is to be regarded as scientifically relevant and what not. And to reiterate, the orthodox strains in critical legal research are no different.

My claim is that this type of normative and 'regulative' tradition that is not complemented by genuine theoretical insights about the discipline in general is not a tradition at all. Even if the demands of a normative tradition of research could be justified from a practical point of view, it is never enough. Without the possibility to address the uniqueness of the discipline, the 'idea' of law, if you will, the researcher is lost blindly following externally imposed rules and regulations like methods without knowing why they are there. And in addition, one must also be able to question the very notion of a tradition.

What is, then, tradition? How does tradition display itself in a discipline like law that is to a large extent based on interpreting texts?

Hans-Georg Gadamer (1900–2002) is considered to be the founder of philosophical hermeneutics, that is, the philosophy of understanding and interpretation. It is well known that Gadamer modelled his philosophical hermeneutics on how lawyers intuitively work with their legal texts:

> Legal hermeneutics is able to point out what the real procedure of the human sciences is. Here we have the model for the relationship between past and present that we are seeking. The judge who adapts the transmitted

law to the needs of the present is undoubtedly seeking to perform a practical task, but his interpretation of the law is by no means on that account an arbitrary re-interpretation. Here again, to understand and to interpret means to discover and to recognise a valid meaning. He seeks to discover the 'legal idea' of a law by linking it with the present.[40]

It is this linking of past and present that Gadamer understands as tradition. And he has often – too hastily, in my mind – been accused of conservatism because of this.[41] Indeed, the word 'tradition' easily invokes such thoughts. But this tradition is something quite different. In one of his rare poetic moments, Gadamer describes how the interpreter becomes aware of tradition in the process of understanding. When we confront any given text, we approach it within a particular situatedness that Gadamer calls a horizon. No one can read texts in a vacuum, and our understanding is always conditioned by both our social and our individual circumstances. A horizon may always be changing, but it includes within itself all the prejudices and expectations with which the interpreter approaches her text. For example, I am an educated white man from a Northern European middle-class background, and that will inevitably affect the way in which I relate to lay participation in law. If we are, for example, reading legislation on lay participation in law, a self-professed legal critic will be looking for different emphases than her more conformist counterpart. For my part, I may not see it as a uniquely positive phenomenon or as something contributing towards democracy. Because of my situatedness in the ideals of the Scandinavian welfare state, I have seen how a well-educated and socially representative career judiciary has been able to promote those ideals, and I may be less keen to see uninformed lay interference than someone from, say, Britain, who may have an innate distrust of an elite judiciary. Although we all approach texts from our particular horizons, Gadamer insists that if the interpreter genuinely wishes to understand her text, she must first isolate and suspend her prejudices until they have properly demonstrated their worth: Is lay participation really 'uninformed'? Does a socially representative career judiciary really endorse welfare state values? And so on. Structurally, this suspension is what Gadamer calls a 'question':

The essence of the question is the opening up, and keeping open, of possibilities. If a prejudice becomes questionable, in view of what another

40 H.-G. Gadamer, *Truth and Method* [1960], trans. J. Weinsheimer and D. G. Marshall, London and New York: Continuum, 2004, 292–93.
41 See, e.g., J. D. Caputo, *Radical Hermeneutics: Repetition, Deconstruction, and the Hermeneutic Project*, Bloomington, IN: Indiana University Press, 1987, 108–19.

or a text says to us, this does not mean that it is simply set aside and the other writing or the other person accepted as valid in its place. It shows, rather, the naiveté of historical objectivism to accept this disregarding ourselves as what actually happens. In fact our own prejudice is properly brought into play through its being at risk. Only through its being given full play is it able to experience the other's claim to truth and make it possible for he himself to have full play.[42]

Not, then, by discarding my personal prejudices from the outset as the requirement for scientific objectivity usually requires, but by putting them to the test in a question. So not by bracketing out my personal views on the political benefits of a trained legal bureaucracy merely because they are 'personal', but by setting them up against contrasting views on, for example, how that legal bureaucracy in fact emphasises certain middle-class values and policies to which I may be blind.

How does the question unravel itself?

A text, even if it may be distant in time or in space, suddenly speaks to us. The pledge of a victim to crime in her statement to the court, a feminist analysis of how gender configures in the world of law, even a work of literature like a tragedy by Sophocles or Shakespeare; suddenly a text 'resonates'. It 'makes sense', and the interpreter becomes aware of a connection even if a conventional understanding of who she is and what she does would suggest that the text in question is rather distant in relation to what the legal researcher should be doing. The prejudices of the legal researcher's own normative tradition may want to resist the resonance through exclusion, but the legal critic may be willing to risk her own prejudices by putting them into play and by allowing the other to have her say. Face to face with such seemingly distant familiarities, the legal researcher can do one of two things. She can either disregard them because her discipline informs her that they are 'unscientific', 'irrelevant', 'methodologically unsound' or what have you, or, as Gadamer suggests, she can embrace them and put them to the test against her own prejudices before deciding about their worth.

But this can work in the opposite way, as well. Being politically impatient as we often are, we may feel tempted to discard the 'baggage' of a tradition that seems to be preventing us from getting on with things. But engaging with, for example, the pure theory of law may also clarify how the tradition of legal positivism more generally exercises its normative hold over the production of legal knowledge. We may be able to question the hostility of legal

---

42 Gadamer, *Truth and Method*, 266.

positivism towards certain approaches in law, its corresponding fascination with regulated knowledge and the method that will supposedly produce it, its belief in the explicative power of formal concepts, and so on. And by putting such issues into play in the question, we may well get a valuable glimpse of where we ourselves could be heading.

Perhaps it is unusual to suggest that a 'humanist' approach like hermeneutics could offer a model for the legal critic that goes beyond mere criticism. But even some approaches that are more commonly associated with critical legal research share a certain kinship. For example, Silja Freudenberger suggests that Gadamer's hermeneutics offers an inspiration and ally – but not necessarily a model – for feminism on many interrelated levels.[43] I will re-formulate Freudenberger's more general observations here with specific reference to legal research. Firstly, feminist approaches to law and hermeneutics both depart from a critique of the propositional concept of knowledge and reject the methodological ideals of modern science that underpin that concept. The starting point of both more conventional approaches to legal research and Kelsen's pure theory of law is, of course, quite the opposite: to construct legal propositions and concepts by adhering to a scientifically sound methodology. Secondly, feminist approaches to law and hermeneutics both endorse a non-patronising and open relationship with the other and what she may have to say, whereas conventional approaches to legal research do not seem to include any such dialogical elements. The tone of conventional legal research is exclusive rather than inclusive, as Kelsen's notion of 'purification' already reveals. Thirdly, feminist approaches to law and hermeneutics both include a fundamental recognition of the historical, cultural and social situatedness of interpreters rejecting any claims to the type of universal and unattached perspective that the 'objective' ideal of conventional approaches suggests. Fourthly, feminist approaches to law and hermeneutics both recognise that, on account of the fundamental situatedness of all interpreters, the existence of differing voices is not considered as a flaw or a weakness, but, rather, as an inevitability, whereas Kelsen's brand of positivism would rather 'purify' legal research from all such deviations. Finally, feminist approaches to law and hermeneutics both call for reflection on one's own position and one's vested interests in research and academic work, whereas the only explicit aim of conventional approaches to law is the supposedly disinterested pursuit of knowledge.

---

43 S. Freudenberger, 'The Hermeneutic Conversation as Epistemological Model', in L.Code (ed.), *Feminist Interpretations of Hans-Georg Gadamer*, University Park, PA: Pennsylvania State University Press, 2003.

So, the legal researcher does not partake in tradition by prudently following the normative demands of her discipline and by enclosing herself in its limited world, but, as Gadamer expresses it, by allowing the other to speak. This is by no means an uncritical encounter. Far from it. Within tradition, the legal researcher encounters the other with her own prejudices, and the encounter takes place in the form of a question. The legal researcher's prejudices are the 'legal baggage' that she by necessity carries with her, and through questions she evaluates whatever it is that she has encountered by understanding it in a particular way: she unravels history 'as a legal researcher', she conceptualises society 'as a legal researcher', she reads literature 'as a legal researcher' and so on. But at the same time, she develops an awareness of the baggage that she is carrying with her. Instead of throwing it all hastily overboard and proceeding to criticise perhaps prematurely, the encounter invites her to review what her position 'as a legal researcher' involves and whether it contributes anything valuable to her understanding of the world.

Resonance

In other words, the legal researcher is part of a tradition only if she can question the other and be herself put into question by it. So, one possible response to the question 'How can critical legal research change law?' could well be: the legal critic can change law by partaking in its tradition. But this requires that tradition is not understood in a normative way. The normative tradition of legal positivism in general and Kelsen's pure theory of law in particular both oblige the legal researcher to follow prescribed conceptual, epistemological or methodological rules. Research into, for example, lay participation in law must be conducted in particular ways, and the sanction for doing otherwise is a negative assessment of the results. As such, these rules do not allow for the resonance of the question. On the other hand, a dialogical tradition such as the legal critique that I am advocating here offers the researcher the possibility to allow that resonance to grow into ever new questions, the answers to which lead to yet new questions.

Tradition, then, reveals itself to the legal researcher in this resonance, in the seemingly unlikely familiarities that she first questions through her own prejudices and that consequently also put her and her prejudices into question. Through the resonance of tradition, the legal critic can become aware of the self-imposed limitations that prevent her from seeing the wider picture. But her response is not an alternative 'critical' legal method that would limit her in more or less similar ways, but, rather, an attitude and a willingness to continuously question and to be put into question.

So hopefully my own fascination for the Germans is at least partly justified. There may very well be more conventional or established critical perspectives like Marxist or feminist approaches that I should at least consider as my starting points. But there is also an argument to be made for developing critical departures from the tradition that one comes from by engaging with it in critical dialogue. Otherwise, the legal critic runs the risk of unwittingly carrying that tradition with her by blindly swapping one normative tradition for another.

Recommended reading

Douzinas, C. *The End of Human Rights: Critical Legal Thought at the Turn of the Century*, Oxford: Hart, 2000.

Kavanagh, A. and Oberdiek, J. (eds), *Arguing about Law*, London and New York: Routledge, 2009, in particular, Part 5: Critical Approaches to Law.

Kelman, M., *A Guide to Critical Legal Studies*, Cambridge, MA: Harvard University Press, 1987.

Kennedy, D. and Klare, K. E., 'A Bibliography of Critical Legal Studies', *Yale Law Journal* 94, 1984, 461.

Tushnet, M., 'Critical Legal Studies: An Introduction to Its Origins and Underpinnings', *Journal of Legal Education* 36, 1986, 505.

Tushnet, M., 'Critical Legal Studies: A Political History', *Yale Law Journal* 100, 1991, 1515.

Unger, R. M., 'The Critical Legal Studies Movement', *Harvard Law Review* 96, 1983, 561.

Ward, I., *Introduction to Critical Legal Theory*, 2nd edn, London: Cavendish Publishing, 2004.

8 Economic analysis of law, or economically informed legal research

Albert Sanchez-Graells*

> For the rational study of the law ... the man of the future is the man of statistics and the master of economics. It is revolting to have no better reason for a rule of law than that so it was laid down ... and the rule simply persists from blind imitation of the past.
>
> Oliver Wendell Holmes, Jr[1]

In this chapter, I reflect on the topic of 'lay decision-making in the legal system' from the perspective of the *economic analysis of law*. Or, in other words, I look at the ways in which economic theory and insight can help resolve issues of legal decision-making by providing both a methodology for the analysis of the legal reality to which the decision relates (i.e. contributing to the decision-making process by structuring it and helping us focus on relevant factors), and a normative framework and workable criteria to favour some alternatives over others (i.e. providing a decision-making benchmark). Broadly, then, I am concerned with the question of how economic analysis can help us improve legal decision-making. After this broad overview, and in order to stress the link with the rest of the contributions to this book, I briefly focus on the potential application of some of these theories to research that aims to assess specific issues of lay decision-making in the legal system. Some final thoughts stress the importance of carrying out economically informed legal research more generally.

* I am grateful to Professor Jesús Alfaro Águila-Real, Pierluigi Cuccuru, Professor Francisco Marcos Fernández, Dr Jule Mulder and Dr Sebastian Peyer for their comments on an earlier draft. I am also grateful to Dr Dawn Watkins and Professor Mandy Burton for their invitation to contribute to this book and their editorial work. The standard disclaimer applies.
1 O. Wendell Holmes, Jr, 'The Path of the Law', *Harvard Law Review* 10, 1897, 457, 469.

Introduction

The economic analysis of law (also generally known as *law and economics*)[2] is probably the dominant legal methodology in US scholarship, and one that is slowly growing in importance in Europe,[3] although it is still a far from mainstream methodology in most EU and UK law schools.[4] As aptly put, it 'uses economic theory to analyse the legal world. It examines that world from the standpoint of economic theory and, as a result of that examination, confirms, casts doubt upon, and often seeks reform of legal reality'.[5] Or, in even clearer terms, the '[e]conomic analysis of law seeks to answer two basic questions about legal rules. Namely, what are the effects of legal rules on the behaviour of relevant actors? And are these effects of legal rules socially desirable?'.[6] Therefore, the economic analysis of law serves two main purposes. Firstly, it helps describe and explain how the law is and what effects it creates or can be expected to create (positive dimension). Secondly, it provides a framework for critical analysis and an ultimate view of how the law *ought* to be (designed, reformed, interpreted or enforced) for it to achieve specific goals that are socially desirable (normative dimension). Both functions can be controversial, but the normative dimension of the economic analysis of law – which ultimately rests on the pursuit of economic efficiency as a proxy for the maximization of social welfare,[7] as discussed below – has probably been its most debated aspect,

---

2 In this chapter, I use the expressions law and economics and economic analysis of law interchangeably. However, distinguished scholars have made important attempts to establish differences between the two; see, e.g., G. Calabresi, *The Future of Law and Economics: Essays in Reform and Recollection*, London: Yale University Press, 2016. I do not ignore their work, but the discussion here remains at a level of generality where such distinctions are not needed.

3 N. Garoupa and T. S. Ulen, 'The Market for Legal Innovation: Law and Economics in Europe and the United States', 59 *Alabama Law Review* 59, 2007–08, 1555–633.

4 For discussion on current developments on legal methodology, see R. van Gestel, H.-W. Micklitz and M. Poiares Maduro, *Methodology in the New Legal World*, EUI Working Paper LAW 2012/13, 2012, http://cadmus.eui.eu/bitstream/handle/1814/22016/LAW_2012_13_VanGestelMicklitzMaduro.pdf (accessed 7 March 2017); and R. van Gestel and H.-W. Micklitz, 'Why Methods Matter in European Legal Scholarship', *European Law Journal* 20(3), 2014, 292–316.

5 Calabresi, *The Future of Law and Economics*, 2. For a distinction with what he calls *law and economics*, see *ibid.*, 3–4. As Calabresi explains, this largely matches behavioural law and economics, which is not discussed in detail in this chapter.

6 L. Kaplow and S. Shavell, 'Economic Analysis of Law', in A. Auerbach and M. Feldstein (eds), *Handbook of Public Economics*, Vol. 3, Amsterdam: Elsevier, 2002, 1661–784, 1661.

7 P. Bohm, *Social Efficiency: A Concise Introduction to Welfare Economics*, 2nd edn, London: Macmillan, 1987.

and one that has triggered significant resistance and even full-on rejection of this methodology. One extreme line of criticism has even relied on the claim that law and economics may be immoral.[8] These issues may create a smoke screen allowing critics to dismiss the economic analysis of law too quickly as either a neoliberal market-making endeavour, or a methodology only relevant in very limited aspects of commercial or market-based legal sub-fields. My submission is that this is simply not the case and that the economic analysis of law is a fundamental tool with which to try to ensure that the legal system is both effective in achieving its goals (which are by no means predetermined by the law and economics approach) and efficient in doing so (it achieves those goals in the way that makes most members of society better off, which is what the concept of efficiency as a proxy for social welfare ultimately encapsulates). This submission relies on a number of implicit assumptions, which I will unpack later.

It is worth stressing that the economic analysis of law rests on the work of some giants of economic and legal thought,[9] a good number of which were awarded Nobel Prizes in Economics. It is hard to do justice to their work when one tries to strip their theories from technical complication and to present their insights in an accessible way.[10] Thus, I do not aim to present the several technical approaches broadly comprised within the economic analysis of law methodology in a thorough and detailed manner, but rather

8 For discussion, see R. P. Malloy and J. Evensky (eds), *Adam Smith and the Philosophy of Law and Economics*, Dordrecht: Kluwer, 1994; and A. N. Hatzis and N. Mercuro (eds), *Law and Economics: Philosophical Issues and Fundamental Questions*, The Economics of Legal Relationships, London: Routledge, 2015. For an advanced analysis, see W. J. Schultz, *The Moral Conditions of Economic Efficiency*, Cambridge Studies in Philosophy and Law, Cambridge: Cambridge University Press, 2001.

9 It is impossible to cover even just the seminal contributions to the development of this field in a basic discussion such as the one in this chapter, as the relevant authors include distinguished scholars such as Arrow, Becker, Buchanan, Calabresi, Coase, Friedman, Nash, Posner and Stigler. Any enumeration is, however, bound to be unfair due to its incompleteness. For clear points of reference in the existing literature, see: R. Posner, *Economic Analysis of Law*, 9th edn, The Hague: Wolters Kluwer, 2014; and S. Shavell, *Foundations of Economic Analysis of Law*, Cambridge, MA and London: Harvard University Press, 2004; as well as the standard handbook by R. B. Cooter Jr and T. Ulen, *Law and Economics*, 6th edn, Boston, MA: Pearson, 2012. For a simpler introduction, see A. M. Polinsky, *An Introduction to Law and Economics*, 4th edn, Gaithersburg: Aspen, 2011.

10 For an excellent and successful attempt to provide such accessible introduction, see E. V. Towfigh and N. Petersen (eds), *Economic Methods for Lawyers*, Cheltenham: Edward Elgar, 2015. For a thought-provoking introduction, see J. Leitzel, *Concepts in Law and Economics. A Guide for the Curious*, Oxford: Oxford University Press, 2015.

I will only try to explain the usefulness of incorporating economic insights into legal analysis and scholarship, in what I like to call *economically informed legal research*. To push the argument, I am convinced that carrying out legal research without assessing its economic implications and without incorporating the insights of economic theory is ultimately unsatisfactory, just as it is equally faulty not to incorporate the insights derived from political science and other social sciences such as sociology or anthropology, or even beyond, from evolutionary theory and psychology. This is not to say that strict doctrinal legal research has no place in modern academia or that it lacks value,[11] but rather a call for legal scholars to broaden their views and – once their analyses are technically sound from a legal perspective – to consider them in their relevant context, in particular from an economic perspective, as a matter of analytical completeness.[12] Law is not, and probably never has been, an independent field of study. When it was claimed it was, a deeper analysis would show that law scholars were making philosophical or even theological – dogmatic – analysis of normative statements or social norms settled down in a text.[13] Furthermore legal studies can hardly be considered free from normative implications.[14] Thus, doctrinal legal research may (simply) differ from other approaches in presenting itself as aseptic and not being explicit about the social and economic normative assumptions that underlie any specific piece of analysis. If that is true, then, it seems preferable to be sincere and avoid masking and passing as 'technical' evaluative issues that are fundamentally normative. I will also explain this in more detail later.

11 This is linked to the discussion on whether 'doctrinal legal research is dead', in which Eric Posner and Richard Posner, among others, engaged. For discussion, see the contribution by Hutchinson to this book, in Chapter 1.
12 Similarly, Douglas G. Baird stressed that '[a]s long as legal scholars have to worry about the consequences that a new law brings, we shall call upon the tools of law and economics', in 'The Future of Law and Economics: Essays by Ten Law School Scholars', *The Record*, 2011, http://www.law.uchicago.edu/alumni/magazine/fall11/lawandecon-future (accessed 7 March 2017).
13 For extended discussion, see T. Smith, 'Neutrality Isn't Neutral: On the Value-Neutrality of the Rule of Law', *Washington University Jurisprudence Review* 4(1), 2011, 49, http://openscholarship.wustl.edu/law_jurisprudence/vol4/iss1/3 (accessed 7 March 2017).
14 cf. A. Marmor, 'Legal Positivism: Still Descriptive and Morally Neutral', *Oxford Journal of Legal Studies* 26(4), 2006, 683–704. See also R. Banakar, 'Can Legal Sociology Account for the Normativity of Law?' in M. Baier and K. Åström (eds), *Social and Legal Norms*, London: Ashgate, 2012. See also K. M. Ehrenberg, 'Defending the Possibility of a Neutral Functional Theory of Law', *Oxford Journal of Legal Studies* 29(1), 2009, 91; and R. L. Abel, 'Redirecting Social Studies of Law', *Law and Society Review* 14(3), 1980, 805.

I will not cover all aspects of the economic analysis of law and, in particular, I will not discuss in detail its main criticisms and the emergence of *behavioural* law and economics or an *economic analysis of law 2.0*.[15] Focusing strictly on 'classic' economic analysis of law (*law and economics 1.0*, or *'primitive' law and economics*)[16] is simply justified by the need to provide a clear account of what this methodological approach can and cannot do, and to avoid any misrepresentation of the very powerful analytical tools it offers, even when the criticisms are considered – or, even *discounted*, if you wish. Consequently, all the discussion in this chapter will revolve around the basic understanding of law as an institution aimed at regulating the behaviour of the economic man (or *homo economicus*),[17] without engaging in any level of detail with the theories that challenge this conception or seek to refine it.[18]

The importance of the *homo economicus* for the economic analysis of law

In very general terms, it can be said that the economic analysis of law focuses on the study of how changes in the law alter the way people behave, which requires a characterisation of human behaviour. Economic analysis is based on rational choice theory, which ultimately rests on the assumption that humans are rational beings who behave accordingly. Thus, the economic analysis of law revolves around the model of the economic man (or *homo economicus*).[19] This means that, for the purposes of predicting or analysing the behaviour that will result from specific legal rules or reforms, the economic analysis of law *assumes* that we make decisions based on our assessment of the utility we can obtain

15 For discussion, see the special issue of the University of Chicago Law School Alumni Magazine *The Record* in the autumn of 2011, available at http://www.law. uchicago.edu/alumni/magazine/fall11/lawandecon2-0 (accessed 7 March 2017).

16 C. A. Williams, 'A Tale of Two Trajectories', *Fordham Law Review* 75(3), 2006, 1629, at 1657, http://ir.lawnet.fordham.edu/flr/vol75/iss3/21 (accessed 7 March 2017).

17 At this level of generality, the potential connections with socio-legal studies are probably quite apparent, particularly if socio-legal studies are conceptualised in broad terms and the fact that economics is a social science is given proper weight. However, the economic analysis of law is usually not included among the garden variety of socio-legal approaches, at least in UK academia.

18 See C. Jolls, C. R. Sunstein and R. Thaler, 'A Behavioral Approach to Law and Economics', *Stanford Law Review* 50(5), 1998, 1471–550.

19 For discussion, see H. Demsetz, 'Where Economic Man Dwells', in *From Economic Man to Economic System: Essays on Human Behavior and the Institutions of Capitalism*, Cambridge: Cambridge University Press, 2011.

from the different options[20] and that, rationally, we will choose the option that maximises our utility (or, in other words, that we are self-interested). This general assumption leads us, for example, to expect people to have an incentive to breach a contract if they can obtain a benefit from non-compliance (for instance, the seller has incentives to walk away from a contractual commitment and hand over the goods to a higher bidder); or expect them to be more deterred from committing crimes the higher the sanction and/or the likelihood of being caught and convicted; or to pursue their own individual interests if the negative consequences of a given behaviour fall upon somebody else's shoulders (such as slacking at work if the employer cannot monitor effort, or reducing the level of precaution when carrying out insured activities if the insurer cannot detect changes in diligence).

This characterisation of human behaviour as rational allows for the formulation of economic models that can explain the behaviour (as a result of the incentive structure that underlies the expressed rational choice) and, more importantly, aim to predict it (especially in view of changes in the structure of incentives). This is particularly relevant because most legal rules aim at preventing types of behaviour that are considered undesirable, either from a social perspective (e.g. criminal activity) or within the framework of private relationships (such as breaching contracts, causing damages to innocent parties or deceiving trustful partners). It is also useful because sometimes the behaviour that can be considered *privately* undesirable may simultaneously be *socially* desirable, or the opposite. A clear example arises in the area of environmental law, where private parties have rational incentives to minimise their costs (for instance, by acquiring goods or services from highly polluting sources if they are cheaper than environmentally friendly alternatives), despite the fact that this can impose a higher ecological cost on society at large, which is socially undesirable.[21] Conversely, an absolute avoidance of any ecological costs could be socially undesirable if it led to the prevention of economic

---

20 In simple terms, utility is meant to capture the value or the advantage that derives from a given option, which can make it desirable. Or, in other words, it encapsulates 'the capacity of a good or service to satisfy a want, of whatever kind'. For discussion, see R. D. Collison Black, 'Utility', in J. Eatwell, M. Milgate and P. Newman (eds), *Utility and Probability*, London: Macmillan, 1990, 295–302.

21 This relates to the concept of externality, which is a key element of analysis linked to market failure in the so-called *tragedy of the commons*. See J. M. Buchanan and W. C. Stubblebine, 'Externality', in C. Gopalakrishnan (ed.), *Classic Papers in Natural Resource Economics*, London: Macmillan, 2000, 138–54; and E. Ostrom, 'Tragedy of the Commons', in S. N. Durlauf and L. E. Blume (eds), *The New Palgrave Dictionary of Economics*, 2nd edn, Basingstoke: Palgrave Macmillan, 2008.

activity that, overall, could be socially beneficial in terms of generation of employment or the production of necessary goods or services. The economic analysis of law can offer valuable tools that help decision-makers reach a balance of interests that maximises social welfare in the long run (or at least tends to it). Furthermore, it is also relevant because sometimes there will be different ways of promoting the same private behaviour, but they will come at different social costs (such as the difference in costs between raising sanctions and increasing investigative capacity – for example, for the prevention of tax fraud, towards which either option should contribute, as discussed in more detail below).[22] In those circumstances, being able to compare options from a social welfare perspective will be important for decision-makers.

As these basic examples show, the main analytical advantage offered by the economic analysis of law is that, by working on the basis of a characterisation of human behaviour *that closely resembles reality* (at least in most settings or in terms of average expected behaviour), it allows for rather accurate predictions of how changes in legal rules can alter that behaviour so as to promote socially desirable outcomes, as well as to allow the design of private relationships in ways that best serve the interests of the parties involved.[23] The models and the examples do not aim to replicate reality in a perfect way (which would not be possible), but rather to create a workable framework for analysis.[24] In the end, this characterisation of behaviour allows us to identify the incentives created by legal rules and, on that basis, to predict the *likely* behaviour of those subjected to the rules. The immediate implication is that, should the expected behaviour not be the desired one, the same economic analysis of law allows us to design counter-incentives and to assess (both theoretically and empirically) if they are superior in promoting the desired behaviour. All of this ultimately rests on the need to determine what behaviour is desirable, which the economic analysis of law answers by clearly indicating that behaviour will be desirable if it fosters social welfare in the long run. This normative bedrock of the economic analysis of law also deserves further discussion.

22 G. J. Stigler, 'The Optimum Enforcement of Laws', *Journal of Political Economy* 78(3), 1970, 526–36.
23 G. Mitchell, 'Why Law and Economics' Perfect Rationality Should Not Be Traded for Behavioral Law and Economics' Equal Incompetence', *Georgetown Law Journal* 91, 2002, 67.
24 For discussion, see M. Quigley and E. Stokes, 'Nudging and Evidence-Based Policy in Europe: Problems of Normative Legitimacy and Effectiveness', in A. Alemanno and A.-L. Sibony (eds), *Nudge and the Law: A European Perspective*, Modern Studies in European Law, London: Hart, 2015, 61, 75 ff.

Why is this all about efficiency – what about redistribution or fairness?

The economic analysis of law rests on the position that behaviour will be desirable if it promotes social welfare in the long run. Or, in other words, behaviour will be desirable if it is economically efficient. This proposition triggers two issues. Firstly, how to determine what is economically efficient behaviour and, secondly, why alternative goals, such as redistribution of wealth or fairness, are not used as the normative benchmark for analysis.

The first question is relatively easier to answer on the basis of the theoretical work of welfare economists. In strict terms, a situation (or legal rule) will be efficient – i.e. will create the highest possible level of social welfare – if it is not possible to modify it in a way that makes some individuals better off without making anyone worse off or, in other words, a situation will only be efficient if it generates advantages to some to the prejudice of none. This strict approach to efficiency is known as Pareto efficiency.[25] The difficulty with this strict approach is that it would make legal reform almost impossible, in particular if changes to legal rules (e.g. increases in taxation) would negatively affect the rights or legal position of any individual (in the example, that is inescapable because someone would bear the burden of the higher taxes). This makes the strict criterion of Pareto efficiency vulnerable to the criticism that it consolidates existing inequalities and that it prevents legal reform that is socially desirable in a broader sense.

To tackle this issue, a refined concept of efficiency was developed by Kaldor and Hicks.[26] Under Kaldor-Hicks efficiency, there is no increase in economic welfare unless, as a result of the implementation of a given rule or policy, those who gain would *in principle* be able to compensate fully those who lose and still be better off themselves – that is, unless there is a net social gain of economic welfare.[27] Using the same example, increases in taxation can be considered efficient under the Kaldor-Hicks criterion even if some members

25 See V. Pareto, *Manuale di economia politica con una introduzione alla scienza sociale*, Milan: Società Editrice Libraria, 1906, repr. 1919.
26 See N. Kaldor, 'Welfare Propositions and Interpersonal Comparisons of Utility', *The Economic Journal* 49, 1939, 549–52; and J. Hicks, 'The Foundations of Welfare Economics', *The Economic Journal* 49, 1939, 696–712. The seminal ideas behind this approach were advanced by A. C. Pigou, *The Economics of Welfare*, 4th edn, London: Macmillan, 1932.
27 On the desirability of this normative criterion, see R. Posner, 'Ethical and Political Basis of the Efficiency Norm in Common Law Adjudication', *Hofstra Law Review* 8(3), 1980, 487; and J. L. Coleman, 'Efficiency, Utility and Wealth Maximization', *Hofstra Law Review* 8(3), 1980, 509.

of society are worse off due to the higher taxation, provided that the benefits derived from the increased public revenue by those that are on the receiving end (e.g. recipients of social benefits or users of the public health care system) derive a larger advantage, even if there is no actual compensation between these different social groups. This is the concept of social welfare that forms the basis of the (mainstream) economic analysis of law methodology.

A close look at the criterion of Kaldor-Hicks efficiency makes it clear that the analysis under welfare economics is not concerned with whether compensation or redistribution is *actually* achieved by a given rule or legal reform, but it simply focuses on whether that would be possible in economic terms. It also does not express or indicate any preference about who should benefit from the net economic efficiency derived from the legal situation or reform. In that regard, a legal reform whereby the richest in society benefit sufficiently to potentially compensate the poorest that suffer the detriment derived from that legal reform is as desirable as the opposite development, provided both scenarios create the same absolute amount of social welfare. Thus, inequality and its potential increase is not captured by the Kaldor-Hicks efficiency criterion. This has been another focus of criticism of the economic analysis of law, and critics have raised the stylised argument that legal scholarship should be concerned with redistribution and equality or, more generally, with fairness (or justice).[28] Looking forward, this is a criticism bound to carry some additional weight in view of the increasing discussion about the impact of inequality in terms of economic development.[29] However, it is important to stress that economic analysis of law scholars does not necessarily dismiss those concerns in the abstract or in absolute terms. Rather, the consensus is that equality-oriented interventions should be left to specific areas of law and policy specifically designed around the issue of wealth (re)distribution (such as taxation and welfare law), whereas the rest of the legal system (and in particular private law) should not be driven by redistributive considerations because doing so makes the economic analysis either skewed or impossible.[30] The same applies to arguments of fairness,

28 D. Kennedy, 'Law-and-Economics from the Perspective of Critical Legal Studies', in J. Eatwell, M. Milgate and P. Newman (eds), *New Palgrave: A Dictionary of Economics*, 1st edn, London: Macmillan, 1987, 465–74.

29 See T. Piketty, *Capital in the Twenty-First Century*, Cambridge, MA and London: Harvard University Press, 2014, and the debate it has sparked in economic literature and beyond. See also A. Deaton, *The Great Escape: Health, Wealth, and the Origins of Inequality*, Princeton, NJ: Princeton University Press, 2013.

30 For extended discussion, see: L. Kaplow and S. Shavell, *Welfare versus Fairness*, Cambridge, MA and London: Harvard University Press, 2002; and D. A. Weisbach

which are simply impossible to tackle using economic methods.[31] Overall, then, a possible way to conceptualise this is simply to understand that the economic analysis of law ultimately aims at finding ways of making the pie as large as possible, without concerning itself with (nor being able to determine) how the pie is split.[32]

This ongoing discussion and the implicit acceptance of the higher relevance of the economic analysis of law as a powerful methodology where redistribution (or broader *soft* public policy goals) is not the primary concern for legal intervention has had an impact in determining the areas of law where economic analysis has been more developed, which mainly concentrate around commercial law and private law broadly speaking. As clearly summed up:

> Today, economic thinking dominates contract, commercial, bankruptcy, antitrust, corporate, and securities law and related fields. It is also influential if not dominant in tort, criminal, and property law and civil procedure. It has made less progress in the major fields of public law, including constitutional, immigration, administrative, and international law. These areas of law are less closely connected with commercial behavior than most of the others, and so the off-the-shelf economic models do not as clearly apply to them. Economists have produced a large political economy literature, but the models in this literature are more controversial and less usable than models of commercial behavior.[33]

This does not mean that economic analysis of law is necessarily limited to private and commercial law, but it is a fact that these are the fields where its insights may be more powerful and less controversial. Thus, the remainder of the discussion will start by exploring them, and then proceed to other areas of application of the economic analysis of law.

'Should Legal Rules Be Used to Redistribute Income?' 70 *University of Chicago Law Review* 70, 2003, 439. For a criticism of this line of thought, see C. Sanchirico, 'Taxes versus Legal Rules as Instruments for Equity: A More Equitable View', *Journal of Legal Studies* 29, 2000, 797; and C. Sanchirico, 'Deconstructing the New Efficiency Rationale', *Cornell Law Review* 86, 2001, 1003.

31 The difficulty of using other evaluative criteria, such as fairness, was stressed by G. J. Stigler, 'The Law and Economics of Public Policy: A Plea to the Scholars', *Journal of Legal Studies* 1, 1972, 1.

32 For discussion and a different view, see L. A. Bebchuck, 'The Pursuit of a Bigger Pie: Can Everyone Expect a Bigger Slice?' *Hofstra Law Review* 8(3), 1980, 671–709.

33 Eric A. Posner, in D. Baird, 'The Future of Law and Economics'.

The origins of law and economics and its focus on transaction costs

One of the areas where the insights of economic analysis of law are clearly consolidated (and relatively uncontroversial) concerns the analysis surrounding the concept of transaction costs,[34] and the related Coase theorem.[35] Transaction costs are those linked to a given transfer of assets that are necessary for a legal exchange to take place, such as information costs, negotiation costs, enforcement costs, etc. In simplified terms, the analysis based on transaction costs that leads to the Coase theorem indicates that, in the absence of transaction costs (or where they are sufficiently low), assets will be traded in a way that ensures their optimal final allocation (i.e., regardless of any initial allocation of assets, they will be put to their best possible social use). Conversely, where transaction costs are high, economic transactions that would otherwise be efficient will not take place, which causes a loss of (potential) social welfare.[36]

The classic example to illustrate the Coase theorem concerns situations where allowing party A to carry out an activity damages party B, while preventing damage to party B necessarily causes a detriment to party A. For instance, let's think of a situation where party A runs a private school and party B runs a music studio.[37] The school and the music studio are adjacent, so parties A and B are neighbours. Until now, the music studio was only open in the evenings, while the school finished classes in the early afternoon. Thus, until now, the school and the music studio could both develop their activities

34 O. E. Williamson and S. E. Masten (eds), *The Economics of Transaction Costs*, Aldershot: Edward Elgar, 1999.

35 R. H. Coase, 'The Problem of Social Cost', *Journal of Law and Economics* 3, 1960, 1–44.

36 This is ultimately linked to the problem of market failure. See F. M. Bator, 'The Anatomy of Market Failure', *Quarterly Journal of Economics* 72(3), 1958, 351–79. Market failure is one of the main justifications for regulatory intervention. However, any such intervention is affected by potential problems of government failure; see J. J. Pincus, 'Market Failure and Government Failure', in S. King and P. Lloyd (eds), *Economic Rationalism: Dead End or Way Forward?*, Sydney: Allen & Unwin, 1993, 261–76.

37 The qualification that the school is private aims to avoid issues concerning the social value of education, which is certainly difficult to measure. It is generally more accessible (and less controversial) to solely focus on the financial benefits of running a school as a business. This is not intended to pre-empt any other discussion. For some thoughts on the difficulties in measuring the value of public goods, see D. S. Brookshire and D. L. Coursey, 'Measuring the Value of a Public Good: An Empirical Comparison of Elicitation Procedures', *The American Economic Review* 77(4), 1987, 554–66.

unaffected by each other. Imagine that the music studio, in view of increased demand for its services, considers opening all day. If that happens, the school will probably be affected because the noise coming from the studio will distract pupils during their classes.[38] In abstract terms, there are two possible legal rules or models: under option 1, the school is legally responsible to provide a proper (quiet) learning environment to its pupils and, if that is not the case, it must pay the costs to make the situation good or stop its activities altogether. Differently, under option 2, the music studio is responsible for avoiding noise and nuisance to its neighbours, and it is liable to pay damages if it breaches that obligation. Under rule 1, the school has no possibility to sue the music studio, and its only option to avoid discontinuing its activities due to noise is to invest in soundproofing the school. Under rule 2, the music studio is the one having to invest in soundproofing its premises, lest it wants to be open to claims for damages.

An approach to this problem under other research methodologies would probably focus on whether it would be fair for the music studio to take advantage from extended noise hours at the expense of the school, or whether favouring one activity over the other creates the type of social effect that is considered desirable under the relevant normative framework (such as the promotion of regulated school education or the expansion of space for unregulated liberal arts). Differently, under the methodology of economic analysis of law, and in particular under transaction cost analysis, the Coase theorem aims at solving the problem by identifying which solution is more efficient. To understand the insights of this analysis, we need some additional information. Imagine that the private school obtains a profit of £500,000 a year and that it would cost it £100,000 per year to soundproof its premises. In turn, the music studio could increase its annual profit by £250,000 if it extended its opening hours beyond evenings (the current level of turnover of the studio not being relevant), and the cost of soundproofing its premises would be of £200,000 per year. Alternatively, the music studio could risk having to pay damages to the school, which would be the equivalent of £300,000 a year. Under rule 1, the school would clearly decide to invest in soundproofing rather than closing down altogether (hence keeping a profit of £400,000 per year). Similarly, under rule 2, the music studio would rather soundproof its premises and extend its opening hours than keep its activity

---

38 The converse example could be constructed assuming the school intends to offer out-of-hours sports activities and the music studio is concerned that the background noise will disturb its clients or diminish the quality of the musical recordings, so the example is not intended to point towards any specific outcome.

limited to the evenings (thus obtaining an additional benefit of £50,000) or be exposed to damages claims (thus incurring losses of £50,000). Apparently, then, rule 1 is more efficient than rule 2. This derives basically from the fact that the cost of the remedial measure is lower for the school than for the music studio. However, and this is the crucial contribution of the Coase theorem, both rules 1 and 2 are inferior to the solution that parties A and B could reach if they are allowed to cooperate.[39]

In a scenario of possible cooperation (that is, where there are no, or only very low, transaction costs), when the music studio considers the possibility of extending its hours, it could ask the school to provide an estimate of its soundproofing costs. When the music studio realised that it is cheaper for the school to take those measures than for itself, it would be rational for the music studio to ask the school to soundproof and to offer to cover the costs, which would allow for a saving of £100,000 per year in soundproofing costs. It would be equally rational for the school to point out that the music studio should compensate the school for its collaboration, so that they should split the savings equally. The end result would then be that the school would take the soundproofing measures and the music studio would pay it £150,000, thus leaving both parties better off (the school would have a total annual profit of £550,000 and the music studio would increase its annual profits by £100,000). The collaborative solution is superior because both parties are better off than under any other solution.

What this indicates is that, where collaboration is possible, the initial allocation of rights (that is, whether rule 1 or rule 2 controls, or whether the music studio has the right to create noise or the school has the right to a quiet environment) is not relevant and an efficient outcome will be achieved regardless. However, this does not resemble reality because transaction costs are far from zero and because the set of circumstances we have depicted is unrealistic. On the contrary, where collaboration is not possible because transaction costs are sufficiently high (e.g. the cost of negotiating a contract between the school and the music studio exceeds the value of the savings derived from collaboration), the initial allocation of rights is very relevant to the possibility of achieving an efficient outcome and any legal rule devised to adjudicate on disputes runs the risk of being inferior to the collaborative solution that could otherwise emerge.

---

39 We are not concerned here with the analysis of whether cooperation would actually take place, which would be something to assess under game theory, which is briefly discussed below.

The insights that derive from this type of analysis are plentiful, but the most obvious ones are that, when designing legal rules, a clear focus should be on the minimisation of transaction costs, so as to facilitate collaborative solutions that can increase the efficient use of the resources. Further, that in the design of legal rules, the most efficient solutions can be achieved if costs are imposed on the party that can avoid them more efficiently (cheapest cost avoider), even if it is not the obvious party on which to impose a cost from a different perspective (for instance, under fairness or distributive justice considerations). Of course, all these insights result in the need to carry out additional (and increasingly complex) analyses (for instance, to determine who is the cheapest cost avoider in a specific situation, or which rule will tend to impose the risk on the class of agents that are generally the cheapest cost avoiders, and so on) and be sure that all relevant circumstances are taken into account (e.g. are there third parties affected by the noise coming from the studio other than the school?).[40] The work of the legal researcher thus starts with an examination of the rules applicable to the case (Does the school have a right to silence? Are the requirements for a claim, e.g. in tort, met? Is there a general obligation to minimise losses before claiming compensation, or a duty to cooperate with the tortfeasor in minimising the costs of the activity creating the nuisance? etc.), including the way in which they are interpreted and applied by the courts, and then turns towards a consideration of whether these rules are efficient as a final critical assessment, potentially leading to proposals for legal reform.

The extension of the economic analysis of law beyond private law: crimes and sanctions

Beyond the area of private law disputes, the economic analysis of law can also provide useful insights in areas such as criminal law or branches of administrative law that deal with sanctions and fines. In these areas, the concept of deterrence is fundamental in order to get the level of sanctions and the amount of effort put into policing crimes and violations right (or, more realistically, to promote legal reforms that tend towards the optimal level of deterrence). Analysis of these issues under other methodologies can often face difficulties such as assuming that all crimes can be deterred (which is not a truly workable assumption, if nothing else, due to the prohibitive costs it would entail

---

40 For discussion, see G. Calabresi and A. D. Melamed, 'Property Rules, Liability Rules, and Inalienability: One View of the Cathedral', *Harvard Law Review* 85, 1972, 1089–128. Please bear in mind that their contribution has not, however, been uncontroversial.

in terms of policing), or lacking indications as to the appropriate level of criminal and administrative sanctions in view of the (im)moral nature or general undesirability of specific types of behaviour. The economic analysis of law as applied to this area provides some insights that can be useful on both fronts. On the first aspect, it stresses a certain degree of substitution between investing more resources in deterrence and raising the level of the sanctions. However, it also makes it clear that both issues (in particular, increasing the level of sanctions) are subjected to decreasing marginal gains and, consequently, at some point both further investments in deterrence capacity and further increases of the applicable sanctions can be ineffective, or even counterproductive. A useful example can be found in the Singaporean ban on the importation and sale of chewing gum. The punishment for illegal gum trafficking was never corporal, but even for a first offence it can include a fine of up to S$100,000 (£50,000 or €65,000 approximately) and up to two years in prison.[41] Imagine that this measure proved insufficient to completely prevent damages derived from improper chewing gum disposal in the Singapore underground (which was the original goal of the ban) and the Singaporean Government decided to attach corporal punishment, or even the death sentence, for gum traffickers. Would that be a measure susceptible of creating further deterrence, or would it actually undermine the effectiveness of the ban as a whole? That is the sort of thing that can be assessed under general deterrence theory. On the second issue, concerned with the appropriate level of sanctions, by developing an economic theory of crime, law and economics can also provide some indicators as to how to set the sanctions at a level that is efficient (this can, for instance, be useful in terms of choosing whether a given behaviour should constitute an administrative offence liable to the imposition of a fine, or rather be a criminal offence that can carry an imprisonment sentence or some other sort of non-monetary sanction).

Even if it seems counterintuitive at first sight, the economic analysis of law applied to these areas contributes important insights through a theory of rational crime, whereby the incentives and disincentives for the commission of crimes are treated in a way relatively similar to those for the engagement in preventative or corrective measures discussed above. Under this conceptualisation, it is understood that people will commit crimes whenever they expect to gain from them or, maybe in more accurate terms, when the expected

---

41 See L. Benedictus, 'Gum Control: How Lee Kuan Yew Kept Chewing Gum Off Singapore's Streets', *The Guardian*, 23 March 2015, http://www.theguardian. com/lifeandstyle/shortcuts/2015/mar/23/gum-control-how-lee-kuan-yew-kept-chewing-gum-off-singapores-streets (accessed 3 March 2017).

sanction is insufficient to deter them from committing those crimes. A relatively straightforward insight is that the expected sanction for the commission of a given offence is the combined result of the probability of being caught (and convicted) for the offence and of the level or seriousness of the sanction.[42] Thus, it is possible to establish the pay-off that the potential offender would consider in terms that function as prices.

Examples of this are particularly clear if we consider economic offences that are commonly committed as the result of a rational process, such as tax evasion[43] (although the theory applies equally to other crimes and offences). Under this approach, in order to deter the potential offender, it is necessary for the expected sanction to be larger than the expected gain from committing the offence. Imagine an individual subjected to the higher taxation bracket of 40 per cent currently applicable in the United Kingdom, who decides to under-report her income by £10,000. This would lead to an immediate saving of £4,000 in evaded taxes. Imagine that the applicable sanction for that amount of tax evasion was £10,000. The question at this point would be why would she decide to under-report her income, in particular given that the sanction for that behaviour is nominally higher than the amount it plans to evade (in terms of evaded taxes, and equal to the amount of income she plans to under-report). However, maybe counterintuitively, the economic analysis of law demonstrates that this situation would still not ensure deterrence of the under-reporting because not all instances of tax evasion get identified, investigated and successfully sanctioned. Imagine that the tax inspectorate (HM Revenue & Customs) has a probability of sanction of 12 per cent of this type of tax evasion (for instance, because this type of case ranks low in its enforcement priorities, which lead it to concentrate on corporate tax evasion). Then, the expected sanction is the result of multiplying the probability of being sanctioned times the applicable sanction, which means that the expected sanction actually amounts to £1,200 (that is the amount of the fine, £10,000, multiplied by the probability of being caught and sanctioned, which is 12 per cent or 0.12), and falls well below the level needed in deterrence terms. And this is so despite it implying that, in case of being imposed, the £10,000 sanction would represent 2.5 times the evaded taxes (of £4,000) and 100 per cent of

---

42 For an in-depth discussion, see G. S. Becker, 'Crime and Punishment: An Economic Approach', *Journal of Political Economy* 76(2), 1968, 169–217; and Stigler, 'The Optimum Enforcement of Laws'.

43 See M. Allingham and A. Sandmo, 'Income Tax Evasion: A Theoretical Analysis', *Journal of Public Economics* 1(4), 1972, 323–38; and an in-depth discussion in J. Slemrod, 'Cheating Ourselves: The Economics of Tax Evasion', *Journal of Economic Perspectives* 21(1), 2007, 25–48.

the under-reported income (of £10,000), which would ensure that the tax evader keeps no economic advantage whatsoever.

It is important to note that this is the case because the pay-off of the potential offender would be positive. With a probability of 88 per cent (i.e. the reverse of the 12 per cent probability of being sanctioned), she gets to keep the £4,000 in evaded taxes. Taking into account both the benefits of avoiding taxes if not caught and the cost of the fine if caught, this means that her expected pay-off is: 0.88 x £4,000 – 0.12 x £10,000 = £2,320. These calculations still may need to be subjected to adjustments in order to incorporate the potential offender's approach to risk. Risk-averse people will tend to overestimate the probability of being caught (in the example, if she *perceives* the probability of being sanctioned to be any higher than 40 per cent, then she is deterred because at that point her expected pay-off becomes negative), whereas risk-prone people will do the opposite.[44] In any case, though, being able to at least assess the risk-neutral scenario already provides interesting insights – since, otherwise, it could have been quite intuitive to assume that a sanction of £10,000 for the evasion of £4,000 in taxes or £10,000 in taxable income was actually sufficient for deterrence purposes.

Beyond this descriptive power, which can help explain difficult issues such as the perceived ineffectiveness of existing sanctions to deter specific types of behaviour that are considered undesirable (such as tax evasion), the economic analysis of law can also help in normative aspects, such as whether to crimi-nalise a given activity that could otherwise be considered a mere adminis-trative offence (which is clearly relevant in terms of the design of public policy around controversial areas such as drug dealing,[45] or prostitution[46]). The approach under this methodology will usually help structure a cost/benefit analysis[47] of the different options available – which is ultimately oriented

44 Developing the example to capture all the complexities that a full formulation of the economic theory of crime has developed would exceed the possibilities of our discussion. The interested reader can follow the discussion in Cooter and Ulen, *Law and Economics*, chs 11 and 12; and Shavell, *Foundations of Economic Analysis of Law*, chs 20–24.

45 S. Poret, 'Paradoxical Effects of Law Enforcement Policies: The Case of the Illicit Drug Market', *International Review of Law and Economics* 22(4), 2002, 465–93. For a related analysis of the economics of drug dealing, see S. D. Levitt and S. Alladi Venkatesh, 'An Economic Analysis of a Drug-Selling Gang's Finances', *Quarterly Journal of Economics* 115(3), 2000, 755–89.

46 R. Albert, F. Gomez and Y. Gutierrez Franco, *Regulating Prostitution: A Comparative Law and Economics Approach*, FEDEA Working Papers No. 2007-30, 2007, http:// documentos.fedea.net/pubs/dt/2007/dt-2007-30.pdf (accessed 7 March 2017).

47 See S. Chakravarty, 'Cost–Benefit Analysis', in Eatwell et al., *New Palgrave: A Dictionary of Economics*, 1st edn, 1889–97.

towards identifying the option that, on the whole or in net terms, creates the largest surplus or the smallest shortfall – and, more often than not, will allow the researcher to question received wisdom about whether society is better off by following one course of action over the other.

Reaching out to the public law sphere: institutional agency theory and beyond

Together with criminal law, another area beyond private law where economic analysis can offer interesting insights concerns some aspects of public law.[48] Some specific applications of economic theory are well developed and increasingly used in this realm, such as regulatory capture theory.[49] Specifically, I find *agency theory* particularly useful to inform legal issues such as public governance and the management of public resources.[50] Agency theory conceptualises the relationships that arise when one person or entity (agent) is able to make decisions on behalf of, or that impact, another person or entity (principal).[51] The main insight of agency theory is that agency relationships imply an unavoidable risk of conflict of interest because the agent will (always/sometimes) have an incentive to deviate from the behaviour expected by the principal and further its own self-interest. This creates the need for the principal to monitor the agent (which is costly) and the possibility for both parties to reduce the risk of strategic behaviour through (mutual) commitments (involving signalling and bonding, which are also costly), as well as tailor-made systems of

---

48 W. Weigel, 'Why Promote the Economic Analysis of Public Law?' *Homo Oeconomicus* 23(2), 2006, 195–216.

49 This strand of theory has multiple facets, from some closely linked to agency theory, to others conceptualising the problems in terms of rent extraction. For two excellent examples, one in each line of enquiry, see J.-J. Laffont and J. Tirole, 'The Politics of Government Decision-Making: A Theory of Regulatory Capture', *Quarterly Journal of Economics* 106(4), 1991, 1089–127; and F. S. McChesney, *Money for Nothing: Politicians, Rent Extraction and Political Extortion*, Cambridge, MA and London: Harvard University Press, 1997.

50 The commonly accepted initial full formulation of the agency theory was by M. C. Jensen and W. H. Meckling, 'Theory of the Firm: Managerial Behavior, Agency Costs and Ownership Structure', *Journal of Financial Economics* 3(4), 1976, 305–60. In the public law area, institutional agency theory has been significantly influenced by the work of B. M. Mitnick, *The Political Economy of Regulation: Creating, Designing, and Removing Regulatory Forms*, New York: Columbia University Press, 1980.

51 K. M. Eisenhardt, 'Agency Theory: An Assessment and Review', *The Academy of Management Review* 14(1), 1989, 57–74; and J. E. Stiglitz, 'Principal and Agent (II)', in Durlauf and Blume, *The New Palgrave Dictionary of Economics*, 2nd edn.

incentives whereby both sets of interests can be aligned. The most well-known application of agency theory is perhaps in the field of corporate law and governance, where agency theory has been used to conceptualise and regulate the relationship between the owners (shareholders) and managers (directors) of commercial firms.[52]

Agency theory is also very helpful in understanding and designing rules aimed, for example, at controlling the way in which decisions are adopted by politicians or civil servants. The general theory concerned with these issues is known as public choice,[53] and it is a fundamental area of law and economics, as well as public policy studies.[54] One of its core insights – which has been applied to many areas of political and public administration activity[55] – is that when politicians or civil servants make decisions for which they have received a democratic mandate or been invested with public powers, they will have incentives to act in a way that benefits them (personally) rather than in a way that furthers the public interest. This is clear concerning politicians, who will be tempted to act based on their assessment of the path of action that can lead them to re-election (populism), or that can provide them with more immediate personal gains (such as engaging in outright bribery, or rent-seeking behaviour – for example, by trying to obtain appointments to well-remunerated private positions after they step down from office, thus creating problems of revolving doors). It is also clear regarding civil servants, which may also be tempted by personal gain or decide to engage in policy-making that increases their portfolio of influence or power, or that maximises their budget or the size of their operations within the public sector.[56] All of them may also be tempted to slack and avoid making any decisions that can prove unpopular, which is only going to create further problems down the line.

52 E. Fama and M. Jensen, 'Separation of Ownership and Control', *Journal of Law and Economics* 26(2), 1983, 301–25.

53 The seminal work developing the theory is generally understood to be J. M. Buchanan and G. Tullock, *The Calculus of Consent: Logical Foundations of Constitutional Democracy*, Ann Arbor, MI: University of Michigan Press, 1962, available at http://www.econlib.org/library/Buchanan/buchCv3.html (accessed 7 March 2017).

54 See B. G. Peters, *Advanced Introduction to Public Policy*, Cheltenham: Edward Elgar, 2015, 39 and ff.

55 See D. C. Mueller, *Public Choice III*, Cambridge: Cambridge University Press, 2003; and M. Reksulak, L. Razzolini and W. F. Shughart II (eds), *The Elgar Companion to Public Choice*, 2nd edn, Cheltenham: Edward Elgar, 2013. See also J. Cullis and P. Jones, *Public Finance and Public Choice. Analytical Perspectives*, 3rd edn, Oxford: Oxford University Press, 2009.

56 P. Dunleavy, *Democracy, Bureaucracy and Public Choice. Economic Approaches in Political Science*, London: Pearson, 1991; repr. London: Routledge, 2013.

These insights can be usefully exploited under public choice theory and serve the basis of systems of checks and balances, including liability rules, so as to overcome issues derived from the agency problem in the sphere of public governance.

It's not all fun and games, or is it?

A discussion on economic analysis of law, however brief and superficial, cannot end without at least having made a reference to *game theory*,[57] which is another of the main areas of study of law from an economic perspective. In simplified terms, game theory aims to formalise (or create) mathematical models to study the interaction between decision-makers and to predict the potential outcomes of situations where the relevant parties need to make decisions on the basis of their expectations or (limited) knowledge of the behaviour of the other party.[58] The most well-known instance of the type of analysis carried out by game theory is the so-called *prisoner's dilemma*, which conceptualises the incentives for two parties that can either cooperate to their mutual advantage or try to cheat each other to obtain a larger individual advantage, with the constraint that engaging in conflict rather than cooperation makes both parties worse off.

In the standard textbook example, two members of a criminal gang are arrested and imprisoned in solitary confinement, with no means of communicating with each other. The prosecutors lack sufficient evidence to convict them for the commission of specific serious crimes (which would carry a sentence of 20 years in prison), but they are confident that they can convict both of them for their membership of the criminal gang (which is a less serious offence and carries a sentence of one year in prison). In order to try to obtain additional evidence from the suspects, simultaneously, the prosecutors offer each prisoner the possibility to strike a deal if they betray the other by testifying to the major crimes committed by the other prisoner. The conditions of the offer are as follows: if only one of them betrays the other, the one that confesses will be released, whereas the betrayed prisoner will be convicted for the major crime. However, if both confess, they will be jointly convicted

---

57 J. Von Neumann and O.Morgenstern, *Theory of Games and Economic Behaviour*, Princeton: Princeton University Press, 1944.

58 Or, in more formal terms, game theory is 'the study of mathematical models of conflict and cooperation between intelligent rational decision-makers'; R. B. Myerson, *Game Theory: Analysis of Conflict*, Cambridge, MA: Harvard University Press, 1991, 1.

for the more serious crimes, albeit their sentences will be reduced to reflect their cooperation with the investigation, which will result in both of them serving jail sentences of five years. If neither of them confesses, they will only be convicted for the less serious crime – one year. It seems clear that both prisoners have an incentive to cooperate because, if they both remain silent, they are collectively better off.

		Prisoner 2	
		Confess	Remain silent
Prisoner 1	Confess	5, 5	0, 20
	Remain silent	20, 0	1, 1

However, game theory demonstrates that it would be irrational for both prisoners, acting on an individual basis, to remain silent because, by doing so, they risk being cheated by the other prisoner and ending up serving the longer sentence. Thus, not knowing what the other prisoner will do, remaining silent is risky because it leaves one open to being cheated and carries a possibility of serving 20 years in prison. On the contrary, confessing guarantees the prisoner a maximum sentence of five years and the possibility of being let go, which seems a preferable situation. Thus, both prisoners, anticipating that the other one will cheat, will confess and end up serving a five-year sentence each. Of course, all of this analysis relies on the impossibility of the prisoners communicating and cooperating. If cooperation was possible, then we would need to carry out additional assessments concerning the cost of their cooperation, similarly to what we did in the discussion of the Coase theorem above. Where cooperation is structurally impossible or very difficult to operationalise within a legal framework, it is usual to refer to the situation as the tragedy of the commons.[59]

Game theory can tackle much more complex situations of interaction in decision-making than the one discussed in the streamlined scenario of the prisoners' dilemma and is very useful in setting up rules that lead to desired behaviour (such as confessions or collaboration with law enforcement bodies, but also in order to design default legal rules that ensure efficient outcomes when the parties cannot cooperate or coordinate behaviour by themselves), or in assessing the complications in the formation of contracts or the entry into

59 E. Ostrom, *Governing the Commons. The Evolution of Institutions for Collective Action*, Cambridge: Cambridge University Press, 1990.

international treaties, among a myriad of other uses. Therefore, this is another way in which the economic analysis of law can be useful as an analytical tool.[60]

Possible applications to research the topic of 'lay decision-making in the legal system'

After this general discussion of some of the ways in which economic analysis can assist in the analysis of legal institutions and legal decision-making – which are certainly relevant in all areas of law adjudication, regardless of the level of legal training of the decision-maker – it is now time to focus, even if briefly, on the more specific issue of the ways in which this methodology can be applied to the particular topic of 'lay decision-making in the legal system'. For a researcher willing to tackle research questions in this area, this would certainly not be uncharted territory and previous work on juries and their efficiency would necessarily be the point of departure.[61] This line of enquiry under a 'classic' law and economics approach incorporates insights from different, more specific methods, such as transaction cost analysis or game theory, and focuses on questions such as the optimal make-up of the jury and its size (which creates trade-offs between the quality of the fact-finding and the workability of the arrangement), the economics of the decision whether to seek a jury trial over a bench trial (which can be understood as part of a game ultimately leading the parties to settle out of court, whenever possible),[62] the rule that should apply to jury decision-making (unanimity vs majority, or qualified majority, etc.), or whether or not jury duty should be mandatory.[63] More recent studies have started to analyse more specific issues, such as the rules allowing lawyers to veto potential jury members.[64] However, this is an area where *behavioural* law and economics is making increasingly relevant strides,[65] and the researcher may be more interested in that perspective due to the closer links with other socio-legal approaches to the study of law

---

60 D. G. Baird, R. H. Gertner and R. C. Picker, *Game Theory and the Law*, Cambridge, MA: Harvard University Press, 1998.

61 See Posner, *Economic Analysis of Law*, chs 21 and 22, with further references.

62 J. Hersch, 'Demand for a Jury Trial and the Selection of Cases for Trial', *Journal of Legal Studies* 35(1), 2006, 119–42.

63 D. L. Martin, 'The Economics of Jury Conscription', *Journal of Political Economy* 80(4), 1972, 680–702.

64 F. X. Flanagan, 'Peremptory Challenges and Jury Selection', *Journal of Law & Economics* 58(2), 2015, 385–416.

65 For a first approximation to that literature, see K. McCabe, V. Smith and T. Chorvat, 'Lessons from Neuroeconomics for the Law', in F. Parisi and V. Smith (eds), *The Law and Economics of Irrational Behavior*, Stanford, CA: Stanford University Press, 2005, 85–86.

decision-making in the legal system (examples of which are referenced elsewhere in this book). Given the focus of this chapter on 'neoclassical' economic analysis of law methodology, this issue is not discussed in any further detail.

Some final thoughts – what do I mean by 'economically informed' legal research then?

After this quick overview of some of the main applications of the economic analysis of law, it may be worth stressing its relevance for legal research at a postgraduate or advanced level. As mentioned above, and put in its strongest form, I am convinced that carrying out legal research without assessing its economic implications and without incorporating the insights of economic theory is ultimately unsatisfactory, and that all legal research should be economically informed. What I mean by the need to carry out 'economically informed' legal research is that researchers, even if they do not directly engage with economic methods and theories as a core component of their projects, should at least incorporate the insights resulting from previous economic analysis in the relevant research area. That incorporation should at least be by way of discussion, if nothing else, to justify the adoption of a different normative framework or of an approach that may challenge the insights offered by the economic analysis of law, or to offer some rationale as to why economic implications can be neglected in the context of a given research project. This is particularly relevant in areas of law with a clear economic component, such as economic regulation, commercial litigation, securities and finance, etc. But it is also relevant in *any* other area of the law, such as family law,[66] however apparently remote from economic considerations, and even if the main methodology chosen for a specific project is different from law and economics, such as comparative law.[67]

Of course, I recognise that this bold claim may be seen as an attempt on my part to support the imperialism of the economic analysis of law.[68] However,

---

66 See, e.g., M. F. Brinig (ed.), *Economics of Family Law*, Cheltenham: Edward Elgar, 2007; and A. W. Dnes and R. Rowthorn (eds), *The Law and Economics of Marriage and Divorce*, Cambridge: Cambridge University Press, 2010.

67 See U. Mattei, *Comparative Law and Economics*, Ann Arbor, MI: University of Michigan Press, 1999; M. Reimann, 'Comparative Law and Economic Analysis of Law', in M. Reimann and R. Zimmermann (eds), *The Oxford Handbook of Comparative Law*, Oxford: Oxford University Press, 2006, 839–64; and the contributions to T. Eisenberg and G. B. Ramello (eds), *Comparative Law and Economics*, Research Handbooks in Comparative Law series, Cheltenham: Edward Elgar, 2016.

68 The issue is not at all new. See R. D. Cooter, 'Law and the Imperialism of Economics: An Introduction to the Economic Analysis of Law and a Review of the Major Books', *UCLA Law Review* 29, 1982, 1260–69.

I would rather approach this from the opposite perspective and stress the perils of carrying out legal research and engage in legal decision-making in an 'economically disinformed' manner – not to say, 'economically ignorant' way. It seems obvious to me that all legal decision-making has immediate and unavoidable economic effects,[69] and that failing to understand those effects and incorporate them into the decision-making process and/or the process of legal research is bound to result in faulty outcomes or theories and insights that cannot translate into reality in a desirable way.[70] Therefore, the least that legal researchers should do from this perspective is to ensure that their research is economically congruous and that its insights can be related to economic reality and economic theory – even if the main purpose of the research is to criticise them, show any shortcomings, or advocate the adoption of a different paradigm. Otherwise, there is a clear risk of pushing for legal reforms or reaching adjudicative decisions that can be detrimental to social welfare in the long run. To me, this is normatively undesirable. At the risk of accusations of circularity of my arguments, then, I consider all non-economically informed legal research faulty – which, again, is not to say that all researchers necessarily must follow a law and economics methodology, but to stress that all researchers need to engage in an intellectual dialogue with the economic analysis of law.

Recommended reading

Cooter, R. B., Jr and Ulen, T., *Law and Economics*, 6th edn, Boston, MA: Pearson, 2014.

Devlin, A., *Fundamental Principles of Law and Economics*, London: Routledge, 2015.

Miceli, T. J., *The Economic Approach to Law*, 2nd edn, Stanford, CA: Stanford University Press, 2009.

Polinsky, A. M., *An Introduction to Law and Economics (Aspen Coursebook)*, 4th edn, New York: Wolters Kluwer, 2011.

Posner, R. A., *Economic Analysis of Law*, 9th edn, New York: Wolters Kluwer, 2014.

Veljanovski, C., *Economic Principles of Law*, Cambridge: Cambridge University Press, 2007.

---

69 This is clearly recognised in the area of regulatory impact assessment, and should be uncontroversial. See 'Cost-Benefit Analysis and Regulatory Impact Assessment', ch. 15 in R. Baldwin, M. Cave and M. Lodge, *Understanding Regulation. Theory, Strategy, and Practice*, 2nd edn, Oxford: Oxford University Press, 2012.

70 For some additional remarks, see A. Sanchez-Graells, 'The Importance of Assessing the Economic Impact of the Case Law of the Court of Justice of the European Union: Some Exploratory Thoughts', SSRN Working Paper, 2013, http://ssrn.com/abstract=2253346 (accessed 7 March 2017).

9 The master's tools?

A feminist approach to legal and lay decision-making

Vanessa E. Munro*

It is neither possible, nor desirable, within the confines of this chapter to purport to offer any kind of 'instruction manual' for doing feminist legal research. Instead, my aim in the following discussion is to give a brief sketch of key theoretical contributions that feminist analyses have made to our understandings of, and expectations in relation to, law and legal process.[1] Having done so, I explore some of the ways in which feminist methods can be deployed in empirical socio-legal research,[2] and highlight in particular its utility in the context of studying the parameters, content and dilemmas of lay (and quasi-legal) decision-making. As part of this discussion, I also draw attention to some of the tensions that can arise in meeting the demands of access and impact associated with this genre of research while preserving the critical and deconstructive spirit of feminism.

A tentative mapping of (some) feminist theoretical terrain

This chapter inevitably starts with a hefty disclaimer: there is no such thing as a unified feminist jurisprudence, nor a universally shared feminist legal method.

* I am grateful to the ESRC and Nuffield Foundation for funding the research discussed in this chapter, and to Louise Ellison, Sharon Cowan and Helen Baillot, without whose collaboration the projects would not have been possible.
1 For more detailed discussion of the contribution of feminist accounts of knowledge and epistemology to the research process within the social sciences, see, e.g.: S. Hesse-Biber and M. Yaiser (eds), *Feminist Perspectives on Social Research*, Oxford: Oxford University Press, 2004; G. Letherby, *Feminist Research in Theory and Practice*, Oxford: Oxford University Press, 2003; or C. Ramazanoglu, *Feminist Methodologies: Challenges and Choices*, London: Sage, 2002.
2 For a broader discussion of the application of different methods to 'feminist' social science research, see: S. Reinharz, *Feminist Methods in Social Research*, Oxford: Oxford University Press, 1992; and J. Ribbens and R. Edwards, *Feminist Dilemmas in Qualitative Research: Public Knowledge and Private Lives*, London: Sage, 2009.

Aligned under the banner of modern feminism are a diversity of perspectives regarding the causes and consequences of unequal gender power relations, the ways in which the law and state have played a role in their creation and maintenance, and the most effective strategies for their eradication.

For some feminist commentators, women's disproportionate exclusion from positions of political, economic and social power, and their concomitant relegation to private and domestic spheres, reflects a historical legacy of patriarchal privilege that is gradually being eroded by initiatives for equality and non-discrimination. That this is so, proponents argue, is evidenced – among other things – by the increasing numbers of women securing positions of power within the public sphere. But for other feminists, there are more entrenched systems of structural disempowerment that continue to operate notwithstanding some women's ability to successfully 'cheat' the system. Assimilation of women into an unchanged male-defined sphere, or as Iris Young puts it, 'coming into the game after it has already begun, after the rules have been set, and having to prove oneself according to those rules and standards', is not a tenable blueprint for genuine equality.³ Instead, what is required, they argue, is a radical deconstruction of the boundaries between public and private spheres and a de facto revolution in the dynamics of gender power.⁴ While greater recognition and valuation of women's biological and existential connection to care has been posited by some feminists as the route to securing such empowerment for women,⁵ for others any valorisation of this propensity for care serves only to entrench women's disempowerment, tying them to the domestic sphere and affording them status only on the basis of *men's* valuation of their care-giving.⁶

Under-cutting these debates, moreover, have been conflicting understandings of the nature of power and a diversity of perspectives regarding the ways

3 I. Young, *Justice and the Politics of Difference*, Princeton, NJ: Princeton University Press, 1990, 164.
4 See, in particular, C. MacKinnon, *Feminism Unmodified: Discourses in Life and Law*, Cambridge, MA: Harvard University Press, 1987; and C. MacKinnon, *Toward a Feminist Theory of State*, Cambridge, MA: Harvard University Press, 1989. Also A. Scales, 'The Emergence of a Feminist Jurisprudence', *Yale Law Journal* 95, 1986, 1371; and M. Minow, 'Justice Engendered', *Harvard Law Review* 101, 1987, 10.
5 C. Gilligan, *In a Different Voice: Psychological Theory and Women's Development*, Cambridge, MA: Harvard University Press, 1982; V. Held, *Feminist Morality: Transforming Culture, Society and Politics*, Chicago, IL: University of Chicago Press, 1993.
6 Mackinnon, *Feminism Unmodified*; R. West, 'Jurisprudence and Gender', *University of Chicago Law Review* 55, 1988, 1; and D. Rhode, *Justice and Gender*, Cambridge, MA: Harvard University Press, 1982.

in which gendered experiences are reinforced, challenged or overshadowed by myriad 'other' identity markers (including race, class, disability and sexual orientation),[7] as well as by our differential levels of exposure to vulnerability and divergent opportunities to access institutional and inter-personal resources for resilience.[8]

But to focus too much on these feminist 'fault-lines' risks disintegrating any basis for collective action and dismissing the experientially powerful connection that many women share with others on account of their gender. Thus, much recent feminist work has focused instead on identifying points of commonality in the midst of this diversity[9] and on highlighting the extent to which contemporary feminism can rarely be neatly classified exclusively within the bounds of any one conventional 'liberal', 'cultural', 'radical' or 'post-modern' typology.[10] In line with this, I have previously argued that it *is* possible to identify certain 'resemblances' that unite, albeit at times precariously, and often strategically, what are broadly (self-)identified as feminist approaches to law and legal reasoning.[11]

Focusing on the use of feminist legal methods to examine processes and outcomes of lay decision-making, in the remainder of this chapter, I will draw attention to, and build upon, three such feminist 'resemblances' in particular: namely, (1) a rejection of abstraction and commitment to the importance of context; (2) a sceptical approach towards claims of law's rationality and neutrality; and (3) a reflective attitude towards the role of power and the limits of law as a mechanism of social control. But before exploring how these basic premises impact upon, and frame the application of, feminist legal

---

7 K. Crenshaw, 'Demarginalising the Intersectionality of Race and Sex: A Black Feminist Critique of Antidiscimination Doctrine, Feminist Theory and Antiracist Politics', in A. Phillips (ed.), *Feminism and Politics*, Oxford: Oxford University Press, 1998; A. Harris, 'Race and Essentialism in Feminist Legal Theory', *Stanford Law Review* 42, 1990, 581; M. Mahoney, 'Whiteness and Women, In Practice and Theory: A Reply to Catharine MacKinnon', *Yale Journal of Law and Feminism* 5, 1993, 217; and M. Frug, *Postmodern Legal Feminism*, London: Routledge, 1992.

8 For further discussion, see, in particular, M. Fineman, 'The Vulnerable Subject: Anchoring Equality in the Human Condition', *Yale Journal of Law and Feminism* 20(1), 2008, 1.

9 N. Lacey, *Unspeakable Subjects: Feminist Essays in Legal and Social Theory*, Oxford: Hart Publishing, 2008; and J. Conaghan, 'Re-Assessing the Feminist Theoretical Project in Law', *Journal of Law and Society* 27(3), 2000, 351.

10 See, e.g., M. Davies and V. Munro (eds), *The Research Companion to Feminist Legal Theory*, Aldershot: Ashgate Publishing, 2013.

11 V. Munro, *Law and Politics at the Perimeter: Re-Evaluating Key Debates in Feminist Theory*, Oxford: Hart Publishing, 2007.

methods in particular contexts, I will first say a little more about what they each entail.

1. A suspicion of abstraction, and commitment to context

Common to much feminist work is an insistence that social and legal problems cannot be understood by techniques that require abstraction – not only because such abstraction obscures important detail about the concrete particularities of people's daily lives, but because it can disguise the operation of problematic power relations. Key thinkers in mainstream liberal political theory – including John Rawls[12] and Ronald Dworkin[13] – have been criticised from a number of quarters for developing sterile frameworks for justice and rights that require the removal of social actors from their everyday environments.[14] In contrast, a prominent theme among many feminists has been the need to attend to context, to situate legal problems and to understand their purported solutions within the concrete relationships and situations that give them meaning. This requires paying attention to the law in action – how it is interpreted and applied – as much as, if not more than, the law in theory. It demands embracing the complexities and 'messiness' of social interaction, and an understanding of the human individual as a fundamentally relational entity. This is not to say that context and connection are universally perceived as empowering: relational constructions of femininity have been a source of both admiration and denigration, and the socio-economic disadvantages associated with women's caring responsibilities have been significant. But it is to insist that living is a social phenomenon: relationships shape our identities, communities frame the parameters and meanings of our conduct, and, inevitably, the spaces, functioning and potential of law as a social phenomenon are determined by this.[15]

2. A rejection of the 'myths' of legal rationality and neutrality

It is also a common theme in much feminist legal theory that formalist assertions of law's operation as a closed, coherent and distinctive system of

12 J. Rawls, *A Theory of Justice*, Oxford: Clarendon Press, 1971.
13 R. Dworkin, *A Matter of Principle*, Oxford: Oxford University Press, 1985.
14 M. Sandel, *Liberalism and the Limits of Justice*, Cambridge: Cambridge University Press, 1982; A. MacIntyre, *Whose Justice? Which Rationality?* London: Duckworth, 1988; S. Okin, *Justice, Gender and the Family*, New York: Basic Books, 1989; and C. Pateman, *The Sexual Contract*, Cambridge: Polity Press, 1988.
15 West, 'Jurisprudence and Gender'; and E. Frazer and N. Lacey, *The Politics of Community: A Feminist Critique of the Liberal-Communitarian Debate*, Hemel Hempstead: Harvester Wheatsheaf, 1983.

reasoning, with its own language and methods, should be rejected. Alongside prominent Critical Legal Studies scholars,[16] many feminists have insisted that the law, rather than being a seamless web of principles awaiting discovery through legal reasoning,[17] is a patchwork of politically motivated choices, selected on the basis of their ability to support the status quo of (gender) power relations. Legal decision-makers do not neutrally apply legal rules or interpret broader principles to decipher inevitable outcomes; on the contrary, they make partial (and often self-interested) appraisals, which are retrospectively cloaked in the trappings of neutrality through constructed doctrines of precedent and natural justice.

Building upon this, feminist work has often been marked by a commitment to uncover the politics of law's operation, to highlight the biases of its agents, and to deconstruct the systems and discourses that disguise this as legal rationality. Striking incarnations of this critique can be found, for example, in a range of jurisdictionally specific 'feminist judgment projects' in which commentators have taken on the role of 'feminist judge', using the rules and precedents available at the time to re-visit leading cases and explore the extent to which, with different choices, they might have been decided more progressively. Such projects, though operating from the 'inside' of law by adopting its pretensions to precedent and inductive reasoning, provide a powerful counter-illustration of the malleability of legal forms and expose the extent to which, behind a façade of neutrality and rationality, lies a complex amalgam of power, privilege and partisan perspectives.[18]

3. A mindfulness of the power, and the limits, of law

Though feminist legal theorists, by definition, are interested in the ways in which law shapes and legitimates patterns of gender relations, there is a shared ambivalence regarding the extent to which law as a form of social ordering

---

16 D. Kennedy, *A Critique of Adjudication*, Cambridge, MA: Harvard University Press, 1997; and R. Unger, 'The Critical Legal Studies Movement', *Harvard Law Review* 96, 1983, 561.

17 cf. R. Dworkin, *Law's Empire*, Cambridge, MA: Harvard University Press, 1986.

18 See, generally, the Women's Court of Canada; also R. Hunter, C. McGlynn and E. Rackley (eds), *Feminist Judgments: From Theory to Practice*, Oxford: Hart Publishing, 2010; H. Douglas, F. Bartlett, T. Luker and R. Hunter (eds), *Australian Feminist Judgments: Righting and Rewriting Law*, Oxford: Hart Publishing, 2015; K. Stanchi, L. Berger and B. Crawford (eds), *Feminist Judgments: Rewritten Opinions of the United States Supreme Court*, Cambridge: Cambridge University Press, 2016; M. Enright and A. O'Donoghue (eds), *Northern/Irish Feminist Judgments: Judges' Troubles and the Gendered Politics of Identity*, Oxford: Hart Publishing, 2017.

has the capacity to create meaningful change. For the most trenchant critics of the liberal state, the law is deeply implicated within patriarchal structures, operating to legitimate and disguise the myriad violent consequences that they etch upon the lives, and bodies, of women.[19] And yet, at the same time, the impulse to resort to the law – to use 'the masters' tools'[20] – in order to campaign for and bring about reform has a measure of irresistibility. Whether selective critical amnesia or a pragmatic concessionary tactic, feminists have typically been reluctant to abandon altogether what Carol Smart referred to as 'the siren call of law',[21] and have often continued to engage with the state in pursuit of legal reforms. But, for many feminists, this process has been marked by an appreciation of the dangers of ceding too much power to law as a form of knowledge and control. It has been emphasised that feminist-driven reforms, even when *prima facie* achieved within legal frameworks, are at perpetual risk of co-option, capture or undoing by more regressive political, economic and social forces in the process of their translation and application; and that the attendant encroachment of legal authority upon women's lives may have damaging effects.[22]

Lay decision-making: a feminist testing ground

Feminists have engaged with the 'legal' in a variety of contexts and spaces, but lay decision-making provides a particularly apt terrain for feminist analyses that emphasise the relevance of concrete context, the discretionary nature of legal outcomes, and the ways in which 'non-legal' factors influence the application and impact of legal rules. In the rest of this chapter, therefore, I focus on a series of studies that my colleagues and I have conducted, which were designed to explore and critically evaluate the mechanics, processes and outcomes of lay (or, at most, *quasi*-legal) decision-making in relation to rape, across two distinct areas of legal functioning, namely criminal justice and asylum. In a context in which many feminists have pointed to the regulation

19 MacKinnon, *Feminism Unmodified.*
20 A. Lorde, *Sister Outsider: Essays and Speeches*, Berkeley, CA: Crossing Press, 2007.
21 C. Smart, *Feminism and the Power of Law*, London: Routledge, 1989, 160.
22 See, e.g., K. Bumiller, *In an Abusive State: How Neoliberalism Appropriated the Feminist Movement*, Durham, NC: Duke University Press, 2008; V. Munro, 'Violence Against Women, "Victimhood" and the (Neo)Liberal State', in Davies and Munro, *The Research Companion to Feminist Legal Theory*; V. Munro, 'Shifting Sands: Consent, Context and Vulnerability in Contemporary Sexual Offences Policy in England and Wales', *Social and Legal Studies*, forthcoming 2017; but cf. J. Halley, *Split Decisions: How and Why to Take a Break from Feminism*, Princeton, NJ: Princeton University Press, 2006.

of sexuality – both the regimes that determine the parameter of acceptable and unacceptable intrusion, as well as the social tropes about (hetero)sexual desire, mating conventions and (mis)communication that inform them – as a litmus test for gender relations,[23] these studies raise crucial insights about women's embodied experiences under the law, as well as about the ways in which decision-makers cement, enforce, challenge and resist the law's application of patriarchal norms and structures.

In the discussion below, I will first provide a brief account of the research questions, and methods of data collection and analysis, that drove these studies, before moving on to reflect more broadly on the extent and ways in which, consciously or otherwise, they can be characterised as 'feminist'; and on the advantages and disadvantages that such an orientation has brought to bear.

(i) Jury decision-making in criminal rape trials

Across a series of three consecutive ESRC-funded projects, the first of which was conducted in 2003, my co-investigators and I have explored the ways in which (mock) jurors approach the task of deliberating towards a unanimous verdict in contested rape trials, exposing the factors that influence the content, direction and dynamics of those deliberations. Each of these projects had its own distinctive focus – the first explored the approach taken by jurors to a complainant who was intoxicated at the time of the alleged assault, and examined the extent to which evaluations of credibility and responsibility might be affected by the means by which she became intoxicated, the nature of the intoxicating substance and the level of the defendant's intoxication.[24] The second study explored the extent to which providing jurors with 'myth-busting' education (through expert evidence or extended judicial direction) might impact the tone and direction of deliberations involving complainants

23 S. Brownmiller, *Against Our Will: Men, Women and Rape*, New York: Simon & Schuster, 1975; S. Lees, *Carnal Knowledge: Rape on Trial*, London: Penguin, 1993; MacKinnon, *Feminism Unmodified*; L. Gotell, 'Rethinking Affirmative Consent in Canadian Law: Neoliberal Sexual Subjects and Risky Women', *Akron Law Review* 41, 2008, 865; L. Gotell, 'Reassessing the Place of Criminal Law Reform in the Struggle against Sexual Violence', in A. Powell, N. Henry and A. Flynn (eds), *Rape Justice: Beyond the Criminal Law*, London: Palgrave Macmillan, 2015; S. Cowan, 'Freedom and Capacity to Make a Choice: A Feminist Analysis of Consent in the Criminal Law of Rape', in V. Munro and C. Stychin (eds), *Sexuality and the Law: Feminist Engagements*, London: Routledge-Cavendish, 2007.

24 E. Finch and V. Munro, 'Breaking Boundaries? Sexual Consent in the Jury Room', *Legal Studies* 26(3), 2006, 303; E. Finch and V. Munro, 'The Demon Drink and the Demonised Woman: Socio-Sexual Stereotypes and Responsibility Attribution in Rape Trials Involving Intoxicants', *Social & Legal Studies* 16(4), 2007, 591.

who displayed what might otherwise be regarded as counter-intuitive behaviours, namely, failing to physically resist the attacker, failing to report the attack immediately to the police and failing to appear emotionally distraught while giving testimony in the courtroom.[25] And, most recently, the third study explored whether, and in what ways, the fact of a complainant giving testimony with the benefit of 'special measures' (either a screen in the courtroom, a live video-link or pre-recorded evidence-in-chief) influenced jurors' perceptions of her credibility and attendant verdict outcomes.[26]

But individually and collectively, these projects were also engaged in the broader enterprise of charting and interrogating the ways in which popular understandings of what rape looks like, expectations in relation to 'normal' heterosexual mating and dating behaviour, and attributions of responsibility for sexual (mis)communication influenced the substance and outcome of jury deliberations.[27] Moreover, in a context in which observation of, and research about the content of, 'real' jury deliberations is prohibited by the Contempt of Court Act 1981, they provided a glimpse into the discursive dynamics of that process, the ways in which jurors communicate and defend their conclusions to peers, the significance of verdict polls, the impact of the presence of a 'strong' foreperson, and the relevance of gender and other socio-demographics.[28]

In each study, a similar method was adopted to simulate and collect deliberation data. Jury service eligible participants were recruited from the general public and asked to observe a real-time re-enactment of one of a

25 L. Ellison and V. Munro, 'Reacting to Rape: Exploring Mock Jurors' Assessments of Complainant Credibility', *British Journal of Criminology* 49(2), 2009, 202; L. Ellison and V. Munro, 'Turning Mirrors into Windows? Assessing the Impact of (Mock) Juror Education in Rape Trials', *British Journal of Criminology* 49(3), 2009, 363.

26 L. Ellison and V. Munro, 'A Special Delivery? Exploring the Impact of Screens, Live Links and Video-Recorded Evidence on Mock Juror Deliberation in Rape Trials', *Social & Legal Studies* 23(1), 2014, 3.

27 L. Ellison and V. Munro, 'Better the Devil You Know? "Real Rape" Stereotypes and the Relevance of a Previous Relationship in (Mock) Juror Deliberation', *International Journal of Evidence & Proof* 14, 2013, 299; L. Ellison and V. Munro, 'A Stranger in the Bushes or an Elephant in the Room? Critical Reflections on Received Rape Myth Wisdom in the Context of a Mock Jury Study', *New Criminal Law Review* 13(4), 2010, 781; L. Ellison and V. Munro, 'Of "Normal Sex" and "Real Rape": Exploring the Use of Socio-Sexual Scripts in (Mock) Jury Deliberation', *Social & Legal Studies* 18(3), 2009, 1.

28 L. Ellison and V. Munro, 'Telling Tales: Exploring Narratives of Life and Law within the (Mock) Jury Room', *Legal Studies* 35(2), 2015, 201; L. Ellison and V. Munro, 'Getting to (Not) Guilty: Examining Jurors' Deliberative Processes in, and Beyond, the Context of a Mock Rape Trial', *Legal Studies* 30(1), 2010, 74.

series of scripted mini-rape trials that were modified in line with isolated study-relevant variables. Scripts for the trials were created in consultation with a number of criminal justice practitioners, and actors and barristers were recruited to play key roles within the re-enactments. After observing the 'trial', participants were provided with a judicial direction, crafted in accordance with prevailing Bench Book guidance, and then streamed off into juries of eight to deliberate towards a unanimous, or failing that (and only after 75 minutes) majority, verdict. Deliberations were audio- and video-recorded, and then transcribed for analysis. In chapter 3 of this collection, Mandy Burton gives further details regarding the mechanics by which we gathered our deliberation data in these studies, and reflects upon their merits and demerits, as well as their potential to mitigate the chasm of verisimilitude that has often plagued vignette-based simulation studies.[29]

(ii) Home Office decision-making in asylum rape claims

Credibility is frequently acknowledged as the first (and most significant) hurdle to be overcome in the process of successfully securing asylum status,[30] and it is well established that a large proportion of women seeking asylum in the United Kingdom will have, or at least will claim to have, experienced sexual violence in the context of, or as part of their reason for, fleeing from their lives in their home countries.[31] Against this background, this project – funded

29 For further discussion, see also E. Finch and V. Munro, 'Lifting the Veil: The Use of Focus Groups and Trial Simulations in Legal Research', *Journal of Law & Society* 35, 2008, 30.

30 International Association of Refugee Law Judges, 'A Guide on the Assessment of Credibility in International Protection Procedures', 2013, http://www.asylum lawdatabase.eu/en/content/international-association-refugee-law-judges-guide-assessment-credibility-international (accessed 7 March 2017). For further discussion on the challenges of establishing credibility, see also M. Kagan, 'Is Truth in the Eye of the Beholder? Objective Credibility Assessment in Refugee Status Determinations', *Georgetown Immigration Law Journal* 17(3), 2003, 367; D. Bögner, C. Brewin and J. Herlihy, 'The Impact of Sexual Violence on Disclosure during Home Office Interviews', *British Journal of Psychiatry* 191(7), 2007, 75; and J. Herlihy, P. Scragg and S. Turner, 'Discrepancies in Autobiographical Memories-Implications for the Assessment of Asylum Seekers: Repeated Interview Study', *British Medical Journal* 7333, 2002, 324.

31 Asylum Aid, *Unsustainable: The Quality of Initial Decision-Making in Women's Asylum Cases*, London: Asylum Aid, 2011; London School of Hygiene and Tropical Medicine & Scottish Refugee Council, *Asylum Seeking Women, Violence and Health*, London: LSHTM & SRC, 2009; Refugee Council Briefing, *The Experiences of Asylum-seeking Women and Girls in the UK*, London: Refugee Council, 2012.

by Nuffield – examined the ways in which asylum decision-makers handle and evaluate claims of sexual violence made as part of women's claims for refugee status. It explored parallels with the criminal justice system, where presumptions regarding what constitutes a credible victim account are similarly marked by expectations of coherent narratives and complete recall, notwithstanding the disassociative effects of trauma experienced by complainants;[32] but it also highlighted the distinctive ways in which cultural and linguistic factors, and the existence of a 'politics of disbelief', may entrench barriers to being heard and believed in asylum decision-making.[33]

The study involved over 100 semi-structured interviews with key stakeholders, including immigration judges, Home Office case officers and presenting officers, solicitors specialising in asylum and immigration, interpreters involved in asylum proceedings and NGO/support organisations. In addition, we undertook a series of observations of First Tier Tribunal appeal hearings across a number of UK sites, focusing particularly on cases involving female appellants who had previously disclosed an allegation of rape. During these observations, the researcher took detailed notes (often verbatim) of the statements made by Home Office presenting officers and immigration judges, as well as counsel for the applicant (where present) and – far more infrequently – the applicant herself. The researcher also recorded her observations regarding the overall environment of the tribunal centre and hearing room, and the apparent demeanour of, and interaction between, participants. In a number of the cases where tribunal appeals were thus observed, the research team were also able to secure access to surrounding case file documents, including Home Office refusal letters and final tribunal decisions. This provided a valuable context within which to understand the appeal proceedings in the given case, as well as the overall asylum application journey.

The substantive findings of all these studies have been discussed in detail elsewhere, and the aim in this chapter is not to replicate that discussion. Instead, in what follows, I aim to reflect specifically on the ways in which these studies might be seen to be 'feminist' in their orientation, and on the additional insights that this theoretical and methodological approach brought to bear upon their findings. In addition, though, I highlight some of the ways in which their feminist ambitions were frustrated somewhat by the politics and

32 H. Baillot, S. Cowan and V. Munro, 'Reason to (Dis)Believe? Evaluating the Rape Claims of Women Seeking Asylum in the UK', *International Journal of Law in Context* 10(1), 2014, 105.

33 H. Baillot, S. Cowan and V. Munro, 'Hearing the Right Gaps: Enabling and Responding to Disclosures of Sexual Violence within the UK Asylum', *Social & Legal Studies* 21(3), 2012, 269.

pragmatics of research design, and more broadly by the inevitable tensions of using 'the masters' tools'.

Mastery, tools and methods: some feminist reflections

At the heart of each of these projects was a fundamental commitment to 'asking the woman question'[34] – that is, to uncovering and subjecting to critical scrutiny the ways in which legal frameworks impact upon the lives and experiences of women. Although they often also cast light on the handling and evaluation of men's allegations of sexual violence (which can in themselves be an appropriate subject matter for feminist analysis and insight), women were the primary focus – partly as a consequence of the statistically disproportionate levels of sexual violence perpetrated upon women, and partly because the interconnections between victimisation, (hetero)sexualisation and femininity ensure that this continues to represent the paradigm of gender power. But – of course – not all research that is interested in women's experiences can, or should, be assumed to be feminist. 'Asking the woman question' may be the fundamental starting point for much feminist research, but it is by no means a solely determinative feature: resultant data regarding women's experiences must also be situated within broader contexts of (gender) power relations, and so too the precariousness of the constructions of 'reason' and 'normality' upon which these relations are often legitimised by powerful stakeholders must be subjected to critical scrutiny.[35]

Jurors in criminal rape trials are specifically directed by the judge to apply their 'combined good sense, experience and knowledge of human nature and modern behaviour' (*R. v. Olugboja* (1981) 73 Cr App R 344) in evaluating the credibility and probative weight of the testimony with which they are presented, and in applying their individual and collective renderings of 'what took place' to determine a defendant's liability. This 'lay' perspective is often juxtaposed against 'legalistic' rationality as part of a broader narrative by which the centrality of the jury to the pursuit of a socially accountable justice is defended. At the same time, however, the unbridled nature of 'popular wisdom' has provoked much anxiety in the sexual offences context where research

---

34 K. Bartlett, 'Feminist Legal Methods', *Harvard Law Review* 103, 1989, 829; and L. Finley, 'The Nature of Domination and the Nature of Women: Reflections on Feminism Unmodified', *Northwestern University Law Review* 82, 1988, 352.
35 See, further, C. Littleton, 'Feminist Jurisprudence: The Difference Method Makes', *Stanford Law Review* 41, 1989, 751; M. Mossman, 'Feminism and Legal Method: The Difference It Makes', *Australian Journal of Law and Society* 3, 1986, 103; and Bartlett, 'Feminist Legal Methods'.

highlights the existence of problematic public perceptions regarding women's 'appropriate' (that is, non-provocative) sexual and social behaviour, and demanding expectations regarding the 'normal' responses of 'genuine' victims in terms of physical resistance, immediate reporting and so on.[36] The ESRC projects outlined above track the scale and impact of this 'common sense' understanding of sexual assault on the dynamics and outcomes of jury deliberation. They evidence the limited power of legal doctrine – specifically through the imposition of a test of objectively reasonable rather than subjective belief in consent (s. 2 of the Sexual Offences Act 2003) – to shift the balance of responsibility for negotiating and communicating sexual desire from the complainant to the defendant in the minds of lay decision-makers. Moreover, they highlight the tenacity of jurors' impulse to 'fill in the gaps' in the narratives provided by witnesses, often by relying on personal experiences and unfounded presumptions, and to cushion the excesses of hetero-normative sexuality with tropes regarding the ease with which signals can be misinterpreted as consent.

In the criminal justice context, it has long been debated whether evidence of similar preoccupations on the part of police and prosecutors are best attributed to personal or institutional biases in progression decision-making, or to pragmatic predictions of the likelihood of conviction based upon projections of jurors' likely perspectives in these regards. But what is clear is that such 'common sense justice' infiltrates and informs the bureaucratic machinery of the criminal justice process, and often in ways that reduce the prospects of redress for a number of rape complainants. Although the asylum study referred to above emerges in a quite different political, procedural and probative context, its findings also clearly illustrated the extent to which presumptions regarding gender and cultural norms, as well as the bounded parameters of political activity vis-à-vis 'mundane' sexual aggression, influenced – and often determined – the outcomes of asylum decision-making, irrespective of formal rules and protocols. A lower burden of proof is required in asylum contexts, designed to give applicants the benefit of the doubt, in recognition of the difficulties that are often encountered in providing objective evidence to corroborate narratives of persecution and predictions of future threat. Despite this, and notwithstanding the at least formally non-adversarial structure of

36 M. Burt, 'Cultural Myths and Support for Rape', *Journal of Personality and Social Psychology* 38, 1980, 217; K. Lonsway and L. Fitzgerald, 'Rape Myths', *Psychology of Women Quarterly* 18, 1994, 220; H. Gerger, H. Kley, G. Bohner and F. Siebler, 'The Acceptance of Modern Myths about Sexual Aggression (AMMSA) Scale: Development and Validation in German and English', *Aggressive Behaviour* 33, 2007, 422; and J. Temkin and B. Krahe, *Sexual Assault and the Justice Gap: A Question of Attitude*, Oxford: Hart Publishing, 2008.

first instance and appeal asylum decision-making, this study highlighted parallels with the criminal justice system's handling of rape in relation to the suspicion encountered by complainants who failed to conform to expectations in terms of demeanour, behaviour before or after the alleged attack, ability to provide detailed and consistent retrospective accounts and so on. A suspicion that was compounded by a political climate – both in the Home Office, and in the United Kingdom more generally – in which asylum-seekers are seen as presumptively untrustworthy, and a 'problem' to be managed and contained by state officials.

To this extent, both of these projects transcend the immediate parameters of a focus on women's experiences, and the dynamics of sexual domination specifically, to contribute broader feminist insights regarding the limited impact of legal doctrine, the scale and impact of discretion and bias in the application of 'legal' decision-making, and the ways in which the operation of legal structures cannot be meaningfully detached from social contexts and political agendas. The asylum research in particular also highlighted – within the confines of an empirical study – the necessity of consciously engaging with the intersectionality of women's gendered experiences of 'violence', 'protection' and 'voice'. But there are other key ways in which a feminist sensitivity to the role and relevance of power, relationality and context also played out in these studies to produce additional insights. More specifically, these studies – in different ways – highlighted the impossibility of detachment and impartiality in the face of others' narratives of abuse, particularly when one is tasked with the responsibility for attributing blame and bringing about life-changing consequences in their light.

The bureaucratic structures of the asylum process, as much as the investigative and adversarial protocols of the criminal justice system, promote the myth of 'professional' distance and deliberative neutrality. For feminists, such pretensions send alarm bells ringing, and these studies should strengthen their volume. In the jury studies, notwithstanding the fact that participants knew that their involvement in deliberations was 'mock', there was considerable evidence that jurors experienced stress as a consequence of observing the trial, negotiating with peers towards a collective verdict, and returning that judgment upon the parties before them. Disbelief was suspended to the extent that several jurors commented on how emotionally difficult they had found the deliberation process, noting that they felt a burden of responsibility for determining the fate of the defendant and complainant, and suggesting – for example – that they 'won't sleep tonight' as a consequence. There is every reason to suspect that in a 'real' trial, where jurors are exposed to greater amounts of evidence, much of it potentially graphic and brutal, over an extended period marked by numerous disruptions and delays, and are required to reach a verdict upon which there is no doubt that very real consequences will befall the trial parties, the emotional labour referred to by our mock participants will be particularly acute;[37] and yet, jurors continue to be selected at random, provided with very little information regarding what is expected of them and directed at the end of their service that to talk about their experiences in the jury room again would be a contempt of court for which they may face punishment. This has ramifications both for the ethical treatment of lay participants within the criminal justice system, and for our appreciation of the ways in which – under such emotional pressure – jurors may become increasingly susceptible to coping strategies that demonise or depersonalise trial participants, or invoke cognitive shortcuts in order to expedite their emotional exposure.[38]

Similarly, in the asylum study, a prominent theme that emerged from the interview data was the extent to which quasi-legal decision-makers, employed by the Home Office to interpret and apply the provisions of the Refugee Convention and associated doctrine but often without formal legal qualifications, struggled to manage the emotional labour involved in being exposed to, and deliberating upon, narratives of abuse on a recurring basis. The institutional and political context in which asylum decision-making takes place, moreover, increased the sense of 'burn-out' and 'compassion fatigue' exhibited by a number of participants, and threatened to significantly reduce the prospects for justice for individual asylum-seekers. Home Office personnel were seen, in some – but not all – cases to disengage from the specifics of each narrative, viewing them – collectively – as 'stories' that should be met with presumptive suspicion. What was also apparent in this study, and amplified when cast through a feminist lens that is mindful of the politicised nature of personal experience and the significance of relationship and community to personal identity, were the ways in which the background of the interpreter in asylum proceedings can have a considerable impact not only upon the applicant's experience of the process and her prospects for being able to 'tell her story' effectively and convincingly, but also upon the interpreter, and his/her emotional well-being in this interaction. Interpreters – many of whom will have come from the same community as the applicant, and may have experienced, or known family and friends who experienced, the dynamics of

37 N. Robertson, G. Davies and A. Nettleingham, 'Vicarious Traumatisation as a Consequence of Jury Service', *Howard Journal of Criminal Justice* 48, 2009, 1.
38 L. Ellison and V. Munro, 'Taking Trauma Seriously: Critical Reflections on the Criminal Justice Process', *International Journal of Evidence and Proof*, forthcoming, http://journals.sagepub.com/doi/abs/10.1177/1365712716655168 (accessed 27 March 2017).

persecution that the applicant recounts – often reported high levels of emotional upset as a consequence of their professional involvement, with several commenting that they had been reduced to tears after hearings. Meanwhile, it was apparent that – for applicants – the cultural and political orientation of the interpreter (whether actual or surmised) made a crucial difference to their ability to recount experiences openly. This served, in many cases, to increase the emotional challenges already experienced by applicants who are being asked (often on a repeated basis) to narrate traumatic events to satisfy others' evaluation, in unfamiliar and frequently intimidating bureaucratic or tribunal environments.[39]

In both contexts, then, when the veil of law's pretence at neutrality and rationality is – at least partially – lifted, the inherently emotional nature of criminal justice and asylum decision-making, for quasi-legal professional and lay participants alike, begins to emerge; and with it arises a raft of questions regarding how best to acknowledge and attend to that emotionality, and support decision-makers in managing it effectively and productively, in ways that ultimately increase rather than reduce the prospects for a just outcome. In these respects, both studies are indebted to, and influenced by, feminist theories and methods, and can be seen to go beyond merely 'asking the woman question' in specific legal contexts, in order to uncover surrounding power dynamics and their relational ramifications.

But there are also some important ways in which these projects perhaps fell short of their feminist methodological ambitions. The primary focus of the Nuffield study was an exploration of the bases upon which adjudicators assessed credibility and made decisions in relation to women's asylum claims. But to the extent that the processes through which this reasoning was channelled also had profound experiential impacts upon both decision-makers and claimants, the absence of women's voices is lamentable. Women's experiences were represented in this study, but they were mediated in interviews through the lens of NGO support workers' and others' interpretations, and the paper-based format and intimidating environment of the appeal tribunal entailed that women's voices were rarely directly heard in this forum. The research team took a conscious decision – grounded on ethical and pragmatic considerations – not to conduct interviews with women claimants, but this does diminish the texture with which their experiences can be discerned in the study, and raises important questions about representation, authenticity and voice for feminist purposes. But this is a restriction that also speaks to some

---

39 H. Baillot, S. Cowan and V. Munro, 'Second-Hand Emotion? Exploring the Contagion of Trauma and Distress in the Asylum Law Context', *Journal of Law & Society* 40(4), 2013, 509.

of the broader methodological dilemmas – discussed below – that can be faced in conducting feminist empirical legal research, in particular as a consequence of the need to make strategic concessions to gatekeepers, and/or to make the substance of the research 'useful' (which also perhaps entails being palatable) to those with the power to bring about reform.

Feminist dilemmas: access, impact and what lies between

The power dynamics underpinning empirical research are often complicated. In many cases, it involves negotiating with gatekeepers to identify minimally intrusive mechanisms for securing access to required data, and satisfying stakeholder participants of the impartiality of the researchers, the rigour of the analysis process and the uses to which the resultant outcomes will be put. From the outset, these considerations can jar against feminist critical conventions, requiring an abstraction of research questions from the political context in which they originate, and an assertion of 'neutrality' – or at least a postponement of partiality – within the data collection and analysis process. Feminist researchers are often faced, therefore, with the choice of either being at least partially complicit in reaffirming artificial understandings of the social world, including the processes of engaged social research, or failing altogether to secure the empirical data with which to uncover, challenge – and seek to reform – problematic social behaviours. Navigating through this dilemma may involve a strategic 'softening' of feminist edges. So, too, at the end of the research process, while the achievement of 'impact' is often a precarious matter embedded within institutional and political vagaries beyond the control of the researcher, maximising 'pathways to impact' may entail – to some extent at least – a re-packaging of findings into concepts and remedial mechanisms that the 'legal community' already acknowledges, and can more readily digest and action, even where the harms and solutions suggested by the data sit somewhat askew.

In many senses, of course, this is just a replication in the research context of the broader dynamics and challenges encountered in rendering women's perspectives intelligible to powerful (typically male) elites. In the legal environment, these difficulties are amplified, moreover, by the tenacious insistence upon myths of legal rationality, abstraction and neutrality, which feminist work often deconstructs and yet cannot be allowed to entirely move beyond. And in the legal academy, there is reason to suspect that the tensions which this can generate will become even more acute, as increased emphasis is placed upon the need to ensure that the products of research are 'useful' to and liable to generate 'impact'. While such impact can be felt among a variety of constituencies within the community, where research outcomes are directed at bringing about reforms to existing legal institutions, processes and practices, it entails a delicate negotiation of power relationships with those individuals or organisations with the imputed capability to agitate for, or secure, such reforms. What is more, it often involves a strategic forgetting of work that deconstructs this simplistic and linear model and its implicit assumption that any such legal reforms will in turn ensure predicable and effective changes in underlying social practices.

In much the same way as with feminist legal theory more broadly, then, feminist (empirical) legal researchers may ultimately have little choice but to consciously 'play the game'. In the process of ensuring access to data and maximising the impact of our findings, this may, at times, require participating in the perpetuation of half-truths about what the law is, how it operates, and what capacity it has to bring about social change; but staunchly refusing to do so, for all the critical integrity it might bring, may frustrate and potentially paralyse our impulse for pragmatic improvements in the pursuit of social justice. The challenge, then, is to be mindful of the trade-offs that researchers make in this context, of why we make them, the ways in which they skew our analysis, and of what is otherwise at stake.

Recommended reading

Smart, C., *Feminism and the Power of Law*, London: Routledge, 1989.

MacKinnon, C., *Feminism Unmodified: Discourses on Life and Law*, Cambridge, MA: Harvard University Press, 1987.

Davies, M. and Munro, V. (eds), *The Research Companion to Feminist Legal Theory*, Aldershot: Ashgate Publishing, 2013).

Bartlett, K., 'Feminist Legal Methods', *Harvard Law Review* 103, 1989, 829.

Ramazanoglu, C. and Holland, J., *Feminist Methodologies: Challenges and Choices*, London: Sage, 2002.

10 Law and anthropology

Legal pluralism and 'lay' decision-making

Anthony Good

When anthropologists study law, their characteristic approach is to treat lawyers as they would any other exotic group, by trying to understand the distinctive modes of thought that characterise legal specialists and may set them apart from those making use of their services. In some societies or situations, knowledge of law and procedures is widely shared among the population, while in others it has become differentiated from everyday knowledge through professionalisation. However, even when they are studying a hegemonic, state-endorsed legal system managed by specialists, the typical stance of the legal anthropologist is that 'legislation, court judgments and legal scientific publications [are] in the first place "data", "folk systems" having the same status as legal conceptions of religious or traditional authorities elsewhere'.[1]

Almost by definition, the anthropology of law is concerned with legal pluralism in one or more of the senses of that term explored below. So almost by definition, too, the notion of 'lay decision-making' becomes complex and problematic. The lay/professional dichotomy only seems truly straightforward in the context of a single legal system and a single set of legal professionals, a situation which – with all due respect to the legal centralism perspective discussed below – scarcely, if ever, arises in practice. Usually there are parallel, even if hierarchically ranked, legal or quasi-legal systems available, but even if not, there are at least varied forms of 'legal consciousness'.[2]

---

1 F. von Benda-Beckmann, 'Riding or Killing the Centaur? Reflections on the Identities of Legal Anthropology', *International Journal of Law in Context* 85, 2008, 85–110, at 97. For a partly overlapping discussion of some of the issues raised in this chapter, with a specific focus on the work of Franz von Benda-Beckmann, see A. Good, 'Folk Models and the Law', *Journal of Legal Pluralism and Unofficial Law* 47(3), 2015, 423–37.
2 S. Engle Merry, *Getting Justice and Getting Even: Legal Consciousness Among Working-class Americans*, Chicago, IL: University of Chicago Press, 1990, 5.

Broadly speaking, the relationship between law and anthropology as academic disciplines can be seen as analogous to that between different legal orders in situations of legal pluralism, because they provide not merely alternative research methods, but also, more fundamentally, alternative modes of conceptual thought.[3] There are some striking disciplinary differences that need to be taken into account if anthropological methods are to be fruitfully employed in the study of law.

Above all, and of particular relevance here, 'judges have a duty to *decide . . .* scientists and historians mainly *conclude*'.[4] In this connection it is useful to recall Ehrlich's distinction between 'rules for decision' and 'rules of conduct'. Because so much legal education is vocational, designed to train future advocates and judges for their 'tradesman-like' professional roles, legal scholars tend to concentrate on the first of these – the rules by which judges or state officials decide legal disputes.[5] Anthropologists take a broader approach, because as social scientists they seek to explain events in more general terms; their primary focus is not on the faults of particular individuals. While actions and their consequences are assessed normatively by lawyers, social scientists seek to describe and explain them as aspects of local culture and practice. In short, law is prescriptive, while social science is descriptive. A third, related, contrast involves notions of causality. For lawyers, causality involves identifying responsibility, and every injury is presumed to have a human agent as its primary cause. Social scientists, by contrast, while they may recognise individual actions as the immediate causes of particular outcomes, tend to see their ultimate causes as systemic.[6] Finally, in terms of the distinctions dealt with below, the discourse of lawyers is overwhelmingly 'rule oriented', whereas that of social scientists is predominantly 'relationally oriented'.

It is also important to be clear from the start, though, that these differences are not confined to the only-to-be-expected dissimilarities between law as professional practice and anthropology as research discipline. The anthropology of law and the academic *study* of law – what continental European scholars term

3 G. Anders, 'Law at Its Limits: Interdisciplinarity between Law and Anthropology', *Journal of Legal Pluralism and Unofficial Law* 47(3), 2015, 411–22, at 420.

4 W. Twining, *Rethinking Evidence: Exploratory Essays*, 2nd edn, Cambridge: Cambridge University Press, 2006, 253, emphasis added.

5 E. Ehrlich. *Fundamental Principles of the Sociology of Law*, trans. Walter L. Moll, New Brunswick, NJ and London: Transaction, 2002 [1936], 8.

6 R. F. Kandel, 'Six Differences in Assumptions and Outlook between Anthropologists and Attorneys', in R. F. Kandel (ed.), *Double Vision: Anthropologists at Law*, NAPA Bulletin, No. 11, Washington, DC: American Anthropological Association, 1992, 1–4; and A. Good, *Anthropology and Expertise in the Asylum Courts*, London: Routledge-Cavendish, 2007, 29–34.

'legal science' – are also different in crucial ways. Legal science works at the interpretation of law from within the legal paradigm. It is fundamentally normative and dogmatic; concerned with elaborating the 'correct interpretations of general legal abstractions' with regard to particular, concrete cases, together with 'philosophical reflections on what and how law should be'.[7] Indeed, legal science is normative both in focus and in character. That is to say, its subject matter is legal norms, and it takes law itself as the primary object of study, in relative isolation from social and political context.[8] By contrast, legal anthropology is inherently descriptive, comparative and relativistic. Its primary aim is to describe and analyse from the outside, and while, as we shall see in a moment, it is important to understand insiders' concepts and how they are used, the analyses to which these concepts and their associated practices are subjected may draw upon notions that are not only external to the legal sphere, but sometimes depend upon competing or even conflicting premises.

In contrast to the dominant view among legal scholars, therefore, for anthropologists of law it does not matter whether the legal procedures being analysed have the status of 'state law' or 'folk law'; the approach should be the same. Moreover, they should not confine themselves to what, given their emphasis upon ethnographic method, is the most obvious niche for anthropologists studying law – that of describing the 'is', the everyday reality of legal practice. They must also take on the task of explicating the 'ought' – the black-letter law in the law books – rather than leaving such work to academic lawyers and legal philosophers alone. It is especially important for anthropologists of law to avoid the 'expertise-trap' of assuming that where formal state law is concerned they should simply accept what legal experts write about it; quite the opposite, they must always take care not to allow 'legalistic and ideological assumptions' to insinuate themselves within 'anthropological categories and theoretical assumptions'.[9]

Legal centralism and legal pluralism

Arthurs defines legal centralism as the dogma that there exists in common law systems a dominant normative order, defined by a general set of rules and principles ('the law', or the 'legal system') emanating from the state, which applies equally to all members of society and is enforced and applied through the ordinary courts and their associated institutions.[10] Any alternative

7 Benda-Beckmann, 'Riding or Killing the Centaur?', 94.
8 Anders, 'Law at Its Limits', 413.
9 Benda-Beckmann, 'Riding or Killing the Centaur?', 101.
10 H. W. Arthurs, *'Without the Law': Administrative Justice and Legal Pluralism in Nineteenth Century England*, Toronto: University of Toronto Press, 1985.

normative systems, such as religions, or alternate coercive systems, such as the rules enforced by employers upon their workers, are subordinated to the rule of law by means of review in those courts. Consequently, according to this view:

> Any rule-making, dispute-settling, norm-creating group or institution that is not a court or accountable to a court, or required to employ a court as its enforcement arm, or is not part of the state, or is not administered through legal professionals has nothing to do with 'law' in any meaningful sense and has thus . . . no claim on the attention of legal scholars.[11]

By definition, then, in the legal centralist approach 'law' is limited to the hegemonic, state-imposed courts, norms and sanctions. Many scholars therefore portray legal centralism and legal pluralism as 'contending processes'.[12] In fact, though, things are more complicated because the centralist approach is not inconsistent with some situations that social scientists might wish to label forms of legal pluralism.[13] For example, in India and Sri Lanka parallel systems of family law apply to different religious-cum-ethnic groups – Hindus, Muslims, Buddhists – but all of these are sanctioned by the state.[14]

Partly for this reason, Vanderlinden preferred to define legal pluralism as an attribute of a particular social grouping, not of 'law' or a particular legal system; indeed, it did not require the presence of more than one legal 'system' – a problematic notion anyway, since it implies a degree of external closure and internal consistency that can only arise ideologically rather than in practice – but only of multiple legal 'mechanisms':

> (L)e pluralisme juridique est *'l'existence, au sein d'une société déterminée, de mecanismes juridiques différents s'appliquant à des situations identiques'*.[15]

---

11 R. W. Gordon, 'Book Review: Without the Law II – *"Without the Law":
   Administrative Justice and Legal Pluralism in Nineteenth-Century England*, by H. W.
   Arthurs', *Osgoode Hall Law Journal* 24(20), 1986, 421–36, at 421.

12 J. Vincent, 'Law', in A. Barnard and J. Spencer (eds), *The Routledge Encyclopedia of
   Social and Cultural Anthropology*, 2nd edn, Abingdon: Routledge, 2012, 330–33, at
   332.

13 J. Griffiths, 'What Is Legal Pluralism?' *Journal of Legal Pluralism* 24, 1986, 1–55,
   at 5.

14 I. Jaising (ed.), *Men's Laws, Women's Lives: A Constitutional Perspective on Religion, Common
   Law, and Culture in South Asia*, New Delhi: Women Unlimited, 2005; and G. Solanki,
   *Adjudication in Religious Family Laws: Cultural Accommodation, Legal Pluralism, and
   Gender Equality in India*, New York: Cambridge University Press, 2011.

15 'Legal pluralism is *"the existence, at the heart of a given society, of different legal mechanisms
   applicable to identical situations."'* J. Vanderlinden, 'Le pluralisme juridique: essai de

More problematic, though, is his characterisation of legal pluralism as entailing the existence of different legal mechanisms applicable to 'identical' social situations. What does 'identical' actually mean here? Are particular acts (e.g. sales transactions) 'identical' whatever the social identities of the actors (e.g. business corporations or private individuals)? Sameness and difference are not intrinsic to actions themselves, but depend upon how those actions are identified and classified, and are thus ideological rather than empirical labels: they lie in 'the ways in which the "categorizing concepts" of a particular normative order *arrange* social facts, not in the facts themselves'.[16]

One cannot stop there, however, because that distinction between facts and norms is itself too simple. It is not merely that norms lead people to interpret a given set of facts in one way rather than another: more than that, it is largely the normative order itself that determines what counts as a 'fact' in any particular context, and which particular arguments can or cannot be made. Furthermore, ideologies do not arise or persist in a vacuum, but reflect at least to some degree the social and cultural positioning of those who espouse them. In any case, there are situations to which Griffiths' objection does not seem to apply – in which it is not a matter of different kinds of people acting in the 'same' way, but rather of the same person, in a given context, choosing between several alternative courses of action.

The Bohannan-Gluckman debate

The Bohannan-Gluckman debate of the late 1950s provides an ideal point of entry into some core concerns motivating the anthropology of law. It was a key episode in the development of the sub-discipline, and highlighted the centrality of comparison in anthropology more generally. But how, and at what stage of the analysis, should that comparison be carried out?

Two classic ethnographies in the anthropology of law canon, Max Gluckman's account of the jurisprudence of the Barotse in what was then Northern Rhodesia and Paul Bohannan's study of justice and judgment among the Tiv of Nigeria, appeared almost simultaneously, but took different stances on this matter. Gluckman's formalist approach led him to conclude that many Barotse legal concepts could 'without distortion after careful . . . description and discussion, be given English equivalents',[17] whereas Bohannan's substantivist position was

synthèse', in J. Gilissen (ed.), *Le Pluralisme Juridique*, Brussels: Université de Bruxelles, 1971, 19–56, at 19, original quotation marks and emphasis.

16 Griffiths, 'What Is Legal Pluralism?', 13, emphasis in the original.
17 M. Gluckman, *The Judicial Process among the Barotse of Northern Rhodesia*, Manchester: Manchester University Press, 1955, 380–81.

that 'Tiv have "laws" but do not have "law"'.[18] He focused on what he termed the Tiv 'folk model' or 'folk legal system' rather than employing Western legal concepts in his analysis.

The decade-long debate that ensued is therefore generally portrayed as being concerned with the validity of using Western legal categories in the ethnographic study of non-Western legal systems.[19] In fact, though, Gluckman was entirely in agreement with Bohannan over the need to take Barotse legal categories seriously and study them in their own terms; as exemplified below, much of his analysis was conducted with reference to indigenous terminology. However, he did not see this as the end of the analysis, but the beginning. This difference reflected broader differences in national approach. To most British-trained social anthropologists, the degree of focus on indigenous categories in certain branches of American cultural anthropology risked turning anthropology into a solipsistic discipline in which comparison became impossible. Moreover, these cultural analyses often resorted to paradoxically formal, abstract means of representing the supposedly indigenous categories. Thus, Bohannan explicitly aligned his approach to developments in two then-fashionable but quite abstract trends in American cultural anthropology – componential analysis[20] and ethnoscience[21] – and even made what now seem very dated comments about the possibility of simulating socio-cultural systems using computer languages like Fortran![22]

There is the further danger that such 'cultural' approaches may misrepresent the status of indigenous models, which generally do not serve as would-be consistent, philosophical world views. Folk models are better seen as resources that people can use strategically to justify their own behaviour or criticise that

---

18 P. Bohannan, *Justice and Judgment among the Tiv of Nigeria*, London: Oxford University Press, 1957, 57.

19 The debate was not quite so straightforward, not least because it went on for so long. By the late 1960s, the protagonists seemed to be advocating positions rather different from those they had taken at the start, and were actually rather closer than had at first seemed: P. Bohannan, 'Ethnography and Comparison in Legal Anthropology', in L. Nader (ed.), *Law in Culture and Society*, Chicago, IL: Aldine, 1969, 411–18; M. Gluckman, 'Concepts in the Comparative Study of Tribal Law', in Nader, *Law in Culture and Society*, 349–73.

20 W. H. Goodenough, 'Componential Analysis and the Study of Meaning', *Language* 32(1), 1956, 195–216.

21 W. C. Sturtevant, 'Studies in Ethnoscience', *American Anthropologist* 66(3), 1964, 99–131.

22 Bohannan, 'Ethnography and Comparison in Legal Anthropology', 403, 415. Fortran is a computer language developed in the 1950s, used mainly for numerical computing in science and engineering.

of others, rather than as indigenous counterparts to social or legal theory. They are certainly not intended to be comparative in the way anthropological models must always be. This aspect of the debate was neatly characterised by Moore as a disagreement over the significance of legal categories:

> Gluckman sees the concepts and principles of law as part of legal systems, whereas Bohannan is most interested in studying the concepts themselves, because he considers them a reflection of the whole organization of the legal system. To Gluckman, these concepts and principles are manipulable tools within legal systems, part of their equipment, not reflections of their organization.[23]

Bohannan's own use of the term 'folk system' changed markedly over time. By 1969, he was phrasing things very differently:

> I was overeager in *Justice and Judgment* to say that a folk system is what the people think and say . . . [I]f the anthropologist can get the ideas so straight that he can discuss them in detail with informants in their own language . . . then I think he has something that can reasonably be called a folk system [. . .] *a folk system is what an ethnographer thinks and says* that allows him to interact successfully with the people he is studying.[24]

Interaction of this kind is certainly an important aspiration for fieldworkers, as one means of ensuring that they have understood things correctly. But does it make sense to call this a 'folk system'? It seems utterly counter-intuitive to locate the 'folk system' in the mind of the analyst, rather than in the minds of the 'folk' themselves! How, if at all, does this differ from Gluckman's attempt to make sense of Barotse jurisprudence in terms of Western legal categories? At the very least, the seemingly stark contrast between their respective positions became far less apparent as time passed. Even so, this debate raised particularly pressing issues for anthropologists studying law, because – as already noted – their perspective is almost always comparative.

The Bohannan–Gluckman debate raises another question: is it possible to analyse indigenous or 'folk' legal systems in isolation? For Bohannan, it was essential to retain the Tiv term *jir* rather than translate it as 'court', because

---

23 S. Falk Moore, *Law as Process: An Anthropological Approach*, London: Routledge & Kegan Paul, 1978, 143.

24 Bohannan, 'Ethnography and Comparison in Legal Anthropology', 406, emphasis added.

only by so doing could he 'retain the essential ambiguity of the Tiv concept'; likewise, it would 'dissipate its force and truth' to give it several different English translations according to context.[25] Whatever the merits in principle of that position in a wholly isolated society (if such an entity exists), Bohannan's decision had already been overtaken by events in colonial-era Nigeria; indeed, the British had already attempted to administer the area using the very same elders' councils (*jir tamen*) that he was studying. It often happened that European colonists took up what they assumed to be the traditional local legal system, reinterpreted it to suit their own needs, and re-imposed it onto local people in the guise of 'customary law'.[26] Consequently, while it was of course likely that colonisers and colonised would understand the resulting 'legal' processes rather differently, that does not mean that one should or can analyse either understanding in isolation from the other. Moreover, it is crucial – especially in a colonial context – to take into account the power differentials involved in order to understand how the various processes of conflict resolution available to persons in a given social context operate, and how they intertwine or inter-relate with one another.[27] In short, while it is clearly important to understand 'state' law and 'folk' law on their own terms, such an understanding on its own may tell us relatively little.

From our present perspective, it is also interesting to look more closely at these two ethnographic contexts so as to consider whether, or to what extent, Tiv and Barotse legal procedures can be said to involve professional or lay decision-making.

Tiv society is made up of patrilineages and the territory occupied by a given patrilineal segment is called *tar*. Important men of many kinds are known as *ortaregh* (plural *mbatarev*), 'man of the *tar*', but although each *ortaregh* 'represents' a particular *tar*, they are not the 'headmen' of that *tar* as the colonial administration assumed. Partly because of this misunderstanding, a systematic hierarchy of *ortaregh* office-holders had been created, although prior to the 1930s the term had a looser, more general connotation, referring to any person of importance who performed ceremonies or arbitrated disputes. Disputes are said to 'spoil the *tar*' and the process of resolving such disputes through

25 Bohannan, *Justice and Judgment*, 8.
26 J. M. Donovan, *Legal Anthropology: An Introduction*, Lanham, MD: Bowman & Littlefield, 2008, 114–15.
27 F. von Benda-Beckmann, 'Who's Afraid of Legal Pluralism?' *Journal of Legal Pluralism* 47, 2002, 37–82, at 60. Indeed, the notion of 'legal pluralism' was first developed in just such a colonial context, by Dutch scholars working on Indonesia; Cornelis van Vollenhoven, *Miskenningen van het Adatrecht*, Leiden: E. J. Brill, 1909.

arbitration is called 'repairing the *tar*'. Indigenous courts, known as *jir*, range in jurisdiction from 'Grade-A native courts' with full judicial powers, to 'Grade-D courts' limited to minor civil claims and criminal offences. Districts contain from three to eight *mbatarev*, though usually there are four. One duty of an *ortaregh* is to attend the *jir* and contribute to its processes of decision-making and arbitration. Although anyone can attend and participate in a *jir* (the word means 'case' as well as 'court'), the *mbatarev* are its most important members, as shown by the fact that they are seated on chairs. In this capacity, an *ortaregh* is usually called *or-jir* (plural *mbajiriv*), 'man of the *jir*', a term which, says Bohannan, 'can be adequately translated "judge"'.[28]

The Lozi, the dominant group among the Barotse, call their courts *kutas*, while judges are called *indunas*. There is a hierarchy of courts, presided over by judges of appropriate social standing, ranging from 'politically instituted courts' at the apex of the system to 'informal courts of princes or councillors, or of villages or kinship groupings' at the bottom.[29] Only politically instituted courts can actually enforce their judgments, but Gluckman stresses that 'all these courts judge and apply law, and have to be reckoned as part of the juridical system'.[30] There is quite clearly a specifically legal aspect to Lozi governance, as distinct, for example, from its political and moral aspects. Thus, although the king confirms court decisions, he does not usually attend the actual hearing of cases, and even if he *is* present, things proceed as though he were not there. Moreover, Lozi distinguish 'legal' rules that courts have power to enforce from 'moral' rules over which they have no such power – although in practice judges seek ways to avoid fully supporting persons whom they consider 'right in law, but wrong in justice'. Their judgments in such cases are often 'sermons on filial, parental, and brotherly love'.[31]

As one moves up through the hierarchy of courts, from men making rulings as husbands and fathers at the base,[32] through courts presided over by village headmen, to *kutas* in the capital city, judges increasingly take on the character of appointed specialists. In the higher 'politically instituted' courts, three sets of *indunas* are involved, with different levels of seniority, each level being labelled a 'mat' because office-holders have the right to sit on particular mats in the court house:

---

28 Bohannan, *Justice and Judgment*, 1–11; notice how Bohannan's approach leads to a proliferation of indigenous terms, even in this brief account.
29 Gluckman, *The Judicial Process*, 22.
30 *Ibid.*, 26.
31 *Ibid.*, 22.
32 *Ibid.*, 26.

The positions of the titles on each mat are fixed, and if a title-holder is discharged, is promoted, or dies, his successor (who is appointed by the ruler-in-kuta) takes his position on the mat.[33]

The importance of seats for Tiv *mbajiriv*, and of mats for Lozi *indunas*, have obvious superficial parallels with the notion of a judicial 'bench' in English law! But should we regard these functionaries as legal professionals or as lay decision-makers? In the Tiv case, it does seem that a group of quasi-professional legal decision-makers has been brought into being through a kind of self-fulfilling prophecy, because of the assumption by colonial administrators that the degree of order manifest in Tiv society could only be possible if there were officials responsible for administering that order.[34] Yet even under the colonial administration, the role of arbitrator was open to anyone, not the exclusive preserve of *mbajiriv*. They were not the sole decision-makers, merely the most important and influential. Moreover, Tiv processes of dispute settlement are grounded in the *mbajiriv*'s knowledge of Tiv institutions and traditions in general, rather than their expertise regarding a specialised corpus of rules extracted from or regulating those social institutions or traditions.[35] Their authority, in other words, derives from their greater than average mastery of Tiv tradition, rather than their expertise in a specialised body of professional knowledge.

To a large degree, by contrast, Lozi can be said to have always had a specialised and independent judiciary, at least at the higher levels of the system. Yet even at the pinnacle of the hierarchy, *kutas* and *indunas* have other, non-judicial roles too, so Gluckman refers to them more broadly as 'councils' and 'councillors', respectively, except when speaking specifically about legal contexts. As a general rule, indeed, 'judges' in contexts such as these tend to adjudicate in a rather broader sense than is the case in Euro-American legal systems.[36] Nonetheless, it seems appropriate to portray the Lozi system as one in which legal decision-making becomes less a task for 'lay' social figures, and more a task for (supra-)legal professionals, as one moves up through the juridical hierarchy.

Clearly, though, it is no simple matter in either case to differentiate professional and lay decision-making in legal or quasi-legal contexts, although

33 *Ibid.*, 7.
34 Bohannan, *Justice and Judgment*, 9.
35 *Ibid.*, 96.
36 D. Black and M. P. Baumgartner, 'Toward a Theory of the Third Party', in K. O. Boyum and L. Mather (eds), *Empirical Theories about Courts*, New Orleans: Quid Pro Books, 2015 [1983], 84–114.

the posing of the question in those terms does provide us with some analytical purchase with which to examine these two systems. It seems highly likely that comparable complexities will be thrown up by almost any case that anthropologists choose to examine, and that they are by no means confined to the colonial contexts dealt with in this section.

The post-colonial context

It was, however, in the colonial setting that the notion of 'legal pluralism' first arose, which meant that plural legal systems were initially seen as complementary but unequal. Gradually, however, scholars came to put more emphasis on the fact that plural systems may exist in parallel with one another, duplicating many of each other's functions. These parallel systems may offer quite different understandings of and solutions for particular situations while, conversely, in any given situation people may have more than one legal mechanism at their disposal. Their decision to choose one avenue rather than another may then be motivated by many factors such as their overall social values and attitudes and, of course, their perceived self-interest.

In many post-colonial contexts, this plurality is not limited to processes of dispute settlement, but applies also to matters such as land law, natural resource management, property and inheritance, gender relations and governance. As already mentioned, for example, there are parallel – albeit equally state-regulated – systems of family law in India and Sri Lanka; while marriage in Indonesia – which impinges on several of those domains – is institutionalised in three legal systems, *adat* law,[37] Islamic law and state law, which all define marriage differently and have different procedures for establishing legitimate marriages and dissolving them.[38]

Such plurality also arises in the context of transnational post-colonial processes like economic globalisation and mass migration, as in the notable case of trust-based financial arrangements like *hawalas* and *hundis* – so-called 'informal funds transfer' (IFT) systems used by many migrants as alternatives to the international banking system for purposes of trade or to transfer

37 *Adat* is a generic term used to describe customary practices and traditions in Muslim societies, especially in Southeast Asia. It was codified by European colonists in the early twentieth century and remains applicable to wide areas of personal law in Brunei, Malaysia and Indonesia; G. F. Bell, 'Indonesia: The Challenges of Legal Diversity and Law Reform', in A. Black and G. Bell (eds), *Law and Legal Institutions of Asia: Traditions, Adaptations and Innovations*, Cambridge: Cambridge University Press, 2011, 262–98, at 268.
38 Benda-Beckmann, 'Who's Afraid of Legal Pluralism?', 62.

remittances to their countries of origin.[39] These two systems are commonly contrasted in terms of their legal regulation. Payment systems in the official banking sector must conform to a formal body of international and national regulations and legislation, whereas IFT procedures avoid (or evade, depending on one's point of view) many of those requirements, and are often suspected by the hegemonic financial and legal systems of being forms of smuggling or money laundering.[40]

Hawalas are conventionally portrayed as being bound by nothing more than codes of honour and mutual trust among dealers, and certainly they can only operate successfully in environments characterised by high levels of perceived personal integrity. However, as Martin points out, it would be a mistake to understand 'trust' in this context in the narrow sense of 'ethical altruism'. At issue here is what she terms 'calculative trust . . . premised on weighing up the costs and benefits . . . and making a decision based on a number of penalties or fail-safes built into the agreement'.[41] Above all, trust of this kind depends on flows of accurate information about the standing and character of one's trading partners; it is grounded in 'a reputation mechanism among self-interested individuals'.[42]

To distinguish these IFT systems from the state-endorsed banking system as 'informal' and 'formal', respectively, as is done even in the acronym itself, risks underplaying the degree of organization displayed by IFTs, and is a relic of the inability of colonial administrators in the past to comprehend their modes of operation. In many respects, they are more efficient than the so-called 'formal' system; for example, money transfers are often more rapid than in mainstream banking.[43] Martin therefore prefers to refer to *hawalas* and *hundis* as 'indigenous banking systems'.[44] Again, then, we find a situation akin to that described in the previous section, whereby the distinction between formal and informal, like that between professional and lay, requires detailed analysis if it is to aid understanding. In both cases, the primary task for an anthropologist is not to attach labels of these kinds, but to understand the different conceptual logics and procedural arrangements at play – on their own terms first of all, but in the

39 M. B. V. Martin, '*Hundi/Hawala*: The Problem of Definition', *Modern Asian Studies* 43(4), 2009, 909–37.

40 *Ibid.*, 929–32.

41 *Ibid.*, 923.

42 A. Greif, 'Reputation and Coalitions in Medieval Trade: Evidence on the Maghribi Traders', *Journal of Economic History* 49(4), 1989, 857–82, at 858.

43 Martin, '*Hundi/Hawala*', 927.

44 *Ibid.*, 922, 934.

hope, ultimately, of being able to compare the two parallel systems using concepts and criteria external to them both.

'Weak' and 'strong' legal pluralism

Situations like those exemplified by the parallel family law systems of South Asia, mentioned earlier, represent what Griffiths calls 'weak' or pragmatic legal pluralism, in which, although there are 'different rules for different classes of the population', these are 'provided for or recognized by one legal order'.[45] What he terms 'strong' legal pluralism only arises in contexts like those envisaged by Moore, who links legal pluralism to the existence of what she calls 'semi-autonomous social fields'. Unlike Vanderlinden, Moore does not see a 'semi-autonomous social field' as necessarily corresponding to a particular social grouping. Rather, it:

> . . . is defined and its boundaries identified not by its organization (it may be a corporate group, it may not) but by a processual characteristic, the fact that it can generate rules and coerce or induce compliance to them . . . The independent articulation of many different social fields constitutes one of the basic characteristics of complex societies.[46]

So, the key defining features of a semi-autonomous social field are, firstly, that it is not fully autonomous or socially isolated, and, secondly, that it has 'the capacity to generate rules and induce or coerce conformity'.[47] It is only *semi*-autonomous, despite its rule-making and rule-enforcing capacities, because it remains 'set in a larger social matrix which can, and does, affect and invade it'.[48] Its applicability to complex societies is illustrated in Moore's first example, the garment industry in New York City, where the formal legislation impinging upon the various activities directly or indirectly involved in garment production – banking law, labour law and so on – operates alongside other quasi-legal regulations emanating from non-state bodies like trade unions and manufacturers' associations, and yet other even less formal rules generated within the social field itself 'through the interplay of the jobbers, contractors, factors, retailers, and skilled workers in the course of doing business with each other'.[49]

45 Griffiths, 'What Is Legal Pluralism?', 11.
46 Moore, *Law as Process*, 57–58.
47 *Ibid.*, 58.
48 Donovan, *Legal Anthropology*, 190.
49 S. Falk Moore, 'Law and Social Change: The Semi-Autonomous Social Field as an Appropriate Object of Study', *Law and Society Review* 7(4), 1973, 719–46, at 728.

Legislation is one primary means by which centralised governments seek to regulate the social fields within their state boundaries. But legislation often fails to achieve its intended aims, or has unplanned and unexpected consequences, because it is not introduced into a vacuum, but into a situation that already contains complex sets of social arrangements and obligations, which may distort or even defeat its intended purpose. In Moore's second case study, for example, the attempts by the Tanzanian Government to impose a highly centralised form of state socialism upon the Chagga tribe were impeded by two entirely unplanned processes that were already underway: the growing importance of coffee as a cash crop, and the increasingly restricted availability of land because of rapid population growth.[50]

For Griffiths, similarly, 'strong' legal pluralism only arises when:

> . . . law and legal institutions are not all subsumable within one 'system' but have their sources in the self-regulatory activities of all the multifarious social fields present . . . so that the 'law' which is actually effective on the 'ground floor' of society is the result of enormously complex and . . . unpredictable patterns of competition, interaction, negotiation, isolationism, and the like.[51]

The main advantages of Moore's formulation, as Griffiths sees it, are that it is particularly suitable for work in complex societies; and that, as Moore herself noted: 'By definition it requires attention to the problem of connection with the larger society.'[52]

More recently, Moore herself has listed five senses in which the notion of 'pluralism' is employed within the contemporary anthropology of law.[53] Firstly, the state itself is internally complex and diverse, and its official administrative sub-parts compete for legal authority. Secondly, in weak legal pluralism, the state acknowledges diverse social fields within society and organises itself in relation to them, as with South Asian family law. Thirdly, by contrast, in what Donovan terms 'reverse weak pluralism',[54] state law itself may depend upon 'the collaboration of non-state social fields' for its implementation.[55] Fourthly,

---

50 *Ibid.*, 730.
51 Griffiths, 'What Is Legal Pluralism?', 39.
52 Moore, *Law as Process*, 57.
53 S. Falk Moore, 'Certainties Undone: Fifty Turbulent Years of Legal Anthropology', *Journal of the Royal Anthropological Institute* 7(1), 2001, 95–116.
54 Donovan, *Legal Anthropology*, 190.
55 Moore, 'Certainties Undone', 107. Neither Moore nor Donovan give specific examples of this, but presumably they include cases where the state privatises the delivery of services.

the state itself vies with other state legal systems in supra-national arenas like the European Union, or with global institutions like the World Trade Organization.[56] Finally, there is strong legal pluralism itself, where the state is enmeshed with 'non-governmental, semi-autonomous social fields which generate their own . . . obligatory norms to which they can induce or coerce compliance'.[57]

In short, then, legal pluralism is an attribute of a particular social field, not of 'law' or of a 'legal system'. It arises when, within any given social field, 'more than one source of "law", more than one "legal order", is observable', and it 'refers to the normative heterogeneity attendant upon the fact that social action always takes place in a context of multiple, overlapping "semi-autonomous social fields"'.[58] In none of Moore's five situations can we expect the delineation of a professional/lay distinction to be straightforward, and in some cases it may not be possible at all.

Legal consciousness and legal discourse

The discussion so far concerns what Merry termed 'classic legal pluralism', which she characterised as being concerned above all with 'the intersections of indigenous and European law'.[59] She contrasted this with 'new legal pluralism' appearing from the 1970s onwards, especially among anthropologists of law working in the United States, as the result of a series of detailed studies of the American legal system as experienced by ordinary litigants. Classic legal pluralism focused, as shown above, on social fields regulated by more than one legal order, whereas the work of Conley and O'Barr,[60] and Merry herself,[61] showed how different understandings of law coexist within mainstream American society. Thus, while classic legal pluralism concentrates on alternative

---

56 It is partly for this reason that some writers see legal pluralism as universal: the mere characterisation of societies as legally 'plural' therefore becomes analytically trivial; C. J. Fuller, 'Legal Anthropology: Legal Pluralism and Legal Thought', *Anthropology Today* 10, 1994, 9–12; and Donovan, *Legal Anthropology*, 188.

57 Moore, 'Certainties Undone', 107. She actually says 'their own (non-legal) obligatory norms' here, in a paradoxical last-minute lapse into the vocabulary of legal centralism; see Griffiths, 'What Is Legal Pluralism?', 37 for a similar criticism of Moore, *Law as Process*.

58 Griffiths, 'What Is Legal Pluralism?', 38.

59 S. Engle Merry, 'Legal Pluralism', *Law and Society Review* 22, 1988, 869–96, at 872.

60 J. Conley and W. O'Barr, *Rules versus Relationships: The Ethnography of Legal Discourse*, Chicago, IL: Chicago University Press, 1990.

61 Merry, *Getting Justice and Getting Even*.

processes of regulation or dispute settlement, 'new legal pluralism' focuses on what Merry calls 'legal consciousness',[62] that is, on different folk understandings of the same normative order. Every actor in a legal process displays a distinctive and evolving 'legal consciousness', constructed through their ongoing cultural interpretation, as well as their strategic use, of a whole repertoire of particular discourses.[63]

Paradoxically, though, Merry continued to emphasise the official state legal system, which she saw as 'fundamentally different' from other normative orders because 'it exercises the coercive power of the state and monopolizes the symbolic power associated with state authority'.[64] From an anthropological perspective, there seemed no need for Merry to limit herself in this way. Indeed, her approach was criticised[65] for admitting through the back door that very same lawyers' folk ideology of legal centralism that she claimed to have 'vanquished'.[66]

'New' legal pluralists adopt an interpretative approach that often draws upon Geertz's account of law as a cultural phenomenon, a set of 'symbols . . . through whose agency [legal] structures are formed [and] communicated'.[67] Geertz certainly seems right to argue that legal reasoning places particular events into broader contexts, thereby suggesting principled courses of action to be undertaken in response, but he is on far shakier ground when he argues that 'the cultural contextualization of incident' is 'a critical aspect of legal analysis . . . as it is of . . . sociological analysis', and that law 'makes life's nebulous events tangible and restores their detail'.[68] While this may possibly be true of proceedings among the Tiv, for example (and these may have been the kinds of situations Geertz had mainly in mind), what is striking about formal legal proceedings in Western common law and civil code systems is that specific contexts are *downplayed* in the interests of attaching events to general principles of law. Whereas anthropological analyses treat ambiguity and complexity as immanent aspects of all real-life situations, the reasoning in Western courts seeks to prune away 'extraneous' details, so as to identify the abstract, *de*-contextualized legal principles presumed to lie within.

62 *Ibid.*, 5.
63 *Ibid.*, 205.
64 Merry, 'Legal Pluralism', 879.
65 F. von Benda-Beckmann, 'Comment on Merry', *Law & Society Review* 22(5), 1988, 897–902, at 900.
66 Merry, 'Legal Pluralism', 878. This resembles Griffiths' criticism of Moore (see above).
67 C. Geertz, *Local Knowledge*, New York: Basic Books, 1983, 182.
68 *Ibid.*, 181–82.

The professionalisation of the practice of law almost inevitably creates differences in 'legal consciousness' as between legal professionals and lay litigants, but even lay legal actors who broadly share a common cultural background may display widely differing forms of 'legal consciousness'. For example, Conley and O'Barr focused on the strategies used by lay people in small claims and magistrates' courts in the United States, where litigants usually present their own cases directly rather than using lawyers. [69] The ways in which lay persons present their cases to the court lie along a continuum.

At one extreme, some litigants display a strong *rule orientation*, framing their problems in relation to specific laws, rules or regulations that have allegedly been violated. In other words, they:

> . . . evaluate their problems in terms of neutral principles whose applica-
> tion transcends differences in personal and social status. In conceiving
> their cases and presenting them to the court, they emphasize these
> principles rather than such issues as individual need or social worth.[70]

All being equal, this is a relatively successful strategy because it chimes with the perspectives of legal professionals themselves. There is therefore a good chance that their presentation of problems in this way will be fully understood.

At the other extreme are litigants who display a *relational orientation*, characterised by a 'fuzzier' definition of issues, whereby rights and responsibilities are predicated on 'a broad notion of social interdependence rather than on the application of rules'.[71] Their testimony 'contains frequent references to . . . items which are significant to [their] social situation but are irrelevant to the court's more limited and rule-centered agenda'.[72] For example, if the case involves a dispute with a neighbour, they may focus less on the particular event that led to them being in court and more on their moral outrage that someone who has lived beside them for years, should violate the social norms of good-neighbourliness. This is less likely to be a successful strategy. Lawyers tend to view the testimonies of relationally oriented litigants as illogical and unstructured, but in reality it is merely that their arguments reflect a form of 'legal consciousness' very different from that associated with professional

---

69 Conley and O'Barr, *Rules versus Relationships*; J. Conley and W. O'Barr, *Just Words: Law, Language and Power*, Chicago, IL: Chicago University Press, 1998, 67–74.
70 Conley and O'Barr, *Rules versus Relationships*, ix.
71 *Ibid.*
72 *Ibid.*, 61.

legal analysis. Consequently, the courts 'often fail to understand their cases, regardless of their legal merits'.[73]

These are examples not of lay decision-making, but of what might be termed 'lay case-construction'. In contexts where litigants' cases are put on their behalf by their lawyers, by contrast, their submissions will be rule-oriented, as will the questions put to witnesses during cross-examination. Nonetheless, because they are usually unfamiliar with legal proceedings, it is quite likely that litigants and witnesses themselves will display varying degrees of relational orientation in their responses.

Immigration and asylum

One legal field which raises with particular and distinctive force many of the issues discussed so far, is that of immigration and asylum. This has assumed increasing political as well as legal significance right across Europe – where it is widely regarded as the most pressing political and social issue of the day – and in other countries experiencing high levels of would-be immigration or large numbers of asylum claims, like the United States, Canada and Australia. Asylum is clearly an example of legal pluralism in the fourth of Moore's senses listed above. Thus, although the United Kingdom was an early signatory of both the 1951 United Nations Convention Relating to the Status of Refugees and the subsequent 1967 Protocol that made it less narrowly focused on the specific circumstances prevailing in Europe after the end of the Second World War, these were not formally incorporated into UK law until the coming into force of the 1993 Asylum and Immigration Appeals Act.

Pluralism does not end there, however, for at least five different reasons. Firstly, immigration and asylum have been subjected to a growing body of UK national legislation, beginning with the 1971 Immigration Act and added to at an increasingly frantic pace over the past two decades. Secondly, they are also regulated by the Immigration Rules, a hugely complex body of quasi-legislative regulatory material that has undergone even more frequent modification.[74] To a large extent, both the plethora of primary legislation and the rapidly changing Immigration Rules reflect repeated attempts by the state to place yet more national restrictions upon the rights supposedly guaranteed by the international Convention. Thirdly, because none of the key

---

73 *Ibid.*, ix.
74 See https://www.gov.uk/guidance/immigration-rules/immigration-rules-part-11-asylum (accessed 8 March 2017). The Rules 'enjoy a comparable . . . legal status to delegated legislation'; J. A. Sweeney, 'Credibility, Proof and Refugee Law', *International Journal of Refugee Law* 21(4), 2009, 700–26, at 707.

terms defining a 'refugee'[75] are actually themselves precisely defined, either in the Convention itself or in the UNHCR Handbook that provides guidance on its application,[76] these have all undergone processes of legal interpretation across the whole range of British courts, from tribunals hearing first instance appeals right up to the Supreme Court itself. Fourthly, as in the New York garment industry case analysed by Moore (see above), asylum and immigration courts are venues where different professional groups (judges, lawyers, doctors, 'country experts' like myself, public service interpreters and so on) interact in complex ways regulated by all of the above; by the rules of procedure developed by or for the different types of court themselves;[77] by the ethical codes of the specific professional bodies to which they belong; and by the unwritten conventions that have arisen through their day-to-day interactions in and out of court. Fifthly, these courts deal with would-be refugees from all over the world, from a vast range of national and sub-national legal systems, and each asylum applicant carries with them their own legal consciousness – generally not reflecting any prior experience or understanding of the British legal system. In short, the United Kingdom's asylum and immigration system can unequivocally be seen as a nexus for a wide range of semi-autonomous social fields, and as a prime example of 'strong' legal pluralism in the sense described by Griffiths.

At the time of my initial ethnographic research in the early 2000s, the asylum process involved lay decision-making in several respects. First and foremost, initial decisions on asylum claims were made by quite junior

75 Article 1(A)2 of the 1951 Convention, as modified by the 1967 Protocol, defines a refugee as someone who, 'owing to well-founded fear of being persecuted for reasons of race, religion, nationality, membership of a particular social group or political opinion, is outside the country of his nationality and is unable or, owing to such fear, is unwilling to avail himself of the protection of that country'. None of these five 'Convention reasons' is precisely defined, nor are the key notions of 'well-founded fear' and 'persecution'.

76 'Handbook and Guidelines on Procedures and Criteria for Determining Refugee Status', 1979, Annexes updated 2011, http://www.unhcr.org/uk/publications/ legal/3d58e13b4/handbook-procedures-criteria-determining-refugee-status- under-1951-convention.html (accessed 8 March 2017).

77 Such as, but by no means confined to, the Civil Procedure Rules and associated Practice Directions, https://www.justice.gov.uk/courts/procedure-rules/civil/rules; The Tribunal Procedure (First-tier Tribunal) (Immigration and Asylum Chamber) Rules 2014, https://www.gov.uk/government/uploads/system/uploads/attachment_ data/file/367129/immigration-asylum-chamber-tribunal-procedure-rules.pdf; and the Practice Directions: Immigration and Asylum Chambers of the First- Tier Tribunal and the Upper Tribunal, https://www.judiciary.gov.uk/wp-content/ uploads/2014/11/revised-pd-3112014.pdf (all accessed 8 March 2017).

case-workers in the relevant Home Office department,[78] most of whom had no legal training whatever. Secondly, most Adjudicators hearing first instance appeals in what was then termed the Immigration Appellate Authority (IAA), and many Tribunal Chairs at second appeals before the Asylum and Immigration Tribunal (IAT),[79] were part-timers who also still worked as solicitors and barristers in the asylum field or other areas of law. Although not 'lay' decision-makers in the sense of lacking legal training, their primary professional identities were as legal representatives and advocates.[80] Thirdly, IAT hearings typically involved panels made up of one or two lay members and a legally qualified Tribunal Chair. It is unclear how much influence on decision-making these lay members had in practice, especially as decisions were almost always presented as collective and the written determinations were actually drafted by the Chair. However, I was told anecdotes about particular appeals in which lay members allegedly 'out-voted' their legally qualified chair, and on a few occasions this was made explicit through the publishing of split decisions.[81]

Fourthly, there is a more technical issue concerning the nature of decision-making in asylum cases. In *Karanakaran*,[82] the Court of Appeal confirmed that the standard of proof in asylum cases, both for proving past events *and* assessing future risk, is the so-called *Sivakumaran* standard[83] – 'a reasonable degree of likelihood' – rather than the normal 'balance of probabilities' civil

---

78   Terminology and organisation have undergone frequent changes, for political reasons linked to the failure of the asylum administration to 'manage' the perceived 'problems'. During my initial research, the relevant Home Office body was the Immigration and Nationality Directorate (IND); several changes later, these issues are now the responsibility of UK Visas and Immigration (UKVI).

79   Here, too, terminology has changed several times. Adjudicators and Tribunal Chairs were later renamed Immigration Judges and Senior Immigration Judges. Later still, immigration and asylum were assimilated into the wider tribunal system, and the bodies hearing first- and second-tier appeals are now named the Immigration and Asylum Chambers of the First-Tier Tribunal and Upper Tribunal, respectively.

80   In the United Kingdom more generally, even full-time judges are drawn from the ranks of practising lawyers, whereas in much of continental Europe, becoming a judge is a separate career involving a distinct professional identity from the start. Decision-making is thus further removed from the daily practice and experience of most lawyers, so the professional/lay contrast arguably takes on a somewhat different form.

81   See *Sadegh v. Secretary of State for the Home Department (SSHD)*, 13124, 20 March 1996 and, in a rather more complex way, *Jelusic v. SSHD*, *00TH01652*, 4 July 2000; Good, *Anthropology and Expertise*, 243–44.

82   *Karanakaran v. SSHD*, [2000] Imm AR 271, [2000] 3 All ER 449 [CA].

83   *R. v. SSHD ex p. Sivakumaran*, [1987] 3 WLR 1047 [CA], [1988] 1 All ER 193, [1988] AC 958, [1988] 2 WLR 92, [1988] Imm AR 147 [HL].

standard. It also stated that both issues must be considered together in 'a unitary process of evaluation' and that the facts of a case should be considered cumulatively rather than in isolation. Thus, 'proving a well founded fear of persecution is *a single composite question* incorporating past and present facts and risk'.[84] This cumulative process requires decision-makers to add up the weight of *all* the material evidence, however unlikely particular aspects are deemed to be. Sedley LJ argued that asylum decision-makers, whether Home Office case-owners or Tribunal adjudicators, do not make truly legal decisions, which entail making a 'choice between two conflicting accounts', but administrative ones involving 'an evaluation of the intrinsic and extrinsic credibility, and ultimately the significance, of the applicant's case'. He added that:

> Such decision-makers, on classic principles of public law, are required to take everything material into account. Their sources of information will frequently go well beyond the testimony of the applicant and include in-country reports, expert testimony . . . No probabilistic cut-off operates here: everything capable of having a bearing has to be given the weight, great or little, due to it.

Thus, the decision-making process in asylum appeals is not the same as that undertaken by judges in civil law contexts, but rather a form of administrative decision-making. Again, we see that the professional/lay distinction requires considerable refinement if it is to account for the processes of asylum decision-making.

Discourse, interpretation and translation

Legal consciousness (above) is an aspect of personhood, whereas 'legal discourse', like language itself, is a Durkheimian social fact 'rooted in institutional structures'.[85] Not surprisingly, then, one approach adopted by many social anthropologists and socio-linguists is to study the forms of discourse used by judges and lawyers, and by the lay witnesses giving evidence before them. Relevant issues here concern the use of specialised legal language; misunderstandings arising from the different cultural backgrounds of legal professionals and litigants or witnesses; distinctive legal forms of syllogistic reasoning;[86] and the structural peculiarities of verbal interactions in legal processes. All of these

---

84 Sweeney, 'Credibility, Proof and Refugee Law', 721, emphasis added.
85 Merry, *Getting Justice and Getting Even*, 9.
86 N. MacCormick, *Legal Reasoning and Legal Theory*, rev. edn, Oxford: Oxford University Press, 1994, 21–32; and Good, 'Folk Models and the Law', 431.

issues arise with particular force and complexity when court procedures require the use of interpreters, as is true of nearly all asylum appeals.

In non-legal contexts, 'interpretation' is normally taken to mean 'the oral transfer of meaning between languages', whereas 'translation' is the equivalent process for written text.[87] For legal professionals, however, 'interpretation' has a different primary meaning: it refers to the process of determining the 'true meaning' of a legal text or document.[88] This means that lawyers commonly refer to the court interpreter's task as 'translation' rather than 'interpretation'. They also require interpreters to provide literal or verbatim 'translation' even though, as Colin and Morris point out, 'word-for-word or literal translation often produces distorted communication',[89] not least because words depend for their meanings on how they are combined with other words within a given utterance. An understanding of this context is required for an accurate rendering into another language to be possible. As Wadensjö argues, building on the work of Morris:[90]

> established legal systems show little or no readiness to acknowledge the interpreter-mediated situation as essentially different from the ordinary, monolingual one, and the court interpreter's task as truly interpretive. Instead, the court interpreter is defined as a disembodied mechanical device.[91]

Typically, the Immigration and Asylum Chapter's *Handbook for Freelance Interpreters* enjoins them to:

> . . . use the witness's *exact words*. If you cannot make a direct or exact interpretation, interpret it as accurately as possible *in the witness's own words* and then inform the Judiciary what the phrase means.[92]

It is not clear what can possibly be meant by 'in the witness's own words' in this passage. Furthermore, interpreters must not, says the *Handbook*, 'let your

---

87 J. Colin and R. Morris, *Interpreters and the Legal Process*, Winchester: Waterside Press, 1996, 16.

88 *Ibid.*, 16.

89 *Ibid.*, 17.

90 R. Morris, 'The Moral Dilemmas of Court Interpreting', *The Translator* 1(1), 1995, 25–46.

91 C. Wadensjö, *Interpreting as Interaction*, London and New York: Longman, 1998, 74.

92 As quoted in M. Henderson and A. Pickup, 'Best Practice Guide to Asylum and Human Rights Appeals', 2015, para. 34.24, emphasis added. Available at http://www.ein.org.uk/bpg/chapter/34 (accessed 8 March 2017).

own experience or views get in the way of how you interpret the evidence'. The explicit assumption here is that the interpreter's own understanding of what the witness means to say will 'get in the way' of the desired verbatim translation, yet the *Handbook* also contains the potentially contradictory admonition: 'Your duty is to make sure the court understands what the witness is saying.' Such naivety about the translation process is of course not confined to legal contexts, but its stress here seems partly a reflection of the centrality of language to the entire legal process. Law itself, as performed in court, depends heavily on the skilful manipulation of language by lawyers and its incompetent or untrained use by those under cross-examination.

As Atkinson and Drew pointed out in their seminal study of courtroom dialogue, interviews and court hearings are structured to avoid the kinds of problems arising in ordinary conversations, which need 'allocational rules' and 'repair sequences' to help deal with '"breakdowns" in the "one at a time" system'.[93] In normal conversation, it cannot be predicted who will talk next, and although ideally people should speak one at a time, this does not always happen in practice. By contrast, cross-examination is restricted to two parties, for whom *'turn order is fixed*, as is the *type of turn* which each speaker's talk constitutes'.[94] The lawyer asks a question to which the witness supplies an answer, leading to another question, and so on; these sequences are not 'locally managed' like normal conversations, but are 'provided for by court-room procedures'.[95] Cross-examination seeks to 'to challenge or blame the witness' by getting them to agree to the 'facts' progressively brought out during the questioning.[96] Both questions and answers are moulded by expectations over what the interlocutor will say next. For example, barristers expect that their accusations will produce denials, and try to turn that expectation to advantage by choosing forms of words such that witnesses damage their standing or credibility whatever answers they give ('when did you last beat your wife?'). Witnesses themselves may anticipate this and respond by 'hedging' to mitigate any potential admission or nullify the next accusation;[97] instead of a simple 'yes', they reply 'I suppose so', or 'Maybe'. Nonetheless, the power to control the form taken by the cross-examination lies overwhelmingly with the interrogator.

Such hegemonic forms of discourse are far harder to sustain, however, when basic communication requires the use of an interpreter. This disrupts normal

93 J. M. Atkinson and P. Drew, *Order in Court: The Organisation of Verbal Interaction in Court Settings*, London: Macmillan, 1979, 41.
94 *Ibid.*, 61; emphasis in the original.
95 *Ibid.*, 65.
96 *Ibid.*, 105–06.
97 *Ibid.*, 116.

turn-taking processes and removes some of the 'controlling power' normally held by the examining lawyer;[98] it even gives limited power to interpreters themselves, through the practical control they exert over turn-taking. Legal efforts to limit and 'mechanise' the interpreter's role are thus in part attempts to maintain as far as possible the hegemony of the examining lawyer. As Wadensjö notes:

> . . . it would obviously be a challenge to the court if interpreters were . . . allowed to clarify an attorney's deliberately ambiguous question. It would be a threat to the system if interpreters were allowed to improve the image of witnesses . . . by rendering eloquently and precisely statements which were originally voiced carelessly and imprecisely.[99]

As that last point exemplifies, differences in speech register also constitute potential barriers to communication and pose further challenges for court interpreters. The *Handbook* instructs them to 'reflect the type of language being used, whether it is simple, formal, colloquial etc. If abusive or obscene language is used in the source language, you should use the English equivalent'. Yet interpreters often feel in a quandary when applicants speak ungrammatically or rudely, especially if this is far removed from the register in which they themselves normally speak.[100]

When lawyers and litigants come from very different cultural backgrounds, all kinds of miscommunication may occur,[101] and these too may be exacerbated by the involvement of interpreters. In British asylum hearings, for example, ambiguities frequently arise over dates. Any vagueness by an asylum applicant over when a particular event took place is certain to be seized upon by the Home Office as damaging to their credibility as a whole. Quite apart from the normal vagaries of individual memory,[102] one complication that tribunals rarely take into account is that many asylum applicants come from countries

---

98 S. Berk-Seligson, *The Bilingual Courtroom: Court Interpreters in the Judicial Process*, Chicago, IL: Chicago University Press, 2002, 145.

99 Wadensjö, *Interpreting as Interaction*, 75.

100 R. Rycroft, 'Communicative Barriers in the Asylum Account', in P. Shah (ed.), *The Challenge of Asylum to Legal Systems*, London: Cavendish, 2005, 223–44; and R. Gibb and A. Good, 'Interpretation, Translation and Intercultural Communication in Refugee Status Determination Procedures in the UK and France', *Language and Intercultural Communication* 14(3), 2014, 1–15, at 9.

101 W. Kalin, 'Troubled Communication: Cross-Cultural Misunderstandings in the Asylum-Hearing', *International Migration Review* 20, 1986, 230–41.

102 H. Evans Cameron, 'Refugee Status Determinations and the Limits of Memory', *International Journal of Refugee Law* 22(4), 2010, 469–511.

not following the Gregorian calendar, so some apparent discrepancies may arise from inaccurate or approximate conversions of dates from one calendar to another. More insidiously, they may reflect inconsistent – though in themselves perfectly reasonable – translation choices made by interpreters at different stages of the asylum process. One confusion I witnessed myself involved the month of *Avani*, which in the Tamil luni-solar calendar begins in mid-August and ends in mid-September, although the exact Western dates differ each year. If the Home Office interpreter renders *Avani* as 'August' at the asylum interview and the court interpreter translates it as 'September' during the appeal hearing, a credibility-damaging 'discrepancy' may be generated without there having been any inconsistency whatever on the part of the hapless appellant, who will be completely unaware of what has happened.

Variations in kin relationship terminology can also create problems. This is not the trivial point that different words are used in different languages, but the more complex one that relatives are classified differently in different cultures. One example I witnessed stemmed from the fact that Tamil has no composite term for 'brother', only the terms *annan* ('elder brother') and *tampi* ('younger brother'). It is easy to imagine, then, how easily confusion can arise through different translation choices regarding the Home Office's question, 'how many of your brothers were in the Tamil Tigers?', and the answer given. In appeals where almost everything hangs on credibility, apparent discrepancies of these – in themselves quite trivial – kinds may be the last straw.

The key point revealed by the examples in this section is that the interposition of interpreters creates obstacles to communication, irrespective of their technical competence. Moreover, despite the institutional expectation that interpreters be 'invisible' or 'mechanical', in practice they are often active verbal participants in legal proceedings.[103] In many contexts, one important marker of the professional/lay distinction is the professional lawyer's ability to use language in two particular ways: their proficiency in a specialised technical vocabulary; and their mastery of a particular interrogative style. Both these finely honed skills are, however, partly blunted by the need to work through an interpreter. Moreover, because so much key evidence comes to them through the medium of translation – rendered by interpreters who are not legally trained and who (in asylum hearings at least) have no access to the case documents before or even during the hearing, still less to the legislation and rules alluded to by the contending lawyers – immigration judges, too, are heavily dependent in reaching their decisions on the spontaneous lay understanding of the interpreter.

103 Berk-Seligson, *The Bilingual Courtroom*, 64.

The role of culture

Misunderstandings like those arising from dates or kinship terms are straight-forward in the sense that the 'discrepancies' can be fully reconciled if the reasons for them are explained to the decision-maker. Subtler problems are raised by suggestions that certain seemingly odd or illogical actions by an asylum appellant were simply expressions of their indigenous 'traditions' or 'cultures'. On the one hand, judges are enjoined to keep such cultural differences in mind. As Lord Bingham's aphorism has it:

> No judge worth his salt could possibly assume that men of different nationalities, educations, trades, experience, creeds and temperaments would act . . . in accordance with his concept of what a reasonable man would have done.[104]

On the other hand, because there is generally no other evidence available, asylum decisions are so dependent on assessments regarding the credibility of the asylum applicants' narrative that it is hard to see how, in practice, judges can avoid applying 'reasonable man' tests in reaching their decisions.

In such contexts, the expertise of anthropologists is often called upon, but its provision raises difficulties that expose some key epistemological differences between lawyers on one hand, and many social scientists or other experts on the other. Most contemporary anthropologists, in the British tradition at least, see culture as a set of resources used to explain or justify social behaviour, rather than as directing or compelling that behaviour. In other words, culture 'does not *cause* behaviour, but summarizes an abstraction from it, and is thus neither normative nor predictive'.[105] Precisely the opposite is assumed by many legal approaches to 'culture', such as the 'cultural defense', a mitigation strategy employed especially in the United States, which seeks to argue that a criminal defendant, 'usually a recent immigrant . . . acted according to the dictates of his or her "culture," and therefore deserves leniency'.[106] Of course, this argument only appears plausible if it is assumed that their culture left the defendant with no choice. Not surprisingly, then, much of the literature on the 'cultural defence' treats the notion of 'culture' itself as fairly unproblematic[107]

---

104 T. Bingham, 'The Judge as Juror: The Judicial Determination of Factual Issues', *Current Legal Problems* 38, 1985, 1–27, at 14.

105 G. Baumann, *Contesting Culture: Discourses of Identity in Multi-ethnic London*, Cambridge: Cambridge University Press, 1996, 11, emphasis added.

106 L. Volpp, '(Mis)identifying Culture: Asian Women and the "Cultural Defense"', *Harvard Women's Law Journal* 17, 1994, 57–101, at 57.

107 Volpp, '(Mis)identifying Culture'; and A. Dundes Renteln, *The Cultural Defense*, New York: Oxford University Press, 2004.

or depicts it in a reified form that downplays or even rules out individual agency.[108]

In asylum contexts, too, legal practitioners routinely seek to downplay the contested nature of cultural practices, which they see as fatally weakening asylum claims dependent upon persecution resulting from such practices. This strategic consideration is reinforced by the positivistic premises that underlie legal reasoning in any case. The legal resort to cultural essentialism creates a dilemma for anthropologist expert witnesses. Do they accept the lawyer's premise that culture itself is the explanation for strange or questionable behaviour, thereby colluding in what they would otherwise see as an unacceptable reification of culture, or try to explain its optative character, thereby raising doubts over the strength of the appellant's case? For example, I have often been asked to report on asylum claims depending partly on a fear of persecution arising from the claimant having entered into a socially disapproved marriage, perhaps across religious or caste lines. I am then obliged to point out that although such marriages are indeed actively and even violently punished in some cases, there are nonetheless families, and whole communities, that display far greater tolerance. [109]

Concluding comment

This chapter deals, in a variety of contexts, with the implications of the fact that, for anthropologists, virtually every society and social context manifests legal pluralism in some form or other. This inevitably creates complications for attempts to differentiate between legal professionals and lay legal actors in general, and for the specific question of lay decision-making in particular. However, this does not mean that the notion of lay decision-making is without analytical value. Quite the contrary, as illustrated by the brief analyses of Tiv and Barotse material, and the vignettes from the asylum courts, it provides one particular perspective from which to view a given legal context. Rather than being reasons for not employing such notions, the very complexities

---

108 '[Y]outh gangs, new-immigrant traditionalists, religious sects and cults, old working-class communities, and other subcultural enclaves . . . *indisputably foster cultural dictation*', W. I. Torry, 'Culture and Individual Responsibility: Touchstones of the Culture Defense', *Human Organization* 59(1), 2000, 58–71, at 68, emphasis added.

109 For a more detailed discussion of the 'cultural defence' and the problems posed for anthropologists by reified notions of 'culture', see A. Good, 'Cultural Evidence in Courts of Law', in M. Engelke (ed.), *The Objects of Evidence: Anthropological Approaches to the Production of Knowledge*, Chichester: John Wiley & Sons, 2009, 44–57.

created are themselves fruitful tools to think with in the analysis of complex legal situations.

Legal decision-making has two aspects: what is the correct interpretation of the law, and what are the facts of the case? In jury trials, these are the separate provinces of judge and jury, respectively, but in asylum hearings, both responsibilities lie with the judge. Twining has repeatedly argued, though, that legal treatments of factual evidence reflect a 'relatively complacent commonsense empiricism' that pays too little attention to the epistemological complexities involved in collecting, processing and weighing information.[110] Can one say, then, that in the context of a Sri Lankan asylum appeal, for example, even a judge – lacking first-hand experience of that country and highly dependent on the court interpreter when it comes to comprehending the appellant's narrative – is a lay decision-maker when it comes to finding facts?

Recommended reading

Conley, J. and O'Barr, W., *Rules versus Relationships: The Ethnography of Legal Discourse*, Chicago, IL: Chicago University Press, 1990.

Donovan, J. M., *Legal Anthropology: An Introduction*. Lanham, MD: Bowman & Littlefield, 2008.

Good, A., *Anthropology and Expertise in the Asylum Courts*, London: Routledge-Cavendish, 2007.

Griffiths, J., 'What Is Legal Pluralism?' *Journal of Legal Pluralism* 24, 1986, 1–55.

Twining, W., *Rethinking Evidence: Exploratory Essays*, 2nd edn, Cambridge: Cambridge University Press, 2006.

110 Twining, *Rethinking Evidence*, 28.

Index

203; law and anthropology 229,
230–1; socio-legal studies 52–64
trust-based financial arrangements
221–2
Tuan, Yi-Fu 47, 48
Twining, W. 23, 238

United Kingdom 22, 40, 41, 94, 157,
171; city centres and shopping 47–8;
comparative law 122, 123–5, 126–7,
129, 130–7, 138–41, 144; Crown
Court judges 136–7; Crown
Prosecution Service (CPS) 78; law and
anthropology 228–35; law reform 34;
legal history 14, 103–21; magistrates
67, 70, 71–2, 75–80, 94; Ministry of
Justice (MoJ) 78; rape cases 67, 81–4,
199–202, 204–5, 206–7, 208; rape
claims, Home Office decision-making
in asylum 199–200, 202–4, 205–6,
207–8; tribunals 52–6, 57–9, 60–4,
203, 229, 230–1
United States 12, 14, 22, 108, 120,
171; administrative adjudication
58; jurimetrics 25; law and
anthropology 223, 225–6, 227,
228, 236–7
University of Canberra 11

validity 73, 80, 85
Van Gestel, R. 14, 24, 25
Van Roermund, B. 95
Vanderlinden, J. 214–15
Vidmar, N. 67, 72, 82

Wadensjö, C. 232, 234
Ward, I. 90, 92
Watt, G. 88, 100, 101
welfare law 178
West, R.L. 101
Westerman, P. 21–2
Wheeler, S. 42
White, J.B. 92, 100, 101
Wiener, M. 115–16
Wikeley, N. 60–4
Wiles, P. 42, 44
Wilson, G. 41
witnesses 96, 99–100, 135, 228, 231,
233; anthropologist expert 237
World Trade Organization 225
Wren, C.G. and J.R. 12–13

year books 105, 106
Young, I. 195
Young, R. 60–4

Zander, M. 137, 141
Zweigert, K. 129–31